THE
ART
(AND SCIENCE) OF

HR

A Legal Guide for New Managers, CEOs, and Leaders in Between

AMIE MCDANIEL REMINGTON, JD

Disclaimer

Just as no two people are exactly alike, no two employment matters are exactly the same. For that reason, analysis of legal matters is nuanced—and many lawyers' favorite answer is, "It depends." While this book explains how to prevent and correct situations that can lead to litigation, it is intended to provide a road map to creating a healthy workplace—*not* binding legal advice. When in doubt, invest in the wise counsel of an employment lawyer because the correct answer *is* often, "It depends."

Table of Contents

Introduction

Why this book? Why now? These are the two guiding questions I've kept in the back of my mind while writing *The Art (and Science) of HR.* I have been fortunate to have a career centered on helping businesses succeed. What I've learned is that few leaders have any training around HR issues, and there are things even well-intentioned leaders don't know that can get them (and their organization) into legal trouble. That's the "why this book" part.

The "why now" part is that over the past half-decade or so, the workplace has evolved tremendously. Employees are in the driver's seat now—and it's crucial to provide the kind of experience they expect so they'll be happier, stay engaged, feel a sense of belonging, and frankly, *not leave.* (In many industries, retention is the number-one issue right now.) To create this kind of culture, leaders need a lot of training…and that includes training on HR issues.

In my 25 years as an employment attorney, I have worked with all sorts of businesses. Some had 2 employees; the largest had 70,000 employees. While most were private-sector businesses such as law firms, medical practices, banks, dry cleaners, and restaurants, some were public-sector or governmental organizations. A substantial number of the private businesses were non-profits. Some businesses were part of a heavily regulated industry. Most businesses were not unionized, but a few had multiple unions. Working with such a variety of businesses over two decades has given me firsthand opportunities to observe what successful businesses do well…and what less successful businesses could do better.

One thing all of these businesses had in common is that the leaders worked for a particular organization or in a particular industry because they were passionate about their product or service—curating the perfect dinner experience for customers, healing patients, creating art, building boats, working with an underserved population, or selling homes—*not* because they were passionate about the mechanics of running a business. Yet, the mechanics of running the business are critically necessary. Simply stated, poorly run businesses generally don't survive in today's competitive environment.

The goal of this book is two-fold. First, this book is designed to help business owners and managers more fully understand the most important assets of their business: employees and their perspectives. After all, employees are the lifeline of a business; just as great employees can elevate a business, poor employees can sink one. The second goal is to help employers make wise choices while avoiding costly and distracting mistakes by having a better understanding of employment-related laws and regulations.

Engaging Your Most Important Asset: Your Employees

Taking proactive, meaningful actions to ensure that employees are treated fairly, engaged, and feel a sense of belonging positively impacts business in the form of lower turnover, higher productivity, and reduced litigation exposure. The converse is true, too: Treating employees unfairly, paying lower-than-market wages, and failing to support and protect employees negatively impacts businesses in the form of higher turnover, lower productivity, and increased litigation exposure.

Workplace culture and the employee experience have always been important, but today they're more than important—they're imperatives. Employees choose and remain at jobs that provide personal satisfaction, professional fulfillment, belonging, and psychological and physical safety. Employees who are happy with their work and connected to the goals of the organization are more likely to be loyal and productive. They will look for new employment only when their decision is driven by a need for new growth and development (which is, of course, a big reason to make sure you're providing that). Organizations with happy employees experience lower turnover rates and, ultimately, higher profitability.

Unhappy employees, on the other hand, negatively impact organizations. Unhappy employees are less engaged and less productive. They create costly turnover because they are constantly on the lookout for a new position. They also detract from an organization's goals by disrupting employee harmony in the workplace. Most importantly, they may create expensive and time-consuming legal vulnerabilities and damage an organization's reputation.

The trend toward employee empowerment has been building for a while, but COVID-19 magnified it. The availability of remote and hybrid work has given many employees the power to work where and how they want. The Great Resignation gave them more bargaining power and solidified their higher expectations around how they want to work and expect to be treated. Organizations are still feeling the impact as employees continue to rethink their priorities and reinvent their lives. Finally, many industries continue to struggle with talent shortages and higher-than-previous wage expectations.

To ensure success, employers must take steps to help employees feel happy, stable, and confident in the workplace. Leaders must lead in a way that promotes these conditions. Just as important, they must avoid making the kind of off-putting statements that can come from not understanding the employee perspective. Implementing and training on best-in-class human resource practices can help create a culture where the best employees feel connected to the goals of the organization and the work they do.

Unless a business owner or leader has studied human resources, he or she probably does not fully understand what great employees want and need from their employers, how to create a culture where employees are psychologically and physically safe, how to reduce turnover, and how to maximize productivity in a healthy manner. One goal of this book is to help employers and leaders understand these things and maximize positive results.

Protecting Your Organization by Avoiding Mistakes

The second goal of this book is to help employers avoid costly HR mistakes.

The sheer volume of employment-related laws and regulations that govern employment in the United States creates a challenge for the most sophisticated of employers. Not only do employers have to comply with all federal laws, they have to comply with the laws of the states in which they operate—states that may provide different or additional protections to employees. As if that were not difficult enough, employers must also comply with municipal regulations, codes, or ordinances that exist in the geographies in which employees work. While this can overwhelm the most diligent of employers, the matter is further complicated because this body of law continues to increase each year.

For example, in 2023, under new federal laws, employers were required to provide new COVID-19 notices to employees, the Supreme Court changed the landscape of employer-related arbitration agreements, new restrictions regarding cannabis use were implemented, and employers with federal contractors faced changes in minimum wage and wage reporting.

In addition, in 2023, various states passed new laws on almost every employment-law topic imaginable: discrimination and harassment, salary transparency, minimum wage, tip credits, the use of artificial intelligence in the workplace, preemployment background checks, weapons in the workplace, mandatory paid sick leave, mandatory unpaid sick leave, required family leave, vacation payout, meal and rest break requirements, COVID-19, reproductive health, human trafficking, physical privacy, online privacy, data security and responses to data breaches, workers' compensation, and non-disclosure and non-compete agreements.[1] Because many of these new laws allow private rights of action or contain significant financial penalties for non-compliance—even *inadvertent* non-compliance—understanding them is absolutely critical.

This trend continued in 2024 when new federal standards on joint employment were enacted, and a new safety injury and illness law was passed. Many states increased minimum wage. Various states passed laws governing payout of accrued vacation time and the use of cannabis. Several cities passed paid leave laws, as well.[2]

That's where this book comes in. While it does not provide an exhaustive list of all employment laws regulating employment in the United States, it does provide information to help employers identify and correct many common workplace issues, thereby increasing the odds of creating a positive employee experience and avoiding costly and time-consuming litigation.

How to Use This Book

This book is divided into easy-to-read sections, organized by the lifecycle of an employee. Each section is designed to stand alone. This allows readers to choose the chapters most relevant to them, in the order that best fits their current needs.

Perhaps your organization excels at onboarding but needs help in offboarding. You may choose to start toward the end of the "Hiring, Wages, and Termination" section by reading Chapter 8: If You Have to Fire Me, Do It with Heart and

Chapter 9: If You Are Curious Why I Quit, Just Ask Me, and then come back to Chapter 3: If You Want to Reduce Turnover, Focus on My Satisfaction from the Interview Forward at a later time. Perhaps you have a manager with a reputation for talking harshly to employees. You may choose to ask that manager to read Chapter 13: Don't Make Me Deal with Your Bad Behavior to help her consider how her tone is affecting your employees and the business. If you are a new business owner or a new manager, you may choose to read the book cover-to-cover. This book can also be read by groups of leaders in a conversational book club format. Any approach is okay!

Conclusion

All businesses must contend with the reality that employee expectations have changed. To survive, employers and leaders must be creative, flexible, willing to adapt, and able to understand their legal obligations. Organizations must put employee engagement, retention, and legal compliance at the center of their decisions.

While making this shift might sound daunting, in the long run it will pay off as your culture becomes more employee-centric and you begin to see improved organizational performance. By learning the benefits of proactive human resource strategies, reading up on employment laws, and implementing solid human resource practices, it *is* possible to create a win-win for employees and employers alike.

Thank you for reading this book. I am grateful to have learned all that I've learned during my career. It's my hope that by sharing some of these insights with you, your organization will become a better place for employees to work and a more successful version of itself.

Building a Secure Foundation

CHAPTER 1

Surround Yourself with Bold Employees

Margarite and Joe's Story

Margarite owns a grocery store chain and employs about 150 part- and full-time employees in three different store locations. Recently, Margarite noticed that sales in all three stores were declining, but she was not able to identify the reason for this trend because she had not changed anything significant in her stores. To determine why sales were trending downward, Margarite asked each of her location managers, "What could we be doing better or differently?"

Two of the three managers were hesitant to answer Margarite's question. The first manager was intimidated because he had been asked a direct question by the owner. He worried that making suggestions on how to change was akin to criticizing the way things were currently being done. Therefore, he did not provide any feedback at all.

The second manager was comfortable making suggestions, but she knew that change often requires hard work. She did not want to work harder than she already was, and she was content with the status quo. The only feedback she provided was to say that she was sure things would turn around.

The third manager, Joe, reacted differently from his colleagues. Joe viewed Margarite's question as a challenge and an invitation to improve the whole business. Margarite and Joe had a good rapport, and Joe trusted Margarite to listen to his ideas, knowing that he had the best interests of the business at heart—even if his feedback identified things that were not working well.

Joe began doing industry research to learn what products and services customers in their geographic area wanted. Over the course of the next month, he reached out to the state-wide grocery association and asked to read white papers on good store management. He then went to competitor stores and shopped as if he were purchasing a week's worth of groceries for a family of five. He observed other shoppers to see where they lingered and also made note of customer-employee interactions.

Joe's research revealed several things about similarly sized but more successful competitors:

- They had larger staffs, and much of the staff was dedicated to customer service.
- They offered services Margarite's stores did not, such as carrying purchases to customers' cars and grocery delivery services.
- The stores had better lighting and appeared cleaner.
- They carried a wider variety of brands.

Joe presented his findings to Margarite, starting by highlighting what her business was doing well. He then identified areas of opportunity, and pointed out how an additional investment of resources might impact sales and growth.

"Some of these suggestions might fail, but I would like to try regardless," he told Margarite. "I would like to pilot one change per month at my store. If the change yields a positive result, we can implement that change at all three stores."

Margarite thanked Joe for his suggestions and agreed to move forward with his plan.

The Takeaway

Employees tend to believe that their leaders are (or should be) all-knowing: They should know how to create a product, sell the product, manage the finances of the business, select and retain the best employees, make prudent short- and long-term financial decisions, use technology efficiently, *and* remember the name of every customer. This is an impossible standard for any person.

So, how can leaders manage all these areas—and manage them well? They must surround themselves with dependable employees who are capable and proficient—ideally, even experts—at doing their jobs. But that's only part of the equation. These employees must be comfortable proactively giving their leaders the most current and complete information. They should be willing to provide solid, honest, and timely feedback, even when it is not positive. They must be bold enough to challenge their leaders by asking the right questions, even when it is uncomfortable or unpopular to do so. Only when all these elements are in place will leaders have the information and perspective to make the best decisions possible.

In the story above, Joe is such an employee. He had the energy and willingness to do detailed research, provide meaningful feedback to Margarite, and track the results of piloted changes. Joe's positive rapport with Margarite gave him the confidence to provide this honest, timely, and constructive input without fear of retribution.

However, bold employees like Joe can be difficult to find. Many leaders are surrounded by employees who are more similar to Margarite's first two store managers; consequently, these leaders rarely receive all the information they need to make fully informed decisions. Sometimes, whether they realize it or not, they are left completely in the dark. This occurs for a few reasons.

Why Don't Employees Want to Communicate?

Information Inhibitor 1: Leaders hire people who are similar to themselves. As humans, we gravitate toward people who think, act, and live similarly to ourselves. Think of your seven closest friends. Their values, opinions, preferences, likes, and dislikes are probably close to your own. Because you are a human being first and a business leader second, the same may be true in your work life: You are frequently surrounded by employees who think and act like you do. When this is the case, it can be difficult for any leader to receive business-related opinions that differ substantially from their own.

The Solution: Proactively and intentionally surround yourself with leaders and employees whose experiences, backgrounds, perspectives, and opinions are different from yours. For example, you might actively seek input from an employee with a different educational background or work history, or who is from a different generation. If your organization is national, you might seek counsel from leaders who work in different areas of the country. When it comes to filling your board of directors, you might seek members from different industries.

Bold Communication Can Mitigate Legal Risks

Staying apprised of all of the laws related to the employer-employee relationship is a near-impossible standard. According to the U.S. Department of Labor, there are approximately 180 federal laws that protect 150,000,000 employees in 10,000,000 workplaces from discrimination, harassment, or adverse action based on protected factors.[1] Many employers and leaders make mistakes simply because they aren't aware that they are violating a law until after the error has been made. This lack of awareness can be costly to the employer.

To mitigate the risk of non-compliance, it is critical that employers encourage bold communication from their leaders and employees. When any employee raises a concern, employers should take it seriously and determine whether it requires action.

Information Inhibitor 2: Employees feel that leaders are out of touch with their experiences. Employees may withhold their opinions because they believe their leader has never been in their position or, at the very least, has forgotten what it feels like to work on the "front lines." Often, these employees are right!

It's common for organizational leaders to be decades away from their entry-level position, to start their careers midway up the professional ladder immediately after graduating from college, or even to inherit an already-successful family business. Each of these leaders has different experiences and perspectives from many of the employees they manage. Certainly, they have not worked at a line-level, assistant, or staff position in a long time (or maybe ever). As a result, these leaders may be out of touch with the employees doing the day-to-day work of the organization, such as the line cooks, the data entry employees, or the widget-makers.

Whether correctly or not, many frontline employees believe that their leaders do not know what it feels like to support a family on a low hourly wage, navigate taking a day off when it means losing a day of pay, or budget wages to pay a doctor's bill without an employer benefit plan. Is it any wonder that they also assume leaders will not understand and/or care about their feedback and concerns regarding the workplace and the organization?

The Solution: Spend time on the "front lines." To ensure that leaders are empathetic and understanding of the work all employees do, it can be helpful for them to spend at least one day per quarter working next to line-level workers. This gives the leaders an opportunity to put employee opinions, complaints, and suggestions in context, and to see for themselves whether there are things in the working environment that need correction. Here are a few benefits that stem directly from frontline leader participation:

- Leaders will learn whether employees are speaking to clients and each other respectfully; whether correct information is being shared; whether employees are working as efficiently as possible; whether safety protocols are followed; whether additional training, tools, or equipment is needed in particular areas; and whether there is healthy communication in the workplace.

- When employees see their leaders doing the same tasks they are performing, a true "team" dynamic is created. "I won't ask you to do anything I wouldn't do myself" transitions from an empty phrase to a meaningful action. Over time, employees will begin to include their leaders in "us" (i.e., part of *their* team, shift, department, etc.) instead of seeing leaders as "them" (i.e., a separate group who may not understand the front line's concerns and struggles). It's especially impactful when leaders jump in to help during busy or stressful times. Don't underestimate the impact it can have when a leader helps to unload trailers, bus tables, or man a cash register.

- Perhaps most importantly, working alongside frontline employees will help leaders develop rapport and empathy. The more employees see their leaders working alongside them, interacting with them, and caring about them, the more willing they will be to boldly communicate—and the more opportunities they will have to do so. Leaders, meanwhile, will gain the perspective to truly understand what their people are saying and how best to support them.

Information Inhibitor 3: Employees feel intimidated by the power dynamic. Regardless of the level of authority you possess—whether you are the owner of the entire organization or a manager with authority over one person, there is a power dynamic at play. Specifically, there is an inherent imbalance of power: The employer or leader has (almost) all of it, and the employee has (almost) none. The decisions of the leader almost always directly and profoundly impact the employee and his or her family. Rarely is the converse true.

Consider this: If an employer decides to open or close a branch office, to keep or share profits, to increase or decrease employee compensation, to offer or take away benefits, to make risky or conservative business decisions, or to act honestly or dishonestly, employees may be *directly and profoundly* impacted. Each of these decisions can positively or negatively change the personal and financial well-being of an employee. Yet, despite the substantial effect these decisions have on employees, most—particularly line-level or staff employees—have little to no input into these decisions. No wonder employees may feel powerless.

An Employee's Impact

What can a single employee do that will have an equally profound impact on the employer? They cannot unilaterally decide to open or close a branch, to keep or share profits, to increase or decrease their own compensation, or to create a certain benefit package. They cannot force the employer to act in the best interests of the organization. The most impactful thing they can do is quit their job. This might put the employer in a jam for a while, but the impact is temporary; it lasts only until a new employee is hired and trained, or until a new system or process is put into place to absorb the employee's duties.

Sometimes, employees do not share information and opinions with employers not *just* because they are cognizant of their place in the organizational hierarchy, but because—like the first manager in Margarite's story—they are actively intimidated by a leader's power, whether real or perceived. I have known young lawyers who wouldn't dare speak to a senior partner—even though they have the same educational credentials and are working to accomplish the same goal for the same firm. If an employee and employer do not have a personal connection, the employee may view the business owner as they would a celebrity: someone they know but who does not know them.

Unfortunately, I have also known leaders whose behavior—ranging from patronizing to dismissive to abusive—lets subordinates know that they are the "less important" member of the team, and that their input is not valued, or sometimes, wanted at all.

Whatever the particular dynamic in your organization might be, all leaders must understand that employees whose names or positions appear below theirs in an organization chart may be limited in what they feel comfortable saying.

The Solution: Create a culture of psychological safety. To elicit bold communication from your people, all employees must feel that they and their efforts are truly valued, and that they will not be punished, belittled, or retaliated against for volunteering information, making a suggestion, taking appropriate risks, or seeking feedback. Remember, as I shared in the introduction, many employees say their jobs feel tenuous. A culture of psychological safety will help them feel more secure in their positions, and what's more, it will strengthen their loyalty to your organization.

Truthfully, most of this book can be seen as an unofficial manual on how to create a culture of psychological safety. Many of the "dos" and "don'ts" I share are meant to ensure that employees feel recognized, appreciated, fairly treated, respected, and supported. That said, here are a few brief tips to help you nurture an environment where employees feel emboldened and *want* to give feedback:

- **Let employees know you want to hear from them...** Tell leaders and employees that it is okay to make a suggestion for improvement or to disagree with a current practice or policy.
- **...And tell them multiple times.** This message must be given frequently and may be done in writing (in an email or policy, for example) or verbally. Regardless, the most important thing is to make sure the message reaches every leader and every employee.
- **Make sure you are accessible.** Don't just give out your email address; take every opportunity to be present and speak with your people face-to-face. Be a present, active listener in all conversations. (In other words, stay curious...and keep your phone in your pocket!)
- **Respond thoughtfully to every communication.** If an employee volunteers information but the communication is never acknowledged, that person will feel disgruntled, overlooked, and unimportant. Even if their feedback is not valuable or accurate, you can still respond with a sincere, "Thank you for taking the time to let me know." If you are unable

to act on a suggestion or must deny an employee's request, be sure to explain why.

- **Publicly praise employees for giving feedback.** When an employee boldly communicates with you, acknowledge it! Thank them for their suggestion in a meeting. Send an organization-wide email saying, "Emiko brought x, y, z to my attention, and thanks to the information she shared, I am making the following changes." When employees see their peers being recognized for having the courage to come forward, they will want to do the same.

- **Treat employees with compassion when mistakes are made.** It's especially important for leaders to be fully informed when an employee makes a mistake, when a process doesn't work, or when metrics aren't ideal. Yet these are the instances when employees are most reluctant to communicate boldly. Often, they are afraid of being embarrassed, punished, or berated. No one wants to be the bearer of bad news.

  Be very mindful of how you react when someone voluntarily tells you that they made a mistake. If it was an honest mistake (in other words, not the result of negligence or willfully breaking the rules), thank the employee for coming to you. Get curious (but not judgmental) about why the mistake happened, and then work with the employee to fix it. Sometimes this might involve filling in a knowledge or skill gap for the employee or for the entire organization. Bottom line: When employees voluntarily bring you "bad news," you'll know you've achieved a culture of psychological safety.

Information Inhibitor 4: Employees put their own interests ahead of the organization's well-being. This doesn't make them "bad" employees; rather, they may be primarily concerned with retaining their positions. (Who isn't?) These people avoid negative attention that might result in retaliation by agreeing with the top decision-maker, rather than proactively making positive changes that benefit others. (I call these people "Pragmatists"—we'll look at them in more detail soon.)

The Solution: Connect employees with the organization's purpose. Do an honest appraisal of the employees you consult with most frequently to ensure that you are surrounded by leaders with a "team-first" attitude, rather than a "me-first" attitude. The first step in facilitating this attitude shift is creating a culture of psychological safety, which we have just covered. People who don't feel safe will naturally focus on their own survival, not the team's.

The second step is ensuring that employees understand what the organization's goals, mission, and/or purpose are, and how their role directly supports those things. When they see how their jobs support the organization's success—and when their contributions are recognized and valued—they will naturally start to consider what's best for the organization. Here are some ways to help your employees connect to purpose:

- **Invite employees to help create your mission, vision, values, and/or purpose statement.** If this language hasn't already been created, get your people's input. Ask them questions like, *How does our organization help other people or make their lives better? How does our work positively impact the community (be it local or global)? What would you like our organization to be known for? What makes you proud to come to work each day?* Use your employees' responses to craft a statement that they feel is accurate, meaningful, and inspiring.

- **Point out how employees support your organization's purpose as often as possible.** Even after creating a thoughtful purpose statement, some employees may have trouble connecting their daily tasks to that overarching mission. Point out these connections as often as you can. For instance: *Steve, thank you for spending such a long time reconciling the books. Because of your commitment to accuracy, I was able to confidently budget for some updated equipment next quarter. Our technicians will be able to provide faster, less expensive service to our customers.* It's easy to imagine Steve feeling more confident about bringing ideas and concerns to his leader in the future.

- **Keep your purpose front and center.** Consistently remind employees *why* they do what they do. Post your purpose statement in the break room. Print it on promotional t-shirts. Open or close team meetings by repeating it. Publicly recognize employees who go above and beyond to fulfill that purpose, or who boldly provide you with information that allows you to do the same. When the organization's purpose is top-of-mind, employees will be more likely to communicate in a way that advances it.

- **Empower employees to make decisions that impact the business positively.** In other words, give employees—especially frontline employees—the power to proactively help customers and live out your organization's purpose *without* needing to involve a leader. For instance, Chick-fil-A employees can give $5 gift cards to customers who have been waiting in line for a long time. When employees know they are trusted to make good decisions on behalf of the business, they will be more invested in supporting its success. Often, that support will come in the form of authentic communication with leaders.

- **Ask employees to share examples of colleagues who have lived the company's purpose.** Doing so allows two employees to shine, reinforces the company's purpose, and provides a positive example for other employees. Asking employees to recognize one another can be a regular agenda item in all-employee meetings or department meetings. This practice should occur at higher levels, too. For example, members of the board of directors and advisory committee(s) should be able to state the company's purpose, verbalize how decisions made at the board level are consistent with the purpose, and share stories about how the purpose is driving frontline employees' actions. (To that end, collect peer recognition stories that are shared in employee meetings and disseminate them to senior leaders weekly or monthly.)

The Ritz-Carlton: A Team Focused on Bold Service

The Ritz-Carlton is well known for providing the highest level of customer service. In fact, its employees are authorized to spend up to $2,000 of the hotel's money to ensure that guests have the best possible experience—especially if there has been a lapse in service. Talk about empowering employees to ensure their organization's well-being!

I have been the recipient of the Ritz-Carlton's above-and-beyond service twice, albeit on a smaller scale. On one occasion, I asked to purchase some cookies before checking out, but the concierge informed me that they hadn't been baked for the day yet—so the Ritz surprised me by mailing me a dozen.

On the second occasion, the cleaning staff at the Washington, D.C., Ritz accidentally took souvenir glasses that my young daughter Virginia and I had purchased. When the glasses couldn't be located, the Ritz mailed

Virginia a Ritz teddy bear and a pink "Future First Lady" t-shirt. (Virginia was thrilled, but I was a little mystified about why she was relegated to "First Lady." Why not "Future President"? But that's another story…)

My point is, the Ritz's employees clearly feel empowered to make decisions and take actions that enhance the customer experience. With this level of trust from their employer, it's likely that they also feel comfortable boldly communicating their thoughts, suggestions, and concerns.

Four Types of (Not-So-Bold) Employees

As you determine which of these common "information inhibitors" may be preventing bold communication in your organization, remember that employees are human beings with unique emotions, fears, goals, personalities, and abilities. Understanding why they may be unwilling to share information will help you change their behavior, especially on an individual level.

Let's take a closer look at four different types of employees: Peace Makers, Pragmatists, Disengaged, or Detractors.

The Peace Makers. Peace Makers may not tell their leader what they are really thinking because they genuinely care about that leader as a human being. They don't look at their employer and other leaders as "the company." Because they see their leaders as people and don't want to hurt their feelings or create tension in the workplace, they choose not to rock the boat. They know that pointing out mistakes or missteps could be hurtful or embarrassing for the employer.

Peace Makers are loyal, engaged, and care very much about the success of the organization. They value positive organizational changes and personal recognition for a job well done. They tend to be long-term employees, *want* to share their ideas, *want* to be actively engaged in their work, and care deeply about the success of the people who make up the organization. For these reasons, they will benefit the most from being encouraged to share their ideas. Once they realize that their employer truly desires bold communication—even if it isn't positive—this will become one more way for them to deliver their best performance.

The Pragmatists. As I mentioned earlier in this chapter, some employees don't tell their employers and leaders what they are really thinking because they are Pragmatists who choose to fly under the radar. It is often easier, and less risky, for an employee to keep their opinions to themselves than to potentially upset their leader and worry about retaliation. These employees understand that retaliation can result in termination, which in turn would mean:

- The loss of an income (*How will I pay next month's rent/mortgage/day care/ braces/tuition/medical/child support/car payment?*)
- The loss of health insurance (*Can I afford coverage and medical care without an employer-sponsored plan?*)
- The loss of a savings vehicle and/or a complete change in retirement or financial planning (*I am partially—or fully—vested in a 401(k). What would this mean for my retirement? Will I have to dip into my savings if I can't find a new job soon?*)
- The loss of accrued paid time off, vacation time, or sick leave (*My family has a vacation planned for later this year, and I rely on PTO when my child is sick and can't attend school. What if I am unable to find another job with these benefits?*)
- The loss of status or reputation in a community (*Being fired would embarrass me and my family. Most people wouldn't understand what really happened; they would assume it was because I was incompetent.*)
- The loss of their fellowship with coworkers (*I really like the people I work with, and I don't want to let them down by leaving.*)

The good news is, Pragmatists desire to be part of a successful organization and will communicate if they are given a safe opportunity to do so—hence the importance of creating a culture of psychological safety. Once they transition from feeling that their jobs are tenuous to feeling that they are secure, Pragmatists will often become Peace Makers.

The Disengaged. This group of employees are completely discouraged and disengaged—but still employed. They aren't openly aggressive and don't actively try to disrupt operations; they simply don't feel that speaking up would benefit them or the organization. This is your "it's not worth it" group. In their minds, it is easier to go-along-and-get-along than to effect change. These middle-of-the-roaders are the worst producers: They will not leave their jobs but will not be productive.

In the story that opened this chapter, Margarite's second manager was disengaged. Although the manager felt comfortable providing feedback, she simply didn't want to because operational changes would have translated into more work for her.

The good news is that these employees can benefit from open communication and positive organizational changes by their employers and leaders. These employees can be reengaged; they desire a positive workplace and will be receptive to behavior changes by their leaders.

The Detractors. Like the Disengaged, these employees won't communicate what they are really thinking. These employees are unhappy *and* disengaged. Their job is simply a means to an end. They are less productive and therefore less profitable. But unlike their Disengaged peers, Detractors are actively toxic and are probably dragging strong employees down. Their unhappiness may not have anything to do with their employer's behavior. They will likely be unhappy regardless of where they work. Don't sweat it. These employees need to go: Let them be unhappy somewhere else.

The good news is that if you ask, the Peace Makers and Pragmatists will probably tell you who the Disengaged and Detractors are because they like working with like-minded employees. They do not like working with the Disengaged or the Detractors.

The challenge for employers is to reach the Peace Makers, the Pragmatists, and the Disengaged—to ask the right questions and really, really listen to what they have to say…while getting rid of any Detractors. This may, of course, result in uncomfortable conversations. That's okay.

In Conclusion

Employers and other leaders are human and want constructive feedback. They have a desire to improve and, like all employees, need information to do so. Imagine how difficult it would be for a student to assess their mastery of a subject if they went to school for an entire year and never received a grade. Leaders are the same; they cannot improve without honest, constructive, and bold feedback.

The difference is, it is a teacher's responsibility to provide students with feedback. In the workplace, the onus is usually on the leader to solicit it. Sometimes, leaders must put in quite a bit of effort to determine why employees aren't sharing information, and subsequently, what they can do to improve communication. Rest assured, the effort is worth it. You will gain a more accurate perspective of your business, the ability to better plan for the future, and stronger relationships with your people.

CHAPTER 2

Show Me You Care by Investing in Security to Keep Me Safe at Work

Ned's Story

Ned's Sports is a sporting goods store located in a strip mall. The store hours are from 9:00 a.m. to 9:00 p.m., Monday through Saturday. The other businesses in the strip mall close an hour or two earlier, but Ned likes his store to stay open until 9:00 p.m. because the coaches and families who patronize his business often stop by in the evening hours after games, competitions, and practices have ended.

Ned values the safety of his employees and his customers. Before he signed the lease to the store, he negotiated additional lighting in all parking areas. Ned incurred extra expense by installing cameras on the interior and exterior of the building. He also installed a very low-tech system to alert the staff and other customers when someone new enters the building: a bell that rings each time the door opens. This simple little bell causes employees to look at the door and notice the person walking through, creating added situational awareness.

Ned also developed policies specifically aimed at ensuring the safety of employees, such as his "Never Walk Alone" policy. This policy requires at least two employees to exit the building together any time it is dusk or dark outside. During the holiday season, Ned's protocols require two bank deposits per day to avoid accumulating a lot of cash in the store, thereby dissuading would-be thieves.

As a result of Ned's forethought and vigilance, his employees and customers enjoy added safety and security. While many customers take these security measures for granted (if they notice them at all), Ned's employees are very aware that he cares about them and prioritizes their well-being. As a result, they are loyal and committed to putting forth their best efforts.

The Takeaway

When most people think of safety and health in the workplace, work-related injuries are usually the first thing that comes to mind: an employee getting hurt on the job due to a mistake or oversight, for example. These injuries are generally caused by accidents, are unintentional, and often do not rise to the level of OSHA violations. They are often remedied by state workers' compensation programs.

In this chapter, we'll be focusing on a second, often more serious type of harm: intentionally committed workplace violence.

It's an unfortunate truth that any time multiple human beings are in contact with one another, there is a potential—no matter how miniscule—for violence. That certainly holds true in the workplace. It is an employer's responsibility to take reasonable measures to provide employees and customers with a safe, secure experience. (This is something Ned does an excellent job of!)

Not only is prioritizing security the ethical thing to do, it benefits employers financially. When employees like Ned's feel safe, their loyalty, morale, and motivation increase (all of which customers notice and appreciate). Customers themselves are more likely to patronize a business that has taken steps to make them feel physically comfortable and safe.

While investing in security will probably involve a financial outlay, the money you stand to save—through reduced turnover, increased sales, and a decreased likelihood of theft or vandalism—likely outweighs the initial expenditure. And I'm here to tell you that the cost of reasonable security measures is almost always less than what you'll be on the hook for in legal fees and potential damages if you are sued by an employee or customer.

To prevent any type of intentional workplace violence, employers first must understand what workplace violence is and then assess their unique risk based on their industry, employee population, geography, and safety measures. Let's break it down.

What Is Workplace Violence?

First, let's look at the official definition. According to the CDC and the National Institute for Occupational Safety and Health (NIOSH), workplace violence is:

…the act or threat of violence, ranging from verbal abuse to physical assaults directed toward persons at work or on duty. The impact of workplace violence can range from psychological issues to physical injury, or even death. Violence can occur in any workplace and among any type of worker, but the risk for fatal violence is greater for workers in sales, protective services, and transportation, while the risk for nonfatal violence resulting in days away from work is greatest for healthcare and social assistance workers.[1]

Three Federal Agencies Focused on Safety

The United States has several federal agencies committed to ensuring the safety of American employees in the workplace.

- The United States Department of Labor has a division called the Occupational Safety and Health Administration, which is more commonly known as OSHA. OSHA's overarching goal is to protect the safety and health of every single employee in the workplace. This goal is very broad and covers every sort of safety: preventing simple slips and falls, ensuring that workers are provided with personal protective equipment and Safety Data Sheets, and inspecting facilities to ensure that workspaces are safe.
- The United States Department of Labor also oversees the Bureau of Labor Statistics, which provides a wide range of labor statistics. Among them are statistics on employment, wages, inflation, productivity, and (you guessed it!) workplace violence.
- The Centers for Disease Control and Prevention (CDC), based in Atlanta, Georgia, is also concerned with employee safety. Its mission is to protect Americans at work and at home from health, safety, and security threats of all kinds. A super spotlight is placed on the

CDC during times of crisis involving public health, such as during the COVID-19 pandemic.

According to the most recent Bureau of Labor Statistics reports at the time this book was published, 20,050 private sector employees experienced workplace trauma from non-fatal violence in 2020. Within this group:

- 73% were female
- 62% were between the ages of 25 to 54
- 76% worked in the healthcare and social assistance industry
- 22% required 3 to 5 days away from work to recover
- 22% required 31 or more days away from work to recover.[2]

In the same report, the Bureau of Labor Statistics shares that 392 American employees were victims of homicide in the workplace in 2020. Of these:

- 81% were male
- 44% were between the ages of 25 to 54
- 30% were performing retail-related tasks.[3]

One incidence of workplace violence is too many, but 20,050 intentional incidents of harm and 392 deaths seem overwhelming. (And, given that this data was collected in 2020, one wonders if these numbers were smaller than they otherwise might have been due to the widespread COVID-19 lockdowns and business closures.)

What Are the Consequences to Employers If Workplace Violence Occurs?

Harm to an employee, whether caused by intentional workplace violence or an unintentional accident, is generally covered by an employer's workers' compensation insurer. Employers with large loss ratios pay more in workers' compensation premiums.

Workers' Compensation Provides a Win-Win

The workers' compensation system is designed to be a win-win for employers and employees. Workers' compensation laws are created by state legislators. Claims brought by employees against employers for on-the-job injuries are heard by workers' compensation judges, who generally adjudicate only workers' compensation matters.

For employers, the workers' compensation system provides predictability because both the employer and the employee know what to expect. The employer's workers' compensation premium is set by an insurance carrier according to the type of job each employee performs and the employer's experience rating.

For employees, there is no fault assessment. If an employee is injured as a result of an on-the-job accident, the employee's medical expenses and partial wages are paid for a period of time. This period varies from state to state, but the goal of every state is to provide a security net that allows the employee to take the time necessary to heal and then return to work.

That said, *intentional* incidents of workplace violence can be much more costly. In most states, if an employee is harmed as a result of an employer's gross negligence, the employee may seek a legal remedy in tort, *outside of* workers' compensation. A tort claim based on gross negligence would not be heard by a workers' compensation judge and would not be subject to the limits that apply to workers' compensation claims. For these reasons, tort claims based on gross negligence are much riskier than workers' compensation claims.

Gross negligence is understood to have occurred when predictable or intentional harm could have been prevented had an employer acted based on information they knew or should have known. In some states, gross negligence can result in compensatory damages *and* punitive damages, which are monies paid by an employer over and above an employee's direct losses. Punitive damages are calculated to punish the employer at fault, and to deter all employers from the action or inaction that resulted in the harm.

Finally, an employer (or property owner) can also be liable in tort to third parties (e.g., non-employees, such as customers, clients, vendors, patients, etc.) if the third parties are harmed by workplace violence on the employer's property and the predictable or intentional harm could have been prevented had an employer taken action based on information they knew or should have known.

Yes, that's a lot of complex language. But it all boils down to this: It is imperative that employers recognize what workplace violence is and how to prevent it. Failure to do so can be incredibly costly—certainly, from a financial standpoint, but also to your organization's reputation and productivity.

How Can Employers Determine Their Level of Risk?

Knowing your industry's risk is critical. OSHA identifies specific factors that make certain types of employees more likely to experience workplace violence. According to an OSHA directive, you should take focused precautions to proactively prevent workplace violence if you have employees who work in these capacities:

- Contact with the public
- Exchange of money
- Delivery of passengers, goods, or services
- Having a mobile workplace such as a taxicab
- Working with persons in healthcare, social service, or criminal justice settings
- Working alone or in small numbers
- Working late at night or during early morning hours
- Working in high-crime areas
- Guarding valuable property or possessions
- Working in community-based settings, such as drug rehabilitation centers and group homes[4]

These risk factors make sense. Here are a few examples of how they might play out in real-world settings:

- In some retail establishments, cash is frequently used as currency. This can create an opportunity for theft by third parties, which can result in harm to employees. Theft and related violence are particularly likely if the retail business is open late at night; has few employees working at the same time; or is located in a low-traffic, high-crime, or poorly lit area.

- Harm is more likely when employees work in high-stress professions, such as healthcare and law. People visiting healthcare facilities or law firms are generally not there for good news or because they want to be there. Few people visit doctors just to report good health, and few people visit lawyers to determine how to protect their lottery winnings! Instead, people visiting healthcare facilities and law offices are often facing stressful situations and might hear bad news. Employers in those industries would be wise to consider safety measures such as training employees to recognize and respond to patients and clients in distress, and creating communication systems to alert the proper person or authority when a risk is present.

- In the bar, restaurant, and hospitality industries, patrons sometimes consume too much alcohol, which creates opportunities for unsafe situations. Employers in those industries may want to consider safety measures including limiting the amount of alcohol employees are permitted to serve to a customer and hiring off-duty officers to monitor the establishment and handle any customer who becomes intoxicated or belligerent.

If You Aren't Sure of Your Level of Risk, Bring in Outside Expertise!

When it comes to assessing and addressing the risk of workplace violence, there's no need to simply do your best and hope it's enough. If you would like support in determining your organization's level of risk and deciding how to mitigate it, an employment law attorney will be able to help you. Some industries and professional organizations provide resources to help business owners address risk. Finally, there are entire businesses dedicated to assessing risk and consulting with client organizations to mitigate those risks.

How Can Employers Mitigate the Risk of Workplace Violence?

First, implement OSHA's suggested actions. Based on OSHA's suggestions, here are some actions employers can take to reduce the possibility of violence or other intentional harm in the workplace, or to mitigate its impact if it does occur.[5] Not all of these suggestions apply to every workplace, so I encourage you to review this list and determine which safety precautions make sense for your organization. Employers with multiple establishments may determine that some recommendations are appropriate for some locations but not others.

Install physical barriers such as bullet-resistant enclosures or shields, pass-through windows, or deep service counters. If your organization is in a high-risk location, open late at night, or has low traffic, this is an inexpensive and practical way to provide safety. These barriers also help protect employees from and prevent the spread of contagious germs. They became much more widespread during the COVID-19 pandemic and are common during annual flu seasons.

Install alarm systems, panic buttons, and/or radios. These systems are particularly helpful for employees who have direct interaction with the public, such as tellers at banks and credit unions, receptionists, and clerks at retail stores. Panic buttons and radios in particular are often placed discreetly under an employee's desk or on a nearby wall in an easy-to-reach but inconspicuous location.

Provide convex mirrors, an elevated vantage point, and/or clear visibility of service in cash register areas. Product placement and signage are important as well—they should not block the view of employees who need to see people entering and exiting the business. Blocking the view of the interior of the business from the street is not advisable either. It is harder for a person to rob a store with uncovered windows and adequate lighting than it is to rob a store where windows are covered with advertisements.

Install bright and effective interior and exterior lighting. This makes it easier for others to see behaviors inside and outside of the building. The possibility of being observed may be a deterrent to some people who are considering violent behaviors; if not, bright lighting makes it more likely that other employees, customers, or bystanders will notice the behavior and call law enforcement.

In the event of an injury that occurs in a parking lot, storage room, or other company-owned area, the adequacy of lighting will always come up in subsequent investigations.

Ensure that your organization has adequate staffing. Remember what your mom said: "There is safety in numbers." It's 100 percent true. Employees who work alone are more likely to be harmed. If possible, it is always preferable to have more than one person present at a worksite.

Arrange furniture to prevent entrapment. It is easy to test whether furniture creates hurdles, barriers, or bottlenecks for employees. Do an exit-the-building exercise as if there were a robbery or a fire. If all of your employees cannot exit the building swiftly and safely, you may need to reconsider the layout of your furniture and doors.

Establish procedures for cash-handling controls that utilize drop safes, where cash can be inserted (but not removed without a key or code). Not only will this enhance employee safety, it will help prevent employee theft.

Install height markers on exit doors. Would-be criminals do not want to frequent places that have easy methods of identifying them upon entry or exit. Of course, these should be installed correctly. They're useless if they're improperly placed on the wall!

Establish emergency procedures in case of robbery. Employees should be trained on the best way to stay safe in a given situation—which likely includes immediately cooperating with any monetary demands, using the panic button, or calling 911 once it is safe to do so.

In particular, employees should be able to identify hazardous situations and be trained on appropriate responses in emergencies. Employees should understand when to intervene and when to back away. Train and retrain your employees so the responses become second nature. Remember that money can be replaced; people cannot. Your message to employees should be clear: There is no amount of money in a cash register and there is no item in a store that is worth an employee losing his or her life.

Install video surveillance equipment, in-car surveillance cameras, and/or closed-circuit TVs. Video surveillance equipment can deter some individuals from targeting a particular business for theft or other types of violence. And if a crime *does* occur, video footage can help law enforcement identify the perpetrator and prove that a crime took place.

That said, it is critical that employers understand their obligations with respect to recording devices. State law often governs the use of these technologies.

- Some states allow audio and video recording without notice to patrons and/or employees.

- Other states allow some combination of audio or video recording *only* if employees and/or patrons are notified in writing that the recording device is in place.
- Some states allow full audio (without video) as long as one party consents to the recording.
- Other states require two-party consent to audio (without video) recording.
- If you are an employer with establishments in multiple states, you may be allowed to use different technologies and have different notice obligations for each location.

All states have laws regarding preservation of evidence. If there is an incident of violence at work, electronic records must be maintained. They may not be altered, deleted, or modified lest the employer be accused of spoliation of evidence.

Establish a relationship with local police. This is probably the very best advice OSHA or I can give you. Get to know those who took an oath to protect and serve the public. They genuinely care about the safety of their communities, and their very presence can be the best preventive measure.

Determine if additional protective measures are necessary. The above advice was based on OSHA's guidance, and it is sound. Based on my own experience as an employment law attorney, I would like to add a few more actions employers can take to protect themselves, their employees, and their customers from workplace violence. Depending on your industry, geography, and physical structure, you may want to:

Have a written and well-disseminated policy outlining a no-tolerance-for-violence policy. The policy should:
- Specifically state that even jokes about violence, or threats that are camouflaged as jokes, are not allowed in the workplace
- Clearly provide information regarding how to report threats or violence— ideally, you want to include a telephone number or an email address (or even better, both) so that employees can quickly contact a supervisor or owner who has authority to take action
- Contain an anti-retaliation provision to encourage the immediate reporting of meritorious concerns and to discourage the reporting of false claims
- Contain an investigation procedure so employees who make reports will know exactly what action steps will be taken and when

- Provide training on how to recognize and prevent violence from occurring
- Notify employees of the consequences of violating the policy

Offer a free or reduced-cost confidential Employee Assistance Program. The Employee Assistance Program, or EAP, should ideally provide counseling or mental health therapy for employees who are experiencing trauma, financial problems, extreme stress, or any condition that might make them consider harming themselves or someone else. Investing in the mental health of your employees not only helps prevent violence, it also sends a clear signal that you care deeply about their well-being. For more information about EAPs, see Chapter 11: Your Generosity Makes a Lasting Impact.

Where allowed, do legally compliant background checks in accordance with state law. Your goal is to do everything possible to make sure employees are appropriately hired for specific jobs. In some cases, a background check report may indicate that a job candidate has a history of violent behavior. See Chapter 4: My Background Isn't Perfect, But I Will Still Be an Awesome Employee for more information on how to request and properly read background check reports.

Conduct periodic (at least annual) trainings for every single employee on what to do in the event of a safety emergency. While OSHA recommends establishing emergency procedures and training employees on what to do if a robbery occurs, I recommend expanding that training's scope to *all* safety emergencies, be it a belligerent customer, a bomb threat, or something else.

This training should always include a review of the workplace safety policy and a review of the what-to-do-if protocol. Ensure that your employees know how to notify you (or law enforcement) of a problem, and that they know where to go for safety.

If Your Business Is Based in California, Training Isn't Optional

Beginning July 1, 2024, most California employers will be required to implement an interactive workplace violence policy and training program. Senate Bill 553 requires employers to conduct training designed to prevent and react to workplace violence.[6] The first training must occur on or before July 1, 2024, and be conducted at least annually thereafter. The training must be comprehensive and allow employees to ask questions of an employer representative with knowledge about the plan.

The written plan must have specific information, including the name and title of the person(s) responsible for the policy and training program, as well as detailed information on how to respond to violence or a threat of violence.

The law exempts employees who work remotely and some specific industries, such as employers already covered by Cal/OSHA.

This is an overview, not a complete list of the law's requirements. The law is comprehensive and specific, and employers may find it helpful to engage a seasoned human resources leader, an employment attorney, or a third-party professional to draft a compliance policy and plan.

Establish a code word or code phrase that lets other employees know there is the potential for a problem, or an actual problem. The code phrase can be innocuous, such as, "The paper has arrived," or, "I need a green pen immediately." If this phrase is said out loud, texted, or emailed, the employee(s) who receive the message know exactly how to react.

Hire additional security if appropriate. The presence of a security officer or an off-duty law enforcement officer often acts as a deterrent for someone who might otherwise harm an employee. If your organization cannot afford a full-time officer on site, consider hiring a part-time law enforcement officer or security expert on a rotating and unpredictable basis. This person might be in a security uniform, in a law enforcement uniform (if permissible), or in plain clothes.

Require that employees use the buddy system. For instance, if employees are exiting the building at night or in unsafe locations, require them to do so in groups of two or more. Ned had the right idea in the story at the beginning of this chapter!

Most importantly, take all reported concerns about safety seriously. Get your human resource, legal, and/or risk management teams involved immediately, even if the report seems improbable.

Words You Never Want to Hear

The worst thing that can happen after an incident is for an employee to say, "I was afraid, but I didn't know what to do, where to go, or how to make a report."

Wait...I take that back. The worst thing that can happen after an incident is for an employee to say, "I followed the policy and made a report, but no one listened."

In Conclusion

Safety and security are at the heart of employer-employee relations. They are the foundation upon which successful businesses are built. Without a solid foundation, any effort to improve employee retention, create a positive culture, or improve productivity will likely not succeed. Investing in employees' safety is a wise legal strategy because it makes violence less likely to happen. Investing in employees' safety is a wise business strategy because it sends a message to employees that you genuinely care about their well-being.

Hiring, Wages, and Termination

If You Want to Reduce Turnover, Focus on My Satisfaction from the Interview Forward

Sam's Story

Sam is the sole proprietor of a small law firm where she practices criminal defense. Despite her best efforts, she cannot hold on to employees. Sam spends a lot of time advertising, interviewing, and hiring. During interviews, Sam focuses on what the applicants can bring to the organization. During onboarding, she teaches employees the technical portions of their jobs. After the new hires are trained, Sam is most concerned with her employees' productivity and quality of work.

Sam's employees' average tenure is about one year. As a result of this near-constant turnover, Sam is inefficient, frustrated, and short-tempered. She is not able to focus on practicing law.

Sam has never thought to ask what she could do to improve the workplace environment or to measure the satisfaction of existing employees. She has not asked departing employees why they resigned. As a result, Sam is unaware of the things she could do to improve her hiring practices to make better selections. She is also unaware of the things she could do to improve the satisfaction and retention rate of her current employees.

Sam's lack of information is costing her a fortune in time, effort, and expense. It is costing her indirectly as well, because the constant turnover is impacting client satisfaction.

Know Your Leadership Type

There are a few types of employers. One type is genuinely curious about their applicants' and employees' short- and long-term professional goals. This type attempts to select employees with the correct skills and the highest likelihood of long-term success and happiness.

The second type—like Sam—is focused on the technical aspects of the job, to the exclusion of everything else. These employers tend to lose employees at a rapid rate.

And, of course, some employers are a hybrid of these two types.

I want to make it clear that none of these types is inherently better than the others. Each type of employer tends to have particular strengths and weaknesses that play out in different ways beyond the hiring process. What is important is that all leaders be willing to engage in personal introspection about where they fall on the leadership spectrum.

You must be aware of what type of organization you run, what its goals are, what you tend to focus on, and what your employees might need more (or less) of from you. And you must be willing to engage in learning and self-development as you work toward taking a balanced approach to supporting your employees *and* your business. (I'm guessing that's why you're reading this book—so you are already on your way!)

The Takeaway

A lot of research has been done on how costly turnover is. Some research estimates that turnover costs employers one and a half or two times an employee's annual compensation. Other research assigns a specific dollar amount to turnover. There is not *any* research to suggest that turnover is good for morale, does not cost employers anything, or creates positive revenue. The bottom line is simple: Constant change of this nature saps momentum for employees and leaders alike.

Change Isn't Necessarily a Bad Thing

Employees are not against change itself. Change can be very good—when necessary and for good reasons. Employees understand and agree with positive change. Employees do not understand or agree with negative change.

Reducing turnover improves the workplace for everyone and is good for an employer's bottom line. To discover the root cause(s) of turnover, employers should address employee satisfaction at the pre-employment stage, the current-employment stage, *and* the post-employment stage.

Approach Pre-Employment Thoughtfully

Ask Yourself: *What Do I Want in an Employee?*

Before beginning the search for an employee, an employer must know what they are looking for when filling a particular position. An employer must have a clear understanding of the specific skills they are seeking and the day-to-day expectations of the job. This might include specific educational or licensure credentials necessary to perform the job.

For example, Sam needs to consider whether she is looking for a person with a legal assistant or paralegal background; a paralegal certificate or degree; and/or relevant, specific prior experience in the area of criminal law. Sam also needs to determine her expectations related to days and hours of work, whether the position is remote or traditional, and the hourly rate she is willing to pay based on these objective criteria. Finally, Sam needs to consider whether the position will be client-facing. If so, whomever she hires must possess excellent listening skills and a positive customer service attitude.

Interviews with candidates who do not want to work in the criminal law area, who expect higher compensation than Sam is willing to pay, or who do not want to work on the days/hours needed are not a good use of time. Therefore, having these details nailed down and clearly stated in all job postings will help Sam use her time efficiently. Her candidate pool will be limited to qualified applicants who understand her expectations.

Prepare for the Interview

There are several steps to conducting an interview that will result in finding the right employee:

First, make sure interviews are conducted by somebody with experience! This is not necessarily the business owner or even the position's supervisor. To avoid inadvertently asking illegal questions, the interview should ideally be conducted by somebody in the human resources department. If your organization is not large enough to have a human resources department, contact your employment lawyer, who can quickly review the questions you intend to ask to ensure they are all legal. This is a good investment of your time and money because you can use the same interview template each time you interview for this position, which allows you to make an apples-to-apples comparison of candidates.

Get curious about the applicant's goals. During the interview process, interviewers need to ask applicants what *they* are looking for in a position. If an applicant is looking for a part-time position working directly with customers, then a full-time back-office accounting position is not going to be a good fit. (Hopefully your clearly written job posting will have weeded out most mismatches of this sort, but they do happen.)

If an applicant aspires to higher-level positions in a particular company but the open position does not have identifiable steps toward promotion opportunities, then that company may not be a good fit. Learning an applicant's long-term goals can help both parties determine if the applicant and the organization are good matches.

Make sure interview questions are relevant to the job description. If, like Sam, you are interviewing for a paralegal position, you probably don't need to discuss the accounting functions of the firm with candidates. However, questions about an applicant's knowledge of the local court system's online filing system probably *are* relevant to the position.

For instance, Sam might ask:
- "How many filings have you created using (name the specific system)?"
- "How many years have you worked with (name the specific system)?"
- "What challenges have you experienced with (name the specific system)?"

Why Do Interviewers Discuss Topics That Aren't Relevant to the Position?

Here are a few of many possible reasons:
- In my experience, many interviewers just wing it. Because they don't go into the interview with a pre-prepared list of questions, it's easy to get off-track.
- Many interviewers (often incorrectly) assume that the interviewee has done their research, knows what the organization does, and what the role requires.
- The interviewer may not be as familiar as they should be with the job description and what the role requires.
- The interviewer is trying to put the applicant at ease by "making conversation."

Avoid illegal questions at all costs! It is easy to ask an illegal question during a job interview (so easy, in fact, that I decided to give illegal questions their own section in this chapter). Often, interviewers don't realize that a question they're asking violates a state or federal law. Maybe they're simply curious about the candidate's background, or they're trying to put the candidate at ease by asking about the candidate's personal life. It doesn't matter what the interviewer's intentions are—these questions can land your organization in a lot of legal hot water.

Employers who ask illegal questions can easily find themselves being sued under a failure-to-hire theory of discrimination, actionable under federal and state law. For example, suppose Sam asks a candidate whether she has children. Suppose further that the candidate says yes, and then she and Sam have a nice conversation about the children. If Sam's business is located in a state with protection against familial status discrimination, *and* if Sam selects a different, more qualified candidate for the position, the candidate with the children will be able to state a *prima facie* case of discrimination. (*Prima facie* simply means that there is sufficient evidence to proceed to a trial on the merits.)

At trial, it will be up to Sam to prove that the candidate's parental status was NOT the reason for the decision. Sam will have to show that the candidate selected was objectively more qualified. If Sam is not able to do that, she may owe damages. Either way, Sam will likely have to pay an attorney to defend her—a costly proposition.

Even if you don't experience legal consequences after asking illegal questions, you could still alienate a great potential employee. Many illegal questions cross the line from professional to personal curiosity, which can feel intrusive and inappropriate.

What are illegal questions, anyway? Illegal questions can reveal somebody's sex, color, race, religion, national origin, age, marital status, handicap, or other factors that are protected by state or federal law. Avoid those questions at all costs—they are not relevant to the person's skills or ability to perform the job. Let's do a deeper dive into several categories of illegal questions that employers tend to ask:

Do not ask questions about age. For example:
- How old are you?
- When did you graduate from high school?
- When do you intend to retire?
- How much longer do you intend to work?

Employers should not ask an applicant's age, inquire about retirement, or make guesses or assumptions about either. Such inquiries violate the Age Discrimination in Employment Act (ADEA) and the Older Workers Benefit Protection Act (OWBPA) and are irrelevant to how well an applicant can do the job.

Shades of Gray

If you are doubtful that age impacts employability, take a moment and google Lisa LaFlamme, Canada's beloved news anchor who was allegedly fired in 2022 when she decided to stop coloring her hair and allowed it to return to its natural color: gray.

In numerous industries, older employees and job applicants face (often incorrect) perceptions about their grasp of technology, whether their skills are up-to-date, their ability to work with younger generations, and more. Potential employers tend to be especially concerned about older applicants' retirement plans, but increasingly, the reality doesn't match their assumptions.

In particular, the financial effects of the pandemic have changed some Americans' retirement forecasts. Twenty-four percent of Americans who responded to a survey conducted by Northwestern Mutual reported that they intend to work longer than they had before the pandemic.[1]

Accordingly, employers may be interviewing older-than-traditional applicants as people seek to make up savings lost as a result of the pandemic.

Here's the bottom line: No matter how old you *think* an applicant might be, remember that what you are really interested in is not their age; it's the depth and breadth of their *experience*.

Do not ask questions about relationship or familial status. For example:
- Are you married/divorced/single?
- Do you have children?
- Do you have childcare?
- What is the name of your spouse?
- Who do you live with?
- Do you own or rent your home?
- How many people live in your home?

Almost every state has laws preventing questions related to marital status and familial status. Many states also have specific protections for members of the

LGBTQ community. Responses to the above questions are irrelevant to how well an applicant can do the job they are applying for.

Many laws preventing gender- and family-based questions were enacted because their answers often discriminated against women in particular:

- Women who are unmarried (particularly younger women) are sometimes perceived as a high risk. Some employers fear they may quit working once they marry.
- Married women without children may be perceived as high risk; some employers fear they may quit working once they have children. Those employers are hesitant to invest training resources and time into employees who may not work for many years.
- Married women with children may be perceived as high risk because some employers fear they may be distracted at work because they have children who need attention.
- Unmarried women with children are often perceived as high risk because some employers worry they won't be able to balance work and family without spousal support.

If it sounds like women can't win, it's true…at least when employers cling to these outdated and inaccurate perceptions.

Come Fly the Sexist Skies!

Remember, it was not long ago that flight attendants had to be female, unmarried, and retire in their early 30s. Weigh-ins weren't uncommon. And if a flight attendant was pregnant? Forget about it! She was grounded.

These absurd notions need to cease. Women make up nearly half of the American workforce and assume the majority of the parenting and household responsibilities in families.[2]

What if you have concerns about whether an applicant can fulfill the schedule or travel requirements set forth in the job description? First, realize that there are many factors unrelated to gender or family status that might affect a candidate's ability to do so. Second, word your questions carefully. And third, ask these questions to every person you interview. You may ask the following:

- "This job requires that you be present between 7:00 a.m. and 5:00 p.m., Monday through Friday, and often requires evening or overtime hours. Sometimes the need for overtime is not known until the day of. Will that be a problem?"
- "This job requires periodic overnight travel. The travel is often within driving distance but may include multiple-night air travel. Are you able to do that?"

Think Creatively About Accommodations Before Dismissing a Candidate in a Legally Protected Category

Generally, applicants will volunteer the reason they are not able to work outside of normal hours, travel overnight, etc. Some of these reasons place the candidate in a legally protected category. For instance, if an applicant says he or she has to attend religious services at a certain time or on a certain day, or that he or she may not work during certain hours for religious reasons, the employer likely must determine whether it can accommodate the applicant's needs.

The same would be true if the applicant volunteers that he or she has scheduled medical appointments for a disability. Conversations on these topics should be limited to work expectations and scheduling accommodations needed. Before deciding that an accommodation is impossible, the employer should think creatively.

If, however, the applicant offers a reason that is not protected, the employer does not have to accommodate the applicant. We'll look more closely at accommodations in Chapter 21: Please Respect My Religion—But Don't Force Yours On Me.

Do not ask questions about disabilities. For example:
- Are you disabled in any way?
- Why do you have a cane/walker/wheelchair?
- Why are you limping?
- Do you have a (heart/lung/muscular/vision) problem?
- How many days of work did you miss last year because you were sick?
- Have you ever taken leave under the Family and Medical Leave Act, because of a workers' compensation injury, or under the Americans with Disabilities Act?

Unless it can be shown that health is a bona fide occupational qualification, these questions violate the Americans with Disabilities Act and are irrelevant to how well somebody could do the job that they are applying for. An excellent resource to review permissible inquiries under the ADA can be found at www.EEOC.gov/laws/guidance/job-applicants-and-ada.

What Is a Bona Fide Occupational Qualification?

A bona fide occupational qualification, or BFOQ, is an objective standard that an applicant must meet to qualify for a job. For example, an applicant seeking a job as a police officer may have to meet certain vision and fitness BFOQs. Being a member of the Catholic faith may be a BFOQ for teaching applicants at a Catholic school. Some federal contracts may contain citizenship requirements as BFOQs.

When it comes to health and disabilities, bona fide occupational qualifications often exist in fields such as firefighting, law enforcement, and interstate transportation because these fields are regulated by state and/or federal law. Those laws set the standard for health to ensure the safety of both the employee and the public they serve.

Before we move on, here's an important clarification: Being able to perform physical tasks like standing all day or lifting 50 pounds are *not* examples of BFOQs. However, employers *can* ask questions about a candidate's ability to perform these tasks if the job really requires them.

Do not ask questions about race, national origin, etc. For example:
- What is your native country?
- Where were you born?
- What sort of accent do you have?
- What is your national origin?

By now, you can probably guess what I'm going to say. This information is irrelevant…*unless* there is a bona fide occupational qualification related to applicants' and employees' national origin. For instance, some civilian positions on military bases and some positions in national security require employees to be United States citizens.

Don't Forget Form I-9

All U.S. employers must complete a Form I-9 (Employment Eligibility Verification) for each employee they hire in the United States. When completing the form, employees must provide documentation of their identity, citizenship status, and employment authorization—often by submitting documents like passports, driver's licenses, voter registration cards, school records, birth certificates, "green cards," etc. If an employer elects to keep copies of this supporting documentation for one employee, it must keep copies of supporting documentation for all employees.

Employers may elect to participate in the United States' E-Verify program, which allows employers to use a free, quick, and easy website to verify the employment eligibility of all employees.

If a position requires or contains a preference for a bilingual applicant, you may say:
- "As shown in the job description, we are seeking a candidate who is fluent in Spanish and English. Are you able to read, write, and speak both languages fluently?"

Play it safe—stick to the script. Earlier in this chapter, I suggested that you have either your human resources department or an employment lawyer review the questions you intend to ask in interviews. I want to reiterate that advice here. Even if you feel you have great interpersonal skills, even if you work in a "casual" office, even if you believe you are familiar with applicable laws—*don't* wing it. Always structure your interviews using pre-selected questions that directly relate to the job description. You will be less likely to ask an irrelevant or illegal question, and you will be more likely to make a valid, unbiased comparison of candidates' responses.

Onboarding a New Employee

You've hired a great candidate—congratulations! Now it's time to integrate your new team member into your organization as a whole and into their new position in particular. Onboarding is a critical component of a new employee's long-term success. Here are some best practices:

Consider pre-boarding new hires. This means doing all you can to strengthen the bond with a new hire *before* their actual first day. Once an offer has been extended and accepted, take actions to welcome the employee and create a sense of belonging within your organization. Ideas include:

- Providing the new employee's contact information so other team members can send a "welcome" email (Be sure to ask the new employee's permission before giving their personal email out!)
- Mailing the new employee a swag box with branded items
- Including the new employee in a social event, like lunch with team members

Provide relevant background information about your company and its culture. To give an employee an opportunity to succeed, they should be provided clear information about the company's history and origin, the company's culture, and the company's expectations.

Because the onboarding period is a time of first impressions, it is the perfect opportunity to share your company's mission, vision, and values, as well as any other things that make the company unique—such as mentoring programs or training opportunities. Onboarding allows a company to shine!

Make sure to review the compensation package. Onboarding should include a review of the employee's compensation package: salary, payment schedule, commission calculation method, overtime expectations, and a full review of benefits. New employees likely have a lot of questions about these things. Anticipating as many of those questions as you can—and having answers ready—will help solidify the employee-employer relationship from day one because it signals to the employee that your organization values its people and their concerns.

Enact a training schedule. A training schedule ensures that new employees receive all necessary information. In addition to ensuring that each employee is trained on how to perform day-to-day tasks, make sure you're covering categories like:

- **Technology, equipment, machinery, etc.** Remember, something that seems simple and familiar to you—like using your organization's telephone system or your warehouse's inventory management software—can feel overwhelming to a new employee. Onboarding should include training on every technology platform and every type of equipment or machinery the employee will be expected to use.
- **Policies applicable to the new employee's job.** If your organization has policies on important topics such as data or client privacy, the use of artificial intelligence, ownership of intellectual property, sharing or transferring data, telecommuting, use of personal devices during work hours, or any other rule or process you expect your employee to follow, you must share this information with the employee. After all, employees can't be expected to follow rules or policies they aren't aware of.
- **Important topics like privacy and confidentiality.** Training in this area is especially important because relevant laws and policies may not be intuitive. For instance, it is your responsibility to make sure new hires are in compliance with state laws such as the California Consumer Privacy Act or federal laws such as the Health Insurance Portability and Accountability Act.
- **Customer service expectations.** New employees should be paired with more experienced employees for training on customer service expectations. The new employee should know whom to ask if he or she has any questions. If the organization has a mentoring program, the new employee should be

paired with a mentor who will coach him or her on the non-technical aspects of the job on a longer-term basis.

Check in with the new hire regularly. Meeting with the new employee at the end of the first week, and again at the 30- and 60-day marks, will offer the new employee the opportunity to share what he or she has learned, provide feedback to his or her supervisor, and learn how he or she can improve performance.

Here's the bottom line: If an employee feels like onboarding is perfunctory, incomplete, or just another onerous task the organization has to check off, they will feel disconnected from the start. But if they feel that time and consideration were taken to help them adjust to their new role, their engagement and morale will start off at a higher level—and your organization will have created a solid foundation for longer-term satisfaction. All of this contributes to reduced turnover.

Retaining Great Employees

Often, employers *do* put time, thought, and consideration into hiring good employees and integrating them into the organization. But what happens when those employees are no longer considered "new hires," but full-fledged team members? How often do you check in with them to see what's going well and what isn't? To ensure that they feel appreciated and supported? To identify any barriers standing in their way and any goals they are working toward? To confirm that their performance is satisfactory and that they understand expectations?

If employees feel ignored, neglected, or unappreciated (even if it wasn't your intention to convey that message), they will likely also feel that their jobs are tenuous. They probably won't be satisfied in their roles, and sooner or later, they probably *will* begin looking for other positions.

That's why, once an applicant has been hired and onboarded as an employee, employers need to be intentional about periodically connecting with the employee and asking for feedback. I've heard this referred to as "re-recruiting," which is a good way to think about it. There are as many ways to do this as there are types of employers.

Informal feedback can be sought through daily interactions or through scheduled 1:1 meetings. It can be as simple as asking an employee how they are doing—and then pausing to really listen to the answer. Your goal with more casual types of feedback is to make employees feel noticed, appreciated, and valued.

Formal feedback requires more intention. It may occur on a one-on-one basis, in a group setting, or via written surveys. It can be sought bi-annually, annually, quarterly, or more frequently. The important thing is that feedback be sought in a thoughtful, strategic, and intentional manner. To make employees comfortable, employers should consider retaining a third-party vendor that specializes in employer/employee relations to build the questions and gather the feedback. This costs money but is an investment in the business's future.

Before you begin the process of gathering formal feedback, you should determine what will happen with the feedback you receive, and you should communicate that to your employees. When employees participate in surveys, they expect the company to use the information to improve processes and policies. If nothing is done with the feedback, employees will notice and will be less receptive to participating in a similar exercise in the future.

Good generic feedback questions include:

- Do you have the equipment you need to safely and efficiently perform your job?
- Does your supervisor treat you fairly?
- Do you have any safety concerns or know of policies or processes that may cause harm to others?
- Do you feel policies are consistently applied throughout the organization?
- Are you satisfied with your compensation?
- Are you satisfied with your benefit package?
- Do you understand the expectations of your position?
- Does your supervisor communicate with you on a consistent basis?
- Does your supervisor communicate with you in a respectful manner?
- Are you happy working with the organization?
- What would you change about the organization or your job?

You may also want to seek feedback on matters specifically related to your organization:

- Does (name of software) work efficiently? If not, what does it lack?
- Do you feel the (name of policy) is applied consistently?
- Are you adequately cross-trained on (name of task)?

Finally, if you assure employees that responses will be anonymous, the responses must, in fact, be anonymous. If employees learn that you reverse-engineered the responses to determine who might have made a particular statement or if you retaliate against an employee for their participation and candor, you have destroyed the integrity of the entire process and you will lose credibility with your employees. We'll look more closely at constructing and administering effective surveys in Chapter 14: Don't Ask for My Opinion If You Don't Want to Hear It…Or If You Don't Intend to Take Action.

Taking a Closer Look at Departing Employees Can Be Very Helpful

Sooner or later, employees will leave your organization. Some departures will be on positive—or at least neutral—terms, while others will be more negative. Digging into the details may feel uncomfortable at times, but employee resignations and terminations can be a valuable source of information regarding turnover: why it's happening, how often it's happening, and what you can do to reduce it.

First, look at length of employment. Rather than looking at a gross turnover rate, it may be more illuminating to calculate lengths of employment to see whether a pattern emerges.

You might examine this by tenure: Are you losing employees who have been with you less than two months? Are you keeping employees in the short term but losing them after a year? Are they staying longer than a year but less than the average length of employment in your industry? Does the data reveal that you are losing your long-term employees at a higher-than-expected rate?

You might examine this by department: Does the accounting department have consistent turnover while the sales department retains employees for long periods of time?

You also might consider forces outside of your control, such as an economic downturn, the pandemic, or the loss of a contract that necessitated a reduction-in-force.

You should also consider whether the turnovers are (a) voluntary, with notice, (b) voluntary, without notice, or (c) involuntary.

Second, conduct exit interviews. Once you determine whether there is a pattern, you can use exit interviews to learn more and determine what improvements can be made. Exit interviews are critical and, if possible, should be conducted with every employee who leaves an organization. They should also be approached with forethought, handled with sensitivity, and ideally, conducted by someone who has experience in this area. Chapter 9: If You Are Curious Why I Quit, Just Ask Me provides detailed information on conducting exit interviews, including when to conduct these interviews, formats you can use, and questions you can ask.

It is imperative that you consider the feedback you receive with an open mind. Some employee responses may not have merit. Others may. Look for themes or consistencies in what you're hearing. If more than one departing employee raises the same issue, then the issue is probably worth looking into.

As you begin to get a fuller picture of what turnover looks like in your organization and why it is happening, you will be in a position to make systemic improvements that will ultimately reduce turnover and improve the bottom line. Again, Chapter 9: If You Are Curious Why I Quit, Just Ask Me contains more detailed information on common things you might hear from employees and how to proceed.

Consider Customer Turnover, Too

The same strategies can be used by organizations experiencing customer, client, or patient turnover. Often, customers, clients, or patients are happy to share their experiences. This knowledge can help you improve your processes to create happy customers.

In Conclusion

Let's check back in with Sam, who couldn't seem to hang onto employees for much longer than a year at her small law firm. Despite the time and attention Sam puts into her business, her turnover problem was inevitable given that she did not:

- Determine in advance of the interview what she expected from new hires

- Conduct interviews with an eye toward ensuring the right applicant was offered a position
- Offer current employees an opportunity to provide candid feedback
- Ask departing employees their opinions on ways the organization could improve

It boils down to this: You don't know what you don't know. If you want to create an organization where the right people are in the right positions, where employees feel valued and satisfied, and where your time and resources are not constantly siphoned by turnover, you must actively think about and investigate each of these things—and most importantly, be willing to make changes based on what you learn.

It will take time on the front end (and if you're like Sam, you may believe it's time you don't have). But by taking actions that cause you to retain even one employee, it's possible that you'll save yourself thousands of dollars and multiple days of work. Now, multiply that by two, three, or more retained employees. When you look at it from this perspective, you can't afford *not* to focus on employee satisfaction from the interview forward!

CHAPTER 4

My Background Isn't Perfect, But I Will Still Be an Awesome Employee

Pamela's Story

Pamela runs a small dental office that is growing at a positive rate. To keep up, she needs to hire two people: a full-time receptionist to handle the intake of all patient calls and visits, and a bookkeeper to perform basic accounts receivable/ accounts payable tasks, file insurance claims, and communicate with Pamela's outside certified public accountant who conducts quarterly audits.

Several people have applied for the jobs. The most qualified candidate for the receptionist position is Reagan. The most qualified person for the bookkeeping job is Bobbi.

Pamela extends a conditional offer of employment to both candidates, informs them that she plans to run a background check, and provides them the notices required by the Fair Credit Reporting Act. Bobbi does not express any concerns about the background check. Reagan, however, discloses that his background check will reveal a recent driving conviction. He says that he will not make the same mistake twice and that the conviction will not impact his performance at work. Pamela then runs criminal background checks on both candidates.

What Is the Fair Credit Reporting Act?

The Fair Credit Reporting Act requires that candidates consent in writing to any credit or background check and be provided with specific notification about their rights under federal law. For more information and a free copy of the notice that must be provided to applicants and employees, visit www.consumer.FTC.gov.

The penalties for running a background check without the proper authorization may be substantial. To complicate matters, most states have different notice requirements and penalties—so be sure you are familiar with your state's laws and guidelines.

Speaking of the FTC...

Before we move on, here's a bit of bonus information about the Federal Trade Commission, or FTC. It doesn't directly relate to background and credit checks, but this information will be invaluable if your own or your business's good name and credit are ever threatened.

If your identity is ever compromised, the FTC will be your best friend. FTC.gov has a wealth of information related to protecting your personal identity and protecting the credit of your business. It offers specific steps (complete with websites and legitimate links) to take in the event of actual or threatened identity theft. These steps include contacting your state's Department of Motor Vehicles, the Social Security Administration, the Internal Revenue Service, the United States Postal Service, and other state and federal entities that will take proactive steps to create a protective wall around personal and professional identities. FTC.gov also provides links and phone numbers to three credit bureaus that monitor activity associated with you and/or your business so you can verify legitimate activity and dispute incorrect or illegitimate activity.

The background check reveals that Reagan was recently convicted of felony driving under the influence and no longer possesses a valid driver's license. Bobbi's background check shows that she was arrested for, but not convicted of, misdemeanor petty theft of property.

Having extended conditional offers of employment, Pamela is not sure what information she can consider or whether the background check results preclude either candidate from working at her dental office.

The Takeaway

Because employers want to select the best candidate for their organization, it is understandable that they need to know a little bit about potential employees' pasts before extending an offer of employment. Protecting the employer's business, other employees, and clients' personal information are legitimate reasons for running background and/or credit checks to supplement or validate information provided by the candidate in their interview. This is especially true when an employer is required to gather Protected Health Information (PHI) or Personal Identifiable Information (PII), or (as we'll see later in this chapter) where an employee's job requires them to work with a fragile population such as infants and children, or elderly or infirm individuals.

What Are PHI and PII?

Protected Health Information (PHI) and Personal Identifiable Information (PII) are terms used in various state and federal privacy laws to broadly describe information that relates to a specific individual. These privacy laws protect any information that could be used by a fraudster to steal the identify of another person, and they require employers to guard fiercely PHI and PII.

PHI and PII include (but are not limited to) names, social security numbers, dates of birth, bank or credit union account or routing numbers, the identity of beneficiaries, and the like. Protection under privacy laws generally extends not only to employees, but also to any person related to the employee about whom the employer has information (e.g., the identities of children in garnishment matters). A separate, but similar, duty to protect privacy exists with respect to the identity of clients, patients, and customers.

Employers who intend to run credit checks or criminal background checks must make specific disclosures to applicants and employees before obtaining the information. In a pre-hire situation, this disclosure should be provided to the applicant during the onboarding process, as Pamela did. **Under no circumstance should an employer attempt to obtain either type of report without proper written notice to the employee and the receipt of an authorization signed by the employee.**

As a side note—potential employees neglect to mention incidents that will show up on background or credit check reports *all the time*, as Bobbi did. They may be hoping the information will have disappeared (it won't), or that the employer is bluffing and will not *really* run the background check (they usually will). While an applicant's failure to disclose this information isn't necessarily a huge strike against them (they *did* authorize you to run the check, after all), an applicant's up-front honesty regarding their record is a point in their favor.

Running credit checks and/or criminal background checks can be a very effective way to ensure that a person selected for a particular position is an appropriate and safe hire. However, employers often do not know what the Fair Credit Reporting Act and the Equal Employment Opportunity Commission require or allow.

Guidance for Employers

In May 2012, the Obama administration and then-United States Attorney General Eric Holder drafted the Equal Employment Opportunity Commission's Enforcement Guidance on the Consideration of Arrest and Conviction Records in Employment Decisions Under Title VII of the

Civil Rights Act of 1964. With a focus on employment discrimination based on two protected categories—race and national origin—this guidance provided very good information, data, and examples for employers wishing to run criminal background checks on candidates for employment.

It is still in force and available at www.EEOC.gov.

Once credit reports and background checks are obtained, employers often aren't sure how to interpret the information provided, or how to distinguish an arrest from a conviction on a background check report. This is the situation in which Pamela finds herself. Let's break down what she should consider and what her options for moving forward are.

Credit Reports

Credit reports may be run when a candidate's credit is relevant to the job. Prior to advertising a job or interviewing any candidate, the tasks of the job should be listed in a written job description. This will help candidates understand the scope of the employer's expectations for a particular position. It will also identify the legitimate, non-discriminatory reason for requiring credit and background checks.

For example, Pamela is hiring a bookkeeper. If she offers Bobbi the position, Bobbi will have access to Pamela's bank accounts, accounting software, and insurance proceeds. Bobbi will oversee the accounts receivable and accounts payable functions of the entire dental practice. Bobbi will also have access to patients' social security information, check routing numbers, credit card numbers, and insurance identifiers. Pamela has a legitimate reason—and a legal obligation under the Health Insurance Portability and Accountability Act of 1996 (HIPAA)—to protect the financial information of her dental practice and her patients' Personal Identifiable Information. Failing to protect this information could subject Pamela to serious legal consequences under HIPAA.

For these reasons, Pamela can make a strong argument that Bobbi's credit history is directly relevant to the day-to-day tasks associated with the position. Once Pamela has made the decision to run Bobbi's credit history, she needs to ensure she is complying with both the Fair Credit Reporting Act and any relevant state and municipality laws.

Unless the receptionist position for which Reagan is applying has finance responsibilities, access to the office's financial information, or access to patients' Personal Identifiable Information, Reagan's credit history is less relevant.

Can You Run a Credit Check? Depends On Where You Live.

Laws limiting the usage of credit reports are expanding. Currently, the following states have limitations on employers' rights to obtain or examine applicants' and employees' credit reports:

- California
- Colorado
- Connecticut
- Delaware
- District of Columbia
- Hawaii
- Illinois
- Kansas
- Kentucky
- Louisiana
- Maine
- Maryland
- Massachusetts
- Nevada
- New Hampshire
- Oregon
- Vermont
- Washington

New York City and Chicago have similar limitations. Employers should anticipate that other states and municipalities will follow suit. Double-check what is allowable in your state and municipality before requesting a credit check. You might also choose to engage a reputable credit reporting agency with a legally compliant service agreement. This will ensure that only permissible information is reported.

Background Check Reports

Employers have a legal duty to exercise reasonable care in hiring and supervising their employees to prevent harm to employees and third parties. Background check reports are one tool that help employers comply with this duty. Many states have some version of a negligent hiring or negligent supervision statute that applies when a person (usually a third party) alleges that harm resulted because an employer failed to hire or supervise an employee in an appropriate manner.

Mitigate Your Risk by Following the Law

An employer's risk can be mitigated by complying with state laws. For example, Florida's negligent hiring law says that an employer can avoid a claim of negligent hiring and negligent supervision if it can show that it ran a background check report from the Florida Department of Law Enforcement (FDLE), contacted job references to determine suitability for the job, required the applicant to provide written information related to his or her background, interviewed the applicant, obtained proper authorization from the applicant, and correctly determined that none of those revealed information that would indicate that the applicant was not a good fit for the position sought. (See Florida Statute Chapter 768.096 for the precise requirements of the statute.)

(Legal) Greetings from the Sunshine State!

Since my practice is based in Florida and I am a member of the Florida Bar, that is where my expertise lies. Many of the examples I'll share throughout this book feature Florida statutes. These examples may or may not be in accordance with your own state's statutes—so always double-check before proceeding.

While all employers should exercise reasonable care in hiring and supervising employees, it is particularly important in the following instances:

If your organization works with a fragile population. This includes residents in a nursing home, patients in a hospital, or children in a daycare or school. You should carefully consider any arrests or convictions for crimes of violence such as assault, battery, domestic violence, or harm to children or the elderly.

If you are hiring someone whose job will include driving. You should evaluate any arrests or convictions for driving-related offenses, such as driving under the influence, driving without a license or insurance, or leaving the scene of an accident. You should also consider crimes related to possession, use, sale, or distribution of illegal substances.

If you are hiring a person to handle accounting or cash transactions, or who would have access to third party personal information. You should evaluate any crimes of dishonesty or crimes related to theft, embezzlement, or larceny.

If the position provides access to controlled medications. Crimes related to the possession, use, sale, or distribution of illegal substances would be directly relevant.

There are many positions for which background checks aren't just preferred; they're required by federal law—such as positions related to national security. For some jobs, federal law limits the hiring of persons convicted of crimes of financial dishonesty, such as money laundering and embezzlement. Federal law also prohibits the hiring of persons with certain convictions if the job requires driving motor vehicles over certain weights on interstate highways.

Many states also require employers to run background checks when employees' jobs place them caring for fragile populations. (Again, this includes elder caregivers, nursery workers, and teachers.) For example, Florida's Miya's Law requires landlords to perform background checks on prospective employees. The checks must screen criminal history records as well as sexual predator and sexual offender records.

Employment law attorneys can advise employers on the safest course of action. Human resource associations, such as the Society for Human Resource Management (SHRM), and industry associations can be great resources for employers who want to learn more about the laws and requirements specific to their type of organization.

Making an employment decision based on the results of a criminal background check is not discriminatory on its face. Unless there has been a mistake in identity, each criminal background check is unique to an individual person. **The key is to use the background check results in a non-discriminatory manner.** However, this can be difficult because employers often do not understand how to read background check results. It is made more complicated by the fact that states and municipalities use different terms or codes to describe the same conduct.

Here are a few guidelines to help employers avoid using background check results improperly when making hiring decisions.

Know the difference between an arrest and a conviction. That distinction is absolutely critical, because the standard for an arrest is much lower than the standard for a conviction. An arrest is *not* proof that an illegal act has been committed. Instead, an arrest indicates that a member of law enforcement had a reasonable basis to believe that a particular crime was committed.

A conviction, on the other hand, requires a much higher standard. The state must prove to a fact finder—a jury or a judge—*beyond a reasonable doubt* that the person accused committed every single enumerated element of the specific crime with which they were charged. In other words, a conviction serves as evidence that a person *actually engaged* in the conduct they were accused of.

Because the standards for an arrest differ from the standards for a conviction, an employer may consider the fact that an arrest occurred. However, without a conviction of guilt, an arrest alone shouldn't be a dealbreaker.

Disparity in Arrest Rates: A Crucial Consideration in Evaluating Background Checks

It is critical that employers understand that according to the Equal Employment Opportunity Commission's guidance, the likelihood of being arrested is greater for African Americans and Hispanics than it is for White Americans. Statistics also reveal that African Americans and Hispanics are arrested in numbers disproportionate to the general population. To fairly evaluate candidates, employers must be aware of these disparities. They have profound impacts on the lives of the persons impacted.

Consider the following statistics taken from the EEOC's guidance:

- In 2010, 28 percent of all people arrested were African American, even though African Americans comprised only 14 percent of the general population.
- In 2008, Hispanics were arrested for federal drug charges at a rate of approximately three times higher than their proportion in the general population.
- African Americans and Hispanics are more likely than Whites to be arrested, convicted, or sentenced for drug offenses, even though the rate of drug use by African Americans and Hispanics is similar to the rate of drug use by Whites.
- African Americans and Hispanics are also incarcerated at rates disproportionate to their numbers in the general population.
- In 2001, 1 out of every 17 White men (5.9 percent) in the United States could expect to go to prison at some point during his lifetime. This rate is 1 out of every 6 (17.2 percent) Hispanic men. For African American men, the rate of expected incarceration rises to 1 out of every 3 (32.2 percent).
- Based on a state-by-state examination of incarceration rates in 2005, African Americans were incarcerated at a rate 5.6 times higher than Whites. Seven states had African American-to-White ratios of incarceration of 10:1.[1]

Please see the Amie's Required Reading bonus material at the end of this book if you're interested in learning more about race, crime, and justice in America.

Do not have a blanket policy of exclusion, unless such a blanket is specifically allowed by law. A "blanket policy" is a broad policy that says that an employer will not hire someone who has ever been convicted of a crime of any sort, regardless of the individual circumstances of the person or of the crime. Blanket policies are generally allowed only where national security or safety is a concern.

At the time of the publication of the EEOC's guidance, the number of Americans who are probationers, parolees, or incarcerated exceeded 7.3 million adults—more than the populations of Chicago, Philadelphia, San Diego, and Dallas *combined.*[2] If blanket policies were allowed, it would be largely impossible for any of these 7.3 million adults to become gainfully employed. Imagine the cost to the American taxpayers if 7.3 million Americans were never able to secure a job!

Do not engage in disparate treatment or have policies that result in disparate impact. Disparate treatment and disparate impact occur when people are treated or impacted differently because of their race, background, gender, religion, etc., not because of a factor that impacts their ability to do a particular job. Sometimes disparate treatment can stem from information that might be included on a background or credit check, but background and credit checks don't have to be involved for disparate treatment and impact to occur. Here are the basics:

- **What is disparate treatment?** Disparate treatment results when an employer treats people of different races and similar backgrounds differently. In the example at the beginning of this chapter, Reagan's background check revealed that he was recently convicted of felony driving under the influence and no longer possesses a valid driver's license. Disparate treatment discrimination would occur if Reagan was an African American and not offered the job because of the conviction, but the person hired for the position was White and had a similar felony conviction.

To avoid disparate treatment, employers should evaluate their advertising and hiring policies periodically and assess whether certain groups have been unfairly eliminated from consideration.

- **What is disparate impact?** A policy that creates a disparate impact is a neutral (non-discriminatory) policy that—although not intended to do so—results in the elimination of certain groups of individuals from consideration for the job. These policies are discriminatory not because of their language, but because of their impact.

  A good example of a disparate impact policy is one that requires all applicants to submit to a neutral standardized exam that is unrelated to the job, but that has a statistical lower passage rate for certain groups of individuals. Organizations that wish to use examinations to evaluate applicants for hire or employees for promotions should ensure that the examinations are job-related and that they do not have a disparate impact on any group of people.

  Reliance upon the results of background and/or credit checks can also result in a disparate impact on groups of individuals. (Remember the disparity in arrest rates discussed earlier in this chapter.) Therefore, it is important to have a legitimate, non-discriminatory reason to run a background and/or credit check before actually doing so. Furthermore, it is critical to run the same type of check on every applicant applying for the same position. This ensures that you are actually doing an apples-to-apples comparison.

  To determine whether a hiring practice has a disparate impact on certain groups, employers should compare their candidate pool with their hiring results and evaluate whether there is any concerning pattern.

Who Might Be Affected by Disparate Treatment or Disparate Impact?

Disparate treatment and disparate impact discrimination policies are not unique to race or national origin. Employers may not enact policies or practices that result in disparate treatment or disparate impact based on *any* protected category in Title VII of the Civil Rights Act: sex, color, race, religion, or national origin. This also applies to protected categories in other federal laws, such as the Americans with Disabilities Act, the Age Discrimination in Employment Act, the Pregnancy Discrimination Act, or the Genetic Information Nondiscrimination Act.

Here are some examples of policies that might result in disparate treatment or impact:

- Assuming that some positions do not require heavy lifting, a blanket policy that requires people to be able to lift a certain amount of weight might eliminate female candidates or candidates over a certain age.

- An "English-only" policy that says only English may be spoken in the workplace might eliminate non-American-born candidates. While the ability to speak English when interacting with customers, clients, or patients may be a legitimate requirement of a position, employers should *not* require that employees speak only English when they are not working, such as during a meal or rest break.

  EEOC Regulation 29 CFR 1606.7(a) says that requiring employees to speak English at all times is burdensome and presumptively violates Title VII. English-only rules should be narrowly tailored and supported by business necessity. This might include requiring English (1) to communicate with customers, clients, or patients who speak English, (2) when necessary for the safety of employees and customers, clients, or patients, or (3) when necessary in cooperative work assignments in which English-only is needed to promote efficiency.[3] The U.S. Department of Labor has Workplace Equality Compliance Officers (WECOs) available to help employers navigate language issues in the workplace. You can search www.dol.gov to find the most recent WECO contact information.

- Unless lifting, bending, and stretching are day-to-day functions of the job, a lift-bend-stretch-carry policy might unnecessarily eliminate some disabled persons from consideration.

Know what is required to stay in compliance with state and federal laws while being fair to applicants. How do employers remain compliant with federal and state law, consider reported information in a manner that is fair to applicants, and select the most qualified applicant for positions?

According to the EEOC's guidance, if a background check reveals that an applicant has an arrest or conviction, the employer must consider three factors to determine whether the applicant is an appropriate person to hire:

1. The nature and gravity of the offense or conduct
2. The time that has passed since the offense, conduct, and/or completion of the sentence
3. The nature of the job held or sought[4]

Additionally, the EEOC recommends that employers conduct an individualized assessment for each applicant and the job applied for, and consider each of the following:

- The facts or circumstances surrounding the offense or conduct
- The number of offenses for which the individual was convicted
- The age of the individual at the time of conviction and/or release from prison
- Evidence that he or she performed the same type of work, post-conviction, with the same or a different employer and with no known incidents of criminal conduct
- The length and consistency of employment history before and after the offense or conduct
- Any rehabilitation efforts (e.g., education/training) that have occurred
- The results of employment or character references and any other information regarding fitness for the particular position
- Whether the individual is bonded under a federal, state, or local bonding program[5]

This might sound overwhelming. How does an employer gain this sort of detailed personal information? *By having a conversation with the applicant!* Although it can be uncomfortable, this conversation will reveal information to help you determine whether the candidate is an appropriate fit for the specific job sought.

To make all of this less theoretical, let's check back in with Pamela and the two job applicants she is considering. Because of his skill and prior experience, Reagan is the most qualified candidate for the receptionist position. However, his background check revealed that he was recently convicted of felony driving under the influence and no longer possesses a valid driver's license. To evaluate whether Reagan is an appropriate candidate to hire for this position, Pamela should discuss with Reagan:

- The circumstances surrounding the actions that led to his felony conviction
- How long before the first date of employment the event occurred (This is especially relevant if the job requires any driving on behalf of the business)
- Whether the incident was isolated or part of a pattern of conduct
- Whether Reagan completed any court-required actions

Depending on Reagan's answers, Pamela may choose to hire him or tell him his conditional offer is withdrawn. If the receptionist position requires driving, it is likely that Reagan will not be an appropriate candidate for the position. However, if the job duties do not require driving, the fact that Reagan has one conviction for felony DUI may not be relevant to whether he is hired.

An employer like Pamela may ask, "Do you have transportation to get to work?" If the employee says yes, the employer should not inquire further. It doesn't matter whether the employee walks, rides a bike, takes an Uber, uses public transportation, or has a friend drop them off. All that matters is that they are able to arrive at work in a timely manner.

The most qualified person for the bookkeeping job is Bobbi, whose background check shows that she was arrested for, but not convicted of, misdemeanor petty theft of property. To evaluate whether she should hire Bobbi, Pamela should discuss:

- The circumstances surrounding the arrest:
  - If there were multiple arrests for the same or similar crimes, Pamela may inquire as to each arrest.
  - How many people/organizations were harmed as a result of Bobbi's alleged actions?
  - What type of property was allegedly taken?

- How long before the current date the event occurred. This is especially relevant because the alleged crime (petty theft) would be easy to commit in a bookkeeping position.
- Whether the incident was isolated or part of a pattern of conduct.

This is a financial position with direct access to Pamela's accounts receivable and payable. Since the alleged crime is financial in nature, if Pamela is not satisfied with Bobbi's explanation of the events that led to her arrest, Pamela may be justified in choosing to withdraw Bobbi's conditional job offer and hiring a candidate without any arrests or convictions for financial crimes.

Should the background check results reveal that either Reagan or Bobbi lied or intentionally withheld information to deceive Pamela, their dishonesty would also justify Pamela's decision to withdraw their conditional job offers.

IRS Tax Incentives for Hiring

Who doesn't love getting money *from* the IRS? You may be able to hire a new employee with a prior conviction and receive a tax credit for doing so.

Employers who hire "certain individuals from targeted groups who have consistently faced significant barriers to employment" may be entitled to a Work Opportunity Tax Credit (WOTC). The target groups include:

    a. Qualified IV-A Recipients
    b. Qualified Veterans
    c. Qualified Ex-Felons
    d. Designed Community Residents (DCRs)
    e. Vocational Rehabilitation Referrals
    f. Summer Youth Employees
    g. Supplemental Nutritional Assistance Program (SNAP) Benefits Recipients
    h. Supplemental Security Income (SSI) Recipients
    i. Long-Term Family Assistance Recipients
    j. Qualified Long-Term Unemployment Recipients[6]

Businesses that hire such individuals may be entitled to take a credit based on the amount of the business income tax liability or Social Security tax owed on IRS Form 5884-C and/or Form 3800. For more details and to determine whether your business qualifies, visit www.irs.gov and discuss eligibility and filing requirements with your certified public accountant.

In Conclusion

Obtaining, interpreting, and utilizing credit and background check reports is a complex process—but one that's crucial to approach with patience, empathy, and discernment while being careful to comply with federal, state, and municipal statutes.

To stay in compliance with the law, work closely with your organization's HR professionals and/or employment law attorneys. You can also take advantage of resources like the EEOC's guidance on the consideration of arrest and conviction records in employment decisions (referenced earlier in this chapter).

Always remember that each job candidate is a human being with unique life circumstances. If you see an area of concern on an otherwise-outstanding applicant's credit or background check report, it is usually worth talking to the person about what happened. When you get the full picture, you'll be able to make an informed decision about what's best for your organization.

Underpaying Me Now Affects Me for the Rest of My Career: The Importance of Fair Wages

Yvonne's Story

In the 1980s, when my friend Yvonne was a young, single human resource professional, she moved from Miami, Florida, to Pensacola, Florida. She was excited to interview for a human resource position in Pensacola that was equivalent in skill level and responsibility to the one she'd held in Miami. Yvonne was well qualified, and she was ultimately selected for the job. So far so good, right?

Then things took a surprising turn. After offering Yvonne the job, her prospective supervisor asked Yvonne what she expected to be paid. She told him what she had previously earned in Miami in the similar position.

The supervisor's response was, "I don't pay women that much. I don't even pay my men that much if I don't have to." As Yvonne's jaw hit the floor, he followed up with, "And they're married and have families to support. What makes you think I would pay a young, unmarried woman that much money?"

The Takeaway

There is so much to unpack in this scenario. It is hard to decide where to start, but three things jump out at me:

- First and most obviously, the supervisor's statement violated every state and federal law based on gender discrimination, and most state laws regarding age and marital status discrimination. (Look back at Chapter 3: If You

Want to Reduce Turnover, Focus on My Satisfaction from the Interview Forward for more information on these protected categories. We'll look more closely at other protected categories in future chapters.)

- Second, legality aside, Yvonne's marital and gender status had absolutely nothing to do with her qualifications or her ability to do the job. In fact, the interview process revealed that she was the *most* qualified candidate, which is why she was selected for the position.
- Third, making these statements was a terrible business decision. The supervisor did not want to pay Yvonne a salary commensurate with her skills and expected to receive some sort of discount because she was a young, unmarried female.

As a result, Yvonne did not take the job and the organization lost a very qualified candidate.

Paying Employees Less Than They're Worth Leads to a Lifetime of Consequences

There are many reasons why employers might pay people less than their skills and experience merit—both legal and illegal. Even if they aren't as up front as Yvonne's would-be supervisor, many employers allow preconceived notions about a candidate's age, gender, personal circumstances, or other criteria unrelated to the job to influence pay offers. Sometimes, employers legitimately can't afford to pay employees what they are worth…or, as is often the case, they simply don't want to.

No matter what an employer's motivation might be, underpaying an employee begins a legacy of diminished pay that can last an entire career.

Consider this: Suppose the market rate for the position Yvonne applied for was $50,000/year but the supervisor offered Yvonne only $40,000/year based on his hope that he could pay as little as possible. Suppose further that Yvonne accepted the job at $40,000/year, rather than the market rate of $50,000/year, and that she remained with the organization for her entire career.

Yvonne's initial raise would be based on the starting salary of $40,000/year. If her employer offered her a 10 percent annual raise, her new compensation rate would only be $44,000/year—still $6,000 short of the appropriate *starting* rate for the job, and $11,000/year lower than the salary she would earn had she started at the market rate of $50,000/year and received the same 10 percent increase.

Don't Get Hung Up on the Percentage

If you're thinking, *A 10 percent annual raise sounds like a lot—not everyone gets that*, I hear you. Some people receive only a cost-of-living increase in compensation…and unfortunately, others can't even count on that.

I chose 10 percent for this example because it lends itself to easy math, and clearly illustrates what employees have to lose. That said, even small annual raises add up over time when someone is underpaid.

Yvonne's second annual raise would be based on her salary of $44,000/year, rather than $55,000/year. If she received another 10 percent raise based on $44,000, her new salary would be $48,400. After two years of service, she would still earn $1,600/year less than the proper starting wage of $50,000, and $12,100 less than she would have earned had she started at the market rate of $50,000.

After the first two years alone, Yvonne's total pay would be $23,100 less than it should have been.

If Yvonne remains with this organization over the course of her career, the money she could have made will add up to *hundreds of thousands of dollars*, based on a lower beginning compensation. This loss becomes exponential and has lifelong consequences when Yvonne considers that she has fewer dollars to invest in her company's 401(k) plan, in her home, or in other retirement investments—and fewer dollars to contribute to the tax base of her community.

Even if Yvonne works for the organization for only a few years, the diminished starting wage will likely impact her long-term earning potential. If it is legal to ask about prior compensation in Yvonne's state and municipality (more on that later in this chapter), it is probable that her subsequent employers will base any offer of compensation, at least in part, on what she earned when her employment with the first organization ended. Thus, if Yvonne worked at the first organization for five years at the pay rate described above, it is likely that her next employer would consider offering her a starting salary close to $58,560 rather than $73,200, which she would have earned had she started at $50,000.

We Can't Ignore the Gender Pay Gap

The career-spanning consequences of underpayment apply to women and men, but they are especially profound for women because women's wages tend to be depressed. According to the White House, in 2022, women were paid 83 cents for every dollar paid to a man in an equivalent job.[1] If a woman earns $83,000 per year and a man earns $100,000 per year for the same job and both work 40 years, the man would earn $680,000 more than the woman. Imagine the financial impact on the American economy if this $680,000 *per woman* had been invested in the company 401(k), in personal homes, in children's educations, or in the stock market!

The COVID-19 global pandemic exacerbated this problem. In an article published in August 2020, NPR's Greg Rosalsky explains that unemployment for women increased 12.8 percent during the early stages of the pandemic because it impacted service jobs disproportionally held by women—at restaurants and retail outlets, for example, and because school and day care closures forced at least one parent to stay home.[2] The article also predicted that the pandemic would cause the pay gap to widen from a point where women earn 81 cents for every dollar earned by men to a point where women earn 76 cents for every dollar earned by men. Rosalsky quotes Jane Olmstead-Rumsey, an economist at Northwestern University, who says, "We project it's going to take more than 10 years for the gender wage gap to close to what it was before the pandemic."

Studies show that this projection was accurate, at least for women in low-paying jobs that suffered as a result of the pandemic, as well as for women of color.[3]

One Legislative Solution: Prohibiting Inquiries About Prior Compensation

Many states recognize that basing an employee's starting pay on what the employee earned with prior organizations creates a pay disparity that can last a lifetime. Therefore, some states have enacted laws that prohibit employers from asking applicants about compensation earned at prior jobs. If you think about it, the logic makes sense. What an employee earned at a prior job has absolutely nothing to do with the value *you* place on a particular position in your organization or how much the employee should earn doing a job for you. If you base your compensation decision on what a prior employer paid—when that prior employer underpaid the applicant or based their compensation decision on a discriminatory factor—then the legacy of underpayment is perpetuated, regardless of how qualified or skilled the employee is.

As of 2021, the following states have specific legislation limiting what an employer may ask an applicant regarding current or prior compensation:

- Alabama
- California
- Colorado
- Connecticut
- Delaware
- District of Columbia
- Georgia
- Hawaii
- Illinois
- Kentucky
- Louisiana
- Maine
- Maryland
- Massachusetts
- Michigan
- Mississippi
- Missouri
- New Jersey
- New York
- North Carolina
- Ohio
- Oregon
- Pennsylvania
- Puerto Rico
- South Carolina
- Utah
- Vermont
- Washington
- Wisconsin

The exact nature of the prohibitions vary by state. For example, California and Michigan prohibit an employer from asking any questions about prior compensation, Connecticut prohibits employers from inquiring further if an applicant offers the information voluntarily, and in Washington, D.C., the prohibition includes government employers as well as private employers. Finally, some municipalities (e.g., Kansas City, Kansas) allow limited usage of salary history.

If it is necessary to inquire about salary history during the application process, you must determine whether the inquiry is legal in the state and municipality in which you make it. Inquiries allowed in one location may not be allowed in another. An employment law attorney or human resources professional should be able to provide assistance.

A Better Option: Transparency and Fairness

Rather than asking an applicant how much compensation they earned at another organization, the better practice to ensure fair pay is to determine what the job is worth to your organization, using wage bands or tiered compensation plans. Using a wage band allows you to set the low-to-high compensation for a position based on how *you* value it. Putting those wage bands and tiered compensation plans in writing lets an applicant know exactly what to expect, including their maximum earning potential in that particular job.

A written wage band should be tied to the job description for each position. This way, applicants and current employees alike will have an easily accessed "road map" to advancement within the organization. They will be able to ascertain what steps they must take before they qualify to interview for various positions, and what the earning potential of each position is.

For example, assume there are four tiers within the HR department of a large organization.

- The entry-level position might be called HR coordinator. The job description should state the objective skills and education needed to be qualified to interview for the position, such as prior customer service experience and informal HR training.
- The next tier might be HR manager. That job description might state that the position requires at least five years of experience working in an organization's HR department and a specific certification or education level, such as a PHR (Professional in Human Resources) or a bachelor's degree in HR or a related field.
- The third position might be senior HR manager. Like the other job descriptions, this job description should state the specific criteria required to be considered for this position, such as at least seven years working directly in HR, a Senior PHR certification, or a bachelor's degree in HR or a related field, as well as experience working independently to resolve HR-related issues.

- The top position in the organization might be vice president of HR. This position might require at least 15 years of experience, a master's degree in HR, experience overseeing a departmental budget, and experience supervising a team of HR professionals.

Job descriptions for each of these four levels should include a clearly stated wage band.

Providing specific information like this benefits both the employee and the employer: It allows employees to actively participate in their career progression, and it provides legitimate, non-discriminatory criteria for determining whether a candidate is qualified to interview for a particular position.

Are You Required by Law to Provide Compensation Information?

Some states, like Washington, have passed laws like the Washington Equal Pay and Opportunities Act. These laws require employers with 15 or more employees to provide compensation and benefit information in job postings.

From a legal perspective, written wage bands help eliminate the appearance of any improper or discriminatory factors being included in the hiring process. This makes it less likely that you will get sued for discrimination. And if you are sued, written wage bands and tiered compensation plans that are consistently applied make it easier for your employment lawyer to defend your organization.

Beyond including a written description in job postings, you should share during interviews how an applicant's compensation will be calculated if they are hired. This is particularly relevant if compensation is based on or affected by variable factors such as commissions, referrals, piece rate pay, day rate pay, per diem pay, rest periods, or meal periods. This information should be reviewed during onboarding and any time an employee has a question about their paycheck.

Make Sure You Fulfill Your Payment Obligations on Time

If you have a policy stating that you will provide annual reviews that determine pay raises and promotions, then conduct those reviews on time.

If you have a policy governing payment of commissions, bonuses, or referrals, pay those commissions, bonuses, or referrals on time—and without being asked.

If you happen to slip up and let time lapse, then schedule the review or pay what's owed as soon as you realize the mistake. If you do not, employees are left wondering whether they are going to receive the review and/or payment, whether it has been forgotten, whether their own performance is lacking, or whether you do not intend to fulfill your obligations.

In Conclusion

Most employers recognize that if their goal is to pay as little as possible, they will suffer from high turnover, low productivity, and low morale. Long-term, there is no such thing as getting a "bargain" on a quality employee. (Too bad Yvonne's wannabe-supervisor never learned this lesson!)

Good employers seek to pay proper compensation based on objective criteria such as market factors related to individual positions. Not only is this fair to employees, it's an investment in your organization's longevity and success.

CHAPTER 6

Pay Me Now or Pay Me Later: Wage and Hour Basics

Tracy's Story

Tracy is a receptionist at a medical office. She has been employed for two years and reliably arrives on time for work every single day. However, the quality of her work is mediocre at best. She regularly drops calls, forgets patients' names, and misplaces deliveries and mail. Patients frequently complain about the long wait time, which the practice owner, Dr. Smith, attributes to Tracy's disorganization.

Tracy earns $10 per hour. According to her job description, her work hours are eight hours per day, beginning at 8:00 a.m. and ending at 5:00 p.m., with one hour designated for a lunch break. Tracy usually chooses to eat lunch at her desk rather than going out. Dr. Smith would prefer that Tracy leave the office for an hour to take a break, but has never forced her to do so. Patients are not booked during the lunch hour, so there is not much to do. However, if the phone rings or a patient happens to walk in, Tracy assists them.

Frustrated by Tracy's lackluster performance after one too many patient complaints, Dr. Smith finally terminates Tracy's employment. During the termination meeting, Dr. Smith explains to Tracy that she is being terminated for poor performance. Tracy agrees that the job was overwhelming to her.

Three weeks later, Dr. Smith receives a lawsuit filed in federal court alleging that Tracy was not paid for working overtime. Dr. Smith is confused because the office is open only between 8:00 a.m. and 5:00 p.m., and patients are seen only between 8:30 a.m. and 4:00 p.m. Therefore, she reasons, it is not possible for Tracy to have worked more than 40 hours per week.

Through the discovery phase of the litigation, Dr. Smith learns that Tracy is basing her unpaid overtime claim not on any work performed before 8:00 a.m.

or after 5:00 p.m., but on the fact that she regularly worked through her lunch breaks! Dr. Smith defends the practice by arguing that Tracy was not required to stay at her desk for lunch, but chose to do so.

...But How Did Tracy Know She Had Grounds to Initiate Legal Action?

Perhaps you're thinking, *In Tracy's position, I wouldn't have realized that my employer owed me overtime pay. How did Tracy know that? And why didn't she address the issue with Dr. Smith before she was fired?*

The likely answer is that Tracy's attorney advertised in a manner to specifically attract clients in Tracy's position. Why? The Fair Labor Standards Act (FLSA) and almost all state laws include a provision whereby the non-prevailing party is required to pay all or part of the attorneys' fees of the prevailing party. This often means that if an employee can show that an employer failed to pay any of his or her wages, the employer will be required to pay all or some of the employee's attorneys' fees.

Because of this requirement, there are law firms that specialize in wage and hour law. These firms use radio and television to market to potential clients. In Florida, the resulting claims were so prolific that the United States District Court had to create an entire division just to handle the influx.

The Takeaway

Under federal law, work breaks for adults are not required. However, some states *do* mandate break periods. Even where breaks are not required, employers may have a policy requiring employees to take a break during the day. This type of policy often includes a lunch break. Generally, if the break is at least 30 minutes *and the employee is relieved of all duties*, the break is not compensable under federal law.

That said, even when employers have a policy requiring employees to take a lunch break, many employees prefer to work through this time—particularly if leaving the premises is inconvenient. Many employers do not want to "force" employees to take a lunch break because they do not want to micromanage their employees' actions. Plus, they recognize that it might be more comfortable and convenient for an employee to take their lunch break at their desk. However, as Dr. Smith found out, allowing employees to do this can create liability. Even though Tracy voluntarily performed duties during her lunch break, she was never *truly* relieved of all work-related responsibilities.

How Do I "Make" My Employees Take a Break?

I always advise employers to require that their employees step away from their workstations entirely and clock out during breaks. Employers can provide a breakroom, picnic tables outside, or another designated break area. Where possible, employees should be permitted to leave the premises during breaks. Employees who do not follow this rule and remain at their workstations during breaks should be subject to discipline as they would be for failing to follow any other rule.

If your employees ask why this rule is in place, I suggest framing your reasoning around the need to take a "refresh and relax" break (as opposed to highlighting wage and hour laws). After all, people who work for eight or more hours straight are naturally going to become fatigued, and are more likely to make errors. Eventually, they will be at higher risk for burnout.

Working through lunch is just one example of an action that might result in the employer's obligation to pay overtime. Federal law states that a non-exempt employee must be paid for *all* hours worked. (Briefly, a non-exempt employee is one who is eligible for overtime pay—we'll look more closely at this distinction later in the chapter.) So, for example, an employer would be obligated to pay a non-exempt employee overtime if that employee is allowed to clock in early or clock out late.

The same would be true if a non-exempt employee is allowed to answer emails before or after regular working hours. In that instance, the employee's time- and date-stamped emails are evidence of hours worked.

Understanding Federal Wage and Hour Laws

If you don't want to find yourself in a situation like Dr. Smith's, you need to have a foundational grasp of federal wage and hour laws in the United States. To fully understand how this section of the law applies to your organization and specific employees within it, I recommend setting a meeting with your employment attorney. To save you a few bucks, though, I have provided the basics here so you can walk into your meeting prepared.

What is the Fair Labor Standards Act? The Fair Labor Standards Act, or the FLSA, applies to:

- enterprises with an annual gross volume of sales made or business done totaling $500,000 or more
- employees engaged in interstate commerce or in the production of goods for commerce
- all hospitals, businesses providing medical or nursing care for residents, for-profit and not-for-profit schools, and public agencies.[1]

This means that the FLSA applies to (almost) every employer in the United States. In total, it covers more than 143 million workers at more than 9.8 million establishments nationwide.[2]

The FLSA has teeth that other federal laws, such as Title VII of the Civil Rights Act, do not have. Notably, the FLSA allows *individuals* to be personally sued and liable for wage and hour violations when the individual is considered an "employer" under the FLSA. This means that both the organization and the individual employer (e.g., the business owner, the department head, the supervisor, etc.) can be liable for unpaid wages.

There are two types of employees in the United States. You've probably heard of "exempt" employees and "non-exempt" employees, but do you have a good understanding of what each of those categories entails?

Under the FLSA, *exempt employees* are (generally) those who:
- Are exempt from receiving overtime for all hours worked over 40 in a given workweek;
- Are paid a guaranteed weekly salary of at least $684 per week, which is not subject to fluctuation because of quality or quantity of work; and
- Perform duties that qualify for the exemption (such as executive, administrative, professional, computer, or outside sales employees), or who are owners or highly compensated employees. According to the FLSA, highly compensated employees are those who receive at least $107,432 in annual compensation, paid at the rate of at least $684 per week, and any commissions, non-discretionary bonuses, and/or any other non-discretionary compensation earned during the 52-week period.[3]

Let's Define "Workweek"

The term "workweek" means any seven-day, 168-hour period such as Sunday to Saturday or Wednesday to Tuesday.

Every other employee is *non-exempt*. As the name implies, non-exempt employees are not exempt from receiving overtime for all hours worked over 40 in a given workweek. Here are the basics you need to know about paying wages to your non-exempt workers:
- Non-exempt employees qualify for overtime pay at the rate of time-and-a-half for all hours worked in excess of 40 during a given workweek.
- Non-exempt employees may be paid on an hourly basis or on a salary basis.
  - If they are paid on an hourly basis, they are paid for each hour they work.
  - If they are paid on a salary basis, they must receive the same salary per week. It cannot be subject to downward fluctuation due to the quality or quantity of work. This means that salaried non-exempt employees are paid the set salary, even in weeks where they work less than 40 hours. However, if they work more than 40 hours in a

given workweek, they must be paid at least time-and-a-half for the overtime hours.

Should I Classify My Employees as Exempt or Non-Exempt?

Whether a particular position is exempt or non-exempt is a function of the duties and responsibilities of the job—not the title or the method of pay. The U.S. Department of Labor's website (www.dol.gov) is full of resources to help employers navigate compensation obligations by topic or industry. For example, the website contains fact sheets for private sector healthcare, manufacturing, and hospital industries. It also contains fact sheets for public sector industries such as higher education. Finally, the Department of Labor also provides a toll-free number for employers to call if they want to speak with the Wage and Hour Division about any wage and hour issue: 1-866-4-US-WAGE.

Remember, unless an exemption clearly applies, it is safer to identify the position as non-exempt and pay the overtime.

Every single state has its own version of the FLSA. State laws are often more generous to employees than federal law, which sets the "floor" (or the minimum requirements) for the payment of wages. An aggrieved employee may bring a claim under the federal FLSA and/or the state counterpart. State law may provide higher recovery caps, which creates more liability for the employer. Your employment law attorney will be able to point out which, if any, state laws you should be aware of.

Employment Practices Liability Insurance (EPLI) generally does not cover wage and hour claims. EPLI is insurance coverage available for purchase from most commercial insurance brokers. It provides coverage in the event of a claim of harassment or discrimination on the basis of sex, color, race, religion, national origin, or other protected class. It also covers allegations of employment violations such as wrongful termination or failure-to-hire.

Unfortunately, these policies often exclude wage and hour claims. Where wage and hour claims *are* covered, the premium and/or deductible can render coverage unaffordable for many employers. This is because wage and hour claims are so prevalent and the damages can (and often do) include payment of the employee/plaintiff's attorney fees.

Therefore, most employers do not have any insurance protection to provide a defense to an FLSA claim, and would have to fund any legal expenses out-of-pocket. As we'll discuss later in this chapter, your best protection is (you guessed it!) doing everything in your power to prevent wage and hour claims from being made in the first place.

Damages, or monies owed by employers who do not prevail in FLSA litigation, can be extensive. When an employee proves that an employer failed to pay any wages due, the employer can be required to pay:

- *Back pay*. Back pay is the amount of wages not paid to the employee at the time they were earned. The U.S. Department of Labor defines back pay as "the difference between what the employee was paid and the amount he or she should have been paid."[4] Back pay is generally awarded for up to two years, but in the case of a willful violation of the law, back pay can be awarded for up to three years prior to the date of the claim.
- *Liquidated damages*. These damages are often called "double damages" and act as a deterrent for employers who intentionally fail to pay full wages. Basically, they double the amount of back pay awarded to an employee.
- *Interest*. Litigation can take several years. This is particularly true in courts where the docket is flooded with wage and hour cases, such as the United States District Court in the Southern District of Florida.

  If the employee had been paid the wages in a timely manner, the employee could have invested or used the money. However, because the employee was not paid the money owed in a timely manner, the employee has lost the time-value of the money. To make that right, courts often award interest at a statutory rate. The statutory rate begins at the time the wages should have been paid and continues through the time of payment. Many states' statutory rates are better than current market rates and run about 10 percent per year.
- *Attorneys' fees and costs*. The federal Fair Labor Standards Act (and most state laws) contain an attorney fee provision. This means that a prevailing plaintiff party can request that the court make the other party (the

employer) pay some or all of its attorney fees and costs, which can include deposition copy costs, court reporter fees, expert witness fees, filing fees, and similar expenses incurred to litigate the matter.

Want to Save a Lot of Money? Pay Employees What They're Owed Up Front.

Just in case you haven't been running mental calculations, suffice it to say that paying an employee their base pay plus any overtime owed is *a lot less* expensive than what you might owe in legal fees and damages if you don't.

Calculating Tracy's Damages

Now that we've covered the basics of wage and hour laws, let's return to Tracy and the possible outcome of her lawsuit against Dr. Smith.

Tracy is a non-exempt employee, entitled to overtime pay. Even though she was allowed to take a one-hour lunch break, she was permitted to work through her break, and often did so. Therefore, that time is compensable for the days where Tracy can show she performed work during the lunch hour. If Dr. Smith did not intend to pay her for that hour, Dr. Smith should have required her to take the one-hour break each day, rather than allowing her to sit at her desk and perform tasks that benefited the practice.

As a reminder, damages represent the monies that a defendant must pay at the conclusion of a lawsuit. What would Dr. Smith have to pay if Tracy convinces the court or a jury that she worked through lunch every day?

At Tracy's regular rate of $10/hour, her overtime rate would be $15/hour. Let's assume Tracy took two weeks off during the year. If Tracy argued that she "always" worked during lunch and could support this by time-stamped emails, phone messages, patient sign-ins, or the like, she would seek the following in damages:

- *Back pay:*
  - ◦ 5 hours of overtime per week at $15/hour, multiplied by 50 weeks per year, equals $3,750 per year.
  - ◦ Because Tracy alleges to have worked in this manner for two years, she would be entitled to a total of $7,500 in back pay.
- *Liquidated damages:*
  - ◦ A court is likely to liquidate damages, or double them, to increase the amount of back pay to $15,000.
- *Interest:*
  - ◦ If the litigation took two years and the statutory interest rate was 10 percent, the court would likely apply interest in the amount of $1,500 in year one and $1,650 in year two. (If Tracy is owed a total of $15,000, she would get 10 percent of that, or $1,500, in year one. That $1,500 would be added the original principal of $15,000 for a total of $16,500 in year two, resulting in an interest payment of $1,650.)

Thus, Dr. Smith could owe $18,150 *before an award of attorneys' fees.* Tracy's counsel will ask for attorneys' fees and costs should she win the lawsuit, and the court will have to award a reasonable amount based on the attorney's filings during the two years of litigation. Therefore, it is very likely that Dr. Smith will owe in excess of $30,000 before the lawsuit is concluded.

Remember, too, that Tracy may name the practice and Dr. Smith as party-defendants, meaning they would be jointly liable for damages.

Avoid a Lawsuit—Pay Employees Properly!

Rather than facing a lawsuit and paying a large amount of damages, the better practice is to ensure that you are paying all employees properly and maintaining correct timekeeping records. An employment attorney can help with this by conducting a complete audit of all positions to determine which are exempt and which are non-exempt. Then, the employment attorney will look at wage and hour records to ensure that those records are being properly maintained.

This may sound like an expensive proposition; however, you can reduce the expense by being prepared. Familiarize yourself with an employer's recordkeeping obligations by reviewing the Code of Federal Regulations at 29 CFR Part 516 or by visiting www.dol.gov and searching for Fact Sheet #21.[5] You may be able to catch and correct some recordkeeping missteps before an attorney reviews them.

Preparing ahead of time and engaging an employment attorney is a bargain compared to a lawsuit like Tracy's—and it is a drop in the bucket compared to a collective action lawsuit where groups of employees allege their wages were withheld!

If You Want Me to Sign a Non-Compete, Make It Equitable

Gus's Story

Gus has worked for Widgets Inc., a Florida-based company, for 19 years. During his tenure, Gus has seen Widgets Inc. grow from 10 to 90 employees as it expanded from selling widgets made by other companies to designing, outfitting, manufacturing, and selling its own widgets throughout the United States. Widgets Inc. has also begun to manufacture and sell non-widget gizmos and gadgets.

Gus has been an integral part of the company's growth. Over the past 19 years, he has served in almost every role: salesperson, client representative, design, operations, and employee relations. Gus has also established relationships with key players in his industry: vendors, manufacturers' representatives, and even competitors. Gus is often complimented on being a team player and is credited with much of the company's success.

However, Gus has not received an increase in compensation in several years. In fact, due to the company's restructuring of its compensation, several incentive bonus and commission opportunities have been eliminated and Gus's total compensation has decreased (even though the company's profits have increased). Gus is frustrated and feels unappreciated. Yet, as a Peace Maker, Gus continues to work hard for the betterment of the entire company.

Gus wasn't actively looking for a new job, but given his outstanding reputation in the industry, a competitor reached out to Gus and offered him an incredible role in a leadership position. The compensation would be substantially greater, and there would be an opportunity for long-term growth and learning.

When Gus informed Bridget, his direct supervisor, that he accepted a job with the competitor, she was quick to remind him that in year three of his employment, he signed a non-compete agreement in which he agreed never to work for any competitor. She informed him that he simply could not take the new job. Gus verbally promised not to communicate with any existing Widgets Inc. customer, but Bridget replied that if he took the job, Widgets Inc. would enforce the non-compete agreement he signed 16 years earlier and sue him for breach of contract.

Now, Gus feels like he is faced with the following options:

1. Stay with Widgets Inc. at the lower rate of pay, with fewer opportunities for bonuses and fewer opportunities for growth
2. Leave the industry entirely and accept an entry-level job in a completely new field
3. Take the job with the competitor, knowing he might get sued and have to hire an attorney to represent him

All of these options feel terrible to Gus.

Gus's perception is that Widgets Inc. does not trust him. Widgets Inc.'s perception is that it spent a substantial amount of time and money to support and develop Gus—and it does not want to lose his 19 years of institutional knowledge. Widgets Inc. is also concerned that even if Gus does not reach out to his former Widgets Inc. clients, those clients will still choose to follow him to his new employer. This could cause significant financial harm to the company.

The Takeaway

Non-compete agreements serve legitimate purposes. Companies that sell goods or products to targeted audiences, such as Widgets Inc., have a reasonable basis for restricting salespeople from selling a competitor's similar product to their customers. This is especially true if the product or service is unique in the marketplace, the product or service is highly technical, or the customer base is limited.

From an employee's perspective, though, non-compete agreements can feel like handcuffs: Employees are not free to seek employment in the marketplace in their area of expertise, and they may be forced to stay in a job that is no longer a good fit. Because of these limitations, the employees are no longer enthusiastic team players. This is a lose-lose situation for the employer and the now-Disengaged employees.

Is there a way for companies like Widgets Inc. to protect themselves while giving employees like Gus the freedom to move to a competitor?

Gus *and* his current employer can breathe a sigh of relief. There *is* a way to strike a fair balance for both parties. Let's look at how that can be achieved.

Non-Compete Agreements: The Basics

Non-compete agreements can be structured to protect the employer's business interests while being equitable to employees. To accomplish this, employers first need to understand the basic rules of non-compete agreements. Here's a quick crash course in things you should know.

Federal law does not govern non-compete agreements. Instead, non-compete agreements are legal contracts governed by state laws. This means that the substantive state law identified in the agreement generally governs the enforceability of the agreement. For this reason, if your business is located in different states, you should have a different non-compete agreement in each location to ensure that they will all be enforceable.

California Employers, Take Note: Non-Competes Are No Longer an Option

As of January 1, 2024, California *no longer allows* most employers to require a non-compete agreement as a prerequisite for employment. Further, California employers have an obligation to proactively reach out to all individuals whose employment ended during the past two years and inform them *in writing* that any non-compete agreement they previously entered is no longer valid.

The law allows the state to fine any noncompliant business up to $2,500 per violation. This means that an employer with 100 employees could be fined up to $2,500 per employee (a potential total of $250,000) if it fails to notify.

Your state may not use the term "non-compete." Non-compete agreements are called "restrictive covenants" in some states.

This shouldn't be a DIY document. To ensure enforceability, non-compete agreements should be written by an experienced employment law attorney—as should all technical employment contracts (more on employment law attorneys later in this chapter).

A court may be predisposed to side with your employee. Courts often cite public policy as a reason for not enforcing a non-compete agreement. The public has a vested interest in making sure all people are able to work to their highest and best capacity in jobs of their choice. Courts recognize that employees with non-compete agreements are often limited in their job choices. They aren't allowed to seek better jobs with competitors, but their employer does not have to give raises or increase benefits to retain the employees. Public policy supports free enterprise, rather than limitations.

Is There a Better Alternative to Litigation If I Learn an Employee Intends to Work for a Competitor?

Rather than immediately resorting to litigation, employers are well advised to first have an open conversation with the departing employee about intentions and expectations. If an employee wants to leave, it is in the employer's best interest to allow the employee to do so. However, it is reasonable for the employer to determine whether it can comfortably waive some portions of the non-compete.

If an employer is open to enforcing part, but not all, of the non-compete, the employer can outline specifically permitted activities. For example, the employer may inform the employee, "Employee may work for New Widget Company as a salesperson without violating the terms of his non-compete agreement, provided Employee honors all other terms and conditions of his non-compete agreement, including the confidentiality provisions and all terms regarding non-solicitation of current employees, prospects, and clients."

Blanket policies usually aren't the best choice. Courts in many jurisdictions frown on blanket non-compete agreements; in other words, those that prohibit employees from working at *any* competitor in *any* capacity. Your employment law attorney can help you tailor agreements for each position in your organization with respect to the interest you are seeking to protect. This will maximize the chance that the agreement will be enforceable.

Any non-compete should be mentioned as a requirement of the position in all advertisements and job descriptions. The non-compete should be presented to an applicant prior to an offer being made so he or she may consider, and perhaps negotiate, the terms of the agreement. The agreement should be signed along with any other onboarding paperwork. A copy should be provided to the new employee at the time of hire *and* at the time the employee exits the company so he or she will know what was agreed to.

If a non-compete is first presented *after* an offer is made and accepted, the employee could make a strong argument that the non-compete is not valid because they didn't have an opportunity to negotiate. This is especially true if the employee has already left their prior employment.

What Your Employment Law Attorney Brings to the Table

Before telling an employee that their non-compete prevents them from taking a particular job, you should visit with your employment law attorney and review the agreement in light of the job the employee wishes to take.

When It Comes to Employment Law, You Need a Specialist

When I say "employment law attorney," I don't mean your brother's roommate's sister who is a personal injury lawyer or your church friend who is a tax lawyer. I mean a lawyer who specializes in employment law and nerds out on citing 15 different federal employment laws and discussing the new Secretary of Labor's qualifications during a cocktail party. If your lawyer cannot do that, you need to move on to someone who can. This sector of the law is too complex—and the possible consequences are too steep—to take chances.

Your employment law attorney will:

Determine whether harm is likely to result from an employee's taking a new job. If an employee in your data entry department with no client contact wishes to move to a competitor and work in their data entry department with no client contact, enforcement of the non-compete agreement may not be reasonable because harm is unlikely to result. However, if a person in your sales department with direct access to customers wants to move to a competitor's sales department, the chances are higher that the agreement will be enforceable because harm (the loss of existing customers) is more likely to result. Similarly, the risk to the employer is likely different if an employee wants to work for a competitor one mile away than it is if the employee is hired by a competitor in another state. Generally, the closer the relationship and the more influence the employee has with customers, the more likely it is that a non-compete agreement will be enforced.

Identify which portions of the non-compete may be enforceable (or not). If your non-compete agreement was written by someone other than an employment law attorney, an employment law attorney can review the agreement and advise whether portions of the agreement are valid. A few points to keep in mind:

- Only a court or a jury can ultimately decide whether all or part of the non-compete agreement is enforceable—but an employment law attorney will still have valuable insight into what that decision is likely to be. Getting the matter before a court or a jury can be time-consuming and very expensive for both parties. As with most employment law matters, compromise will save everyone a lot of time, money, and effort. Your employment law attorney will often be able to help create an equitable agreement that benefits both parties.
- Specific provisions in the agreement may be enforceable, while others may be unenforceable. When a court or a jury modifies the agreement, it is called "blue penciling." This means that the court or jury literally strikes out the unenforceable portion of the agreement with a blue pencil. The

court may declare the stricken language completely unenforceable, or it may change the language to be equitable. The unstricken or unchanged language remains enforceable.

Consider your history of enforcing non-competes. Your attorney (and ultimately, the court or jury) may consider whether you have enforced the non-compete agreement for prior employees who exited the organization. If you allowed other employees with non-compete agreements to work for competitors, you likely cannot enforce the agreement against another departing employee. The most important rule of employment law applies to non-compete agreements: consistency, consistency, consistency.

Consider whether you have ever hired an employee who was bound by a non-compete. Your attorney will also ask whether you have ever hired an employee from a competitor knowing that the employee had an existing non-compete agreement. If you are in the practice of ignoring your competitors' non-compete agreements, you will have a very difficult time convincing a judge that you expect your non-compete agreements to be enforced.

Evaluate the age and specific terms of the non-compete. Let's check back with Gus, whose 16-year-old non-compete agreement was signed when the company merely sold widgets made by another entity. The agreement was signed in Florida, where Widgets Inc. is located. Therefore, unless the parties agreed that the substantive law of another state applies, the Florida statute applies. Florida law says that non-compete agreements are valid only if the term of the non-compete is two years or less. If Gus's agreement says that in the future he will *never* work for a competitor, the agreement is presumptively invalid and unenforceable.

What if the agreement had been signed in a state with no such statute? If there is no time limit identified in the agreement, or if the agreement states that the term is "indefinite," that *still* may not actually be the case. In general, the older the non-compete is, the less likely it is to be enforced. It is a good practice for employers to periodically ask their employees to sign new, focused non-competes that are relevant to both the employees' current positions and to the employer's business.

However, even if the limitation term is less than two years, it is possible the court may say the length of time is unreasonable. The court may strike the entire agreement or blue pencil the time limitation and replace it with a shorter period of time.

Consider the geographic scope of the agreement. This is the portion of the agreement that says, "Employee agrees not to work within 50 miles of Employer's headquarters." Like the other terms of non-compete agreements, allowable geographic scopes are set by state law.

With respect to Gus's agreement, Florida law applies and says that geographic scopes must be reasonable. Florida courts have interpreted this to mean that geographic scopes cannot exceed 75 miles. Therefore, a Florida court or jury may consider a 50-mile geographic scope reasonable.

What About Remote Workers?

Geographic scopes are relevant to employees who work in a traditional brick-and-mortar office, but they are less relevant to remote workers who may work several states away from a company's headquarters. Companies often mistakenly use a "nationwide" geographic scope that reads, "Employee agrees not to work with a competitor in the United States." Except in extraordinary cases, this is unenforceable, even for nationwide companies.

Sometimes employers do not include a geographic scope at all, and, as a consequence, employees assume they are prohibited from working anywhere. That assumption is often incorrect. If the agreement does not contain a geographic scope at all, part or all of the non-compete agreement may be considered invalid by the court or jury.

When drafting a non-compete agreement for remote workers, it is advisable to focus on terms that are *not* tied to geography.

Determine whether there is a legitimate business reason for the non-compete agreement. Some states require that employers identify in writing a specific reason that the non-compete agreement is necessary to preserve and protect the employer's legitimate business interests. This frequently occurs in medical practices where patients feel a very personal connection to their healthcare provider. These practices are legitimately concerned that a departing provider might take a significant portion of the practice's patients with them.

In our example, if Widgets Inc. can show that it would lose clients to the competitor as a direct result of Gus's departure *because the clients only wanted to work directly with Gus*, then Widgets Inc. might have a legitimate business interest for requiring the non-compete agreement.

Of course, if Gus departs Widgets Inc. and clients report that Gus has been soliciting their business on behalf of the competitor, Gus's credibility before the court would be diminished. Widgets Inc. would have a better chance of prevailing in a lawsuit.

Creating the Win-Win for the Employer and the Employee (Yes, It *Can* Be Done)

If you're thinking, *Non-competes are WAY more complicated than I thought*, or even, *There are so many things that could make a non-compete unenforceable. What's the point of creating one in the first place?*…I get it. The truth is, statutes and standards governing non-compete agreements *are* complex, and there are a lot of variables. (Again, that's why it's so important to work with an employment law attorney.)

The good news for employers and employees is that there *are* several ways to draft fair and enforceable non-compete agreements. There are also equitable alternatives to non-compete agreements. Here are some options that may work for your organization.

Proactively identify employees who should sign a non-compete. Some companies require every single employee to sign non-compete agreements, but this is rarely necessary—and can lead to an equally unnecessary court case. A better alternative is to identify employees whose departure might cause clients to leave and ask only those employees to sign non-compete agreements. (If your goal is to protect information, I recommend using a different type of document, which we'll look at shortly.) For instance:

- A receptionist who works at an ophthalmologist's office should be permitted to work as a technician at another ophthalmologist's office.
- An ophthalmologist who wishes to work for a competitor may be required to abide by an agreement because the ophthalmologist likely has close,

personal relationships with patients. Her departure is more likely to result in the loss of patients, which would directly harm the organization.

Tailor non-compete agreements to each employee. You can request that employees sign narrow non-compete agreements, tailored for each person based on that employee's particular position and access to information.

For example, an architect who designs residential buildings should be permitted to work for a competitor who designs commercial structures. If that competitor also designs residential structures, it is reasonable that the architect not work on any residential structures for a specific period of time. It is also reasonable for the first employer to require that the architect not perform work for existing clients.

Consider creating a non-solicitation agreement… Another alternative to a total non-compete agreement is a different legal document: a non-solicitation agreement. In a non-solicitation agreement, an employee may agree not to solicit or interfere with the employer's existing customers, clients, or patients for a designated period of time. This agreement is equitable because it protects the employer's existing relationships but allows the employee to solicit business from other customers, clients, or patients. In this agreement, an employer may also think it prudent to require that a departing employee not solicit an existing employee (i.e., one of the departing employee's current colleagues) for employment with the new employer.

…Or a confidentiality agreement. Confidentiality agreements are an effective and very reasonable way to protect information. In a confidentiality agreement, employees agree that they will be permitted to work for any competitor as long as they agree to maintain any information they learned from their current employer in complete confidence. Confidentiality agreements can protect trade secrets, formulas, patented data, business goals, client lists, pricing structures, marketing techniques, internal processes and policies, sales strategies, and any other non-public information that provides a competitive advantage. A consequence for failure to abide by the agreement may be incorporated as well.

What Should Gus and Widgets Inc. Do?

Let's return to Gus and the dilemma he faces in leaving Widgets Inc. Given these options, what might a win-win for him and his employer look like?

If, after evaluating all of these factors, Widgets Inc.'s employment law attorney concludes that Gus's agreement is likely to be wholly or partially unenforceable, she may advise Widgets Inc. to work out a reasonable, mutually beneficial agreement with Gus. Perhaps Widgets Inc. and Gus agree that Gus can accept the job with the competitor but must agree not to work in a particular area (sales, development, etc.) or in a given geography for a certain amount of time (less than two years—remember Florida law!). If both Gus and Widgets Inc. act honorably, there should be a compromise that allows Gus to remain in the industry while protecting Widgets Inc.'s interest in maintaining its current clients and confidential information.

Another alternative would be for Widgets Inc. to present Gus with a counteroffer that would eliminate his reason for leaving. If Gus is departing for more opportunity, greater responsibility, or higher compensation *and* Widgets Inc. can provide those things in the form of a promotion or raise, that would be an even bigger win-win.

In Conclusion

Losing a valued employee can feel unsettling and stressful, but seeking to enforce a stringent non-compete agreement is unlikely to end well. Even within large industries, it can be a small world. You don't want to burn bridges or establish a reputation of being unfair or vindictive toward departing employees. (Remember, thanks to social media and tools like Glassdoor, a disgruntled employee can tell their side of the story to thousands of job-seekers—and as we'll discuss in Chapter 16: Do Not Friend Me on Social Media, your ability to respond and tell your side of the story is very limited.)

Instead, work with an employment law attorney and make it your goal to always find the win-win. Working toward an equitable compromise that both parties are satisfied with is *always* worth the effort.

CHAPTER 8

If You Have to Fire Me, Do It with Heart

Young Amie's Story

When I was 16, I worked part-time in the security department of a department store. My job was to stand behind a podium at the entrance of the Junior's Department dressing room and give each entering customer a plastic card printed with the number of items the customer was trying on. When the customer exited the dressing room, I was supposed to count the number of items again to ensure that all items were being purchased or returned to inventory.

When I was not handing out number cards or collecting items as a customer exited the dressing room, I was supposed to visually scan the store, looking for anyone who might be shoplifting. These duties were clearly described to me during the interview and onboarding process. They were reasonable and simple to follow. I accepted the job understanding what my tasks were.

I generally worked after school on weeknights when there were very few shoppers. Scanning an empty store was not very interesting, so I often opened a book behind the podium and read.

The first time my supervisor, Marv, saw me doing this, he patiently and kindly explained why members of the security department and other store employees were not allowed to read at work. He told me that all employees were expected to watch shoppers, especially in areas crowded with clothing rounds. He pointed out that the Junior's Department was a high-theft area. The rationale for asking employees to scan the store (rather than read books) as a method of theft prevention made perfect sense. Marv further explained that if I was reading, I was not engaging with the customers.

Nonetheless, on low-traffic evenings, I continued to hide books on the podium and sneak paragraphs in when I thought no one was looking. Of course, Marv caught me again. I didn't see him watching me because I was reading, not paying attention to the store or to any potential shoplifters around me.

The second time Marv saw me reading on the job, he called me into his office and again went over my duties and the reasons why I couldn't read at work. Like many teenagers, I did what I wanted rather than what I was told to do (and what I was being paid to do).

The third time Marv saw me reading a book behind the podium, he again explained that reading on the job prevented me from scanning the store to look for shoplifters. Then, in private and with compassion, he fired me.

Even at 16, I knew Marv was right and I was wrong. I also knew that I deserved to be fired. Finally, I knew that in Marv's position, I would have fired me too!

Marv did everything right: He explained the job duties to me during the interview, gave me two chances to improve, and told me the "why" behind the policy. Marv did not fire me until he witnessed me ignoring the store's policy and his instructions…three separate times. From that first-job experience, I learned the *right way* to fire someone.

The Takeaway

There are a lot of upsides to being an employment lawyer. I love watching employees succeed, learn new things, and receive promotions. And I love watching employees who, at the end of their careers, are proud of their contributions and accomplishments, and retire feeling fulfilled.

The downside to being an employment lawyer is that employees (like me) do get fired, and no matter how much any employee "deserves" to get fired (as I did), it often feels terrible for the person who makes the decision to end someone's employment. I suspect every single employer, employment lawyer, and human resources professional finds this process difficult. (If you don't, you should seriously question whether burnout or another issue is affecting your empathy and integrity as a leader.)

Terminating an employment relationship is especially difficult and uncomfortable if it is the result of forces outside the employer's or employee's control, such as an economic downturn or the loss of a large client that results in a reduction in force, a layoff, or a furlough.

Even if an employee suspects that termination may be on the horizon, most termination meetings result in immediate emotion for the employee being terminated. Rarely does an employee calmly or unemotionally think, *Yeah, I deserved that*. Instead, the employee may feel shock, disbelief, anger, sadness, grief, surprise, worry, or a combination of these and other very human emotions. The employee being terminated may direct all of these emotions toward you. They may, rightly or wrongly, blame you—even when the employee broke rules, did not follow directives, or otherwise deserved to be terminated. In some cases, termination meetings can even cross the line from emotional or litigious to dangerous. This is especially true if the person conducting the termination meeting is unprepared or handles the discussion without sensitivity.

Further, employees who feel they have been wrongfully terminated can quite easily do great damage to your organization's reputation. They are entitled to use social media to share their opinions about their employment and their version of the events surrounding termination. And as we'll discuss in Chapter 16: Do Not Friend Me on Social Media, employers are limited in their ability to respond. This can create a challenge for the organization.

For these reasons, termination meetings need to be handled delicately. How do you end another person's employment with kindness, humanity, and dignity, and in a way that protects you and your organization from liability and (hopefully) retaliation? The answer may depend on whether you are terminating an employee with cause (such as absenteeism, lack of performance, continual mistakes, or insubordination) or without cause (such as a reduction in force where the employee's employment ends through no fault of their own).

How Do I Avoid a Lawsuit? (The Legal Stuff)

First, let's look at what employers should do to protect themselves and their organizations from a legal standpoint. Following these guidelines will help you avoid being sued for wrongful termination, and will also ensure that you are fair and equitable to all employees who may need to be terminated.

First, Perform a Termination Analysis

Prior to making any termination decision, it is critical that the right person perform a thorough termination analysis. This person should be your human resources manager, your employment attorney, or someone else with experience in this area who can evaluate your risk from all angles. This person should be as unbiased as possible (ideally, they should not work closely with the employee) and able to look at the factors leading to termination objectively. Here are some important components of the pre-termination decision analysis:

Is there a legitimate, objective, business-related reason to terminate the employee? You may find it helpful to pretend that you have been sued and are explaining your decision to terminate the employee to a jury:

- What reasons would you provide to the jury to justify the decision to end a person's employment?
- What would the terminated employee say in response?
- Would your documentation support the reason you provided for the termination? (more on this next)
- Who would the jury believe?

An employer should never manufacture a reason for termination, even if the manufactured reason is more palatable than the actual reason. Similarly, a termination should never be called a voluntary resignation, even if you think a voluntary resignation would be better for the employee. In reality, a voluntary resignation might result in the loss of eligibility for unemployment or other state-provided benefits.

If there is any doubt as to the validity of the reason for the termination, another alternative should be explored. This could include retraining the employee to perform a specific task, putting the employee on a written improvement plan, or pairing the employee with a mentor—all while thoroughly documenting the process.

Do you have objective data and documentation to support the termination? Let's walk through an example. You want to terminate a salesperson, Joe, because he failed to meet a quota.

- *First,* you need to ensure that the quota was communicated to Joe (ideally in writing). Put yourself in Joe's shoes: If the job expectations were not clearly articulated, how is it fair to expect him to perform to the organization's standards?

Quotas Are Measured "By the Numbers"

It's important to have objective, measurable data to support terminations—not just subjective evaluations or opinions. The "quota" could be any quantifiable expectation or job duty:

- In sales, it is often the number of closings completed or revenue generated.
- In a legal practice, it is generally the number of billable or collected hours.
- In phlebotomy, it can be the number of "clean sticks" the nurse or tech achieves.
- In claims, quotas are measured by the dollars saved.

- *Second,* you must ensure that the quota was consistent with the quotas of similarly situated employees. In Joe's case, these would be other salespeople in his geographic region. If Joe's quota differed from those of similarly situated sales employees, you need to be able to articulate an objective reason for the difference. In other words, why are you treating Joe differently from the rest of his team? There may be legitimate reasons for having different quotas. Maybe Joe worked in a different vertical, or maybe quotas are based on experience.
- *Third,* to assess your risk of being sued for wrongful termination or discrimination under state or federal law, you need to determine whether all similarly situated sales employees with the same quota met that quota. If Joe has a better sales record than an employee you are retaining, you need to stop and ask yourself why you are terminating Joe and retaining an employee with a weaker sales record. If you fail to do so, Joe's termination may look like favoritism, or worse, discrimination. This is particularly true if Joe and the employee who was not terminated are of different sexes, colors, races, religions, national origins, or other protected characteristics.

Does the employee have a legally protected status under discrimination laws? If the reason you are treating Joe differently has anything to do with the aforementioned legally protected statuses, Joe could bring a Charge of Discrimination before the Equal Employment Opportunity Commission (or state agency), and a subsequent lawsuit. You can avoid potential litigation by ensuring that employment decisions are made for neutral reasons.

Does the employee have any other type of legally protected status? To fully assess your risk of being sued for retaliation or discrimination, you need to do an analysis to determine whether Joe has protections under state or federal laws *other than* discrimination laws.

For example, let's say that Joe has requested, is currently taking, or has recently used protected time under state workers' compensation laws, the federal Family and Medical Leave Act (FMLA) or a state counterpart, or the federal Uniformed Services Employment and Reemployment Rights Act (USERRA). If you terminate him shortly after his request, during his leave, or shortly after his leave, the termination may appear retaliatory. Under most state and federal laws, the temporal—or close in time—relationship between the protected act (Joe's request for protected leave or leave taken) and the adverse act (Joe's termination) can create a presumption that the adverse action was discriminatory or retaliatory.

This presumption is rebuttable, meaning the employer can offer evidence to support the termination. But proving that the adverse action was unrelated to the protected conduct can be time-consuming and costly. It is much more efficient to evaluate and make the proper decision on the front end, rather than trying to prove that your decision was legal after a Charge of Discrimination or lawsuit has been filed.

The same would be true if Joe engaged in an act that made him a whistleblower under state or federal law. In those instances, the same temporal—or close in time—analysis and rebuttable presumption would apply.

What Is a Whistleblower?

The federal Occupational Safety and Health Act of 1970 provides protections for employees (known as whistleblowers) who report unsafe conditions in a private workplace through the enforcement of over 20 different federal laws. State OSHA laws mirror (and often broaden) federal laws. Both state and federal OSHA laws contain anti-retaliation provisions. This means that an employer *may not take* an adverse action against an employee who is a whistleblower, or against an employee who makes a report to a state or federal agency like OSHA.

An adverse action is any action that materially changes the terms or conditions of an employee's employment for the worse. This can be an actual action or an action that creates the perception of reduced status. Adverse actions include demotions; changes to geographic territory; unreasonable, unattainable, or unexplainable increased quotas; reprimands; threats of reducing (or actually reducing) an employee's title or status; moving an employee to a less-impressive branch or office; or, of course, termination of an employee.

Rather than *responding* to a whistleblower claim (or any sort of lawsuit, for that matter), an employer's time, money, and energy are better spent *preventing* safety and health issues in the workplace. If it is revealed that safety or health issues do exist, it is far more efficient to cooperate in an open spirit with OSHA (or any government agency) and work to solve any legitimate problem than it is to litigate. In no case should an employer threaten the employee or play "hide the ball" with OSHA—or any other state or federal government agency.

It is important to note that being in a protected category does not give an employee the right to behave in an unacceptable manner. The same standard of conduct should be applied to every person on your payroll. If anything, the fact that so many employees fall into one or more protected categories underscores the need for consistent treatment and thorough documentation of any event that may lead to discipline or termination.

The Termination Is Justified—Now What?

Once you have completed your legal due diligence and made the decision that a termination is justified, follow these steps:

Ensure that you are prepared to follow any state law regarding notice at the time of termination. Many states require employers to give specific notices to employees at the end of employment—some states require specific forms or pamphlets, and others require employers to provide general information. Some notices must be provided upon termination, and others must be provided within a certain number of days after the last day worked. For example, in Colorado, employers must notify employees in writing that unemployment insurance benefits may be available. To do so, they must give the employee a form called Notice of Potential Availability of Unemployment Insurance Benefits. For a current copy of the form, visit the webpage of the Colorado Department of Labor and Employment.

Ensure you are prepared to follow all state laws regarding timing and manner of final pay for terminated employees. If you are terminating an employee in Iowa, their final pay is due on or before the next regular pay date. If you are terminating an employee in Minnesota, you must be prepared to make final payment on the next regular payroll or within 24 hours of the employee demanding his or her final pay—whichever comes first. In Montana, however, final pay is due immediately. In my state of Florida, final pay must be tendered on the next regularly scheduled payroll. Be sure you're familiar with the laws that apply to your organization.

Determine *how* the termination will be conducted and schedule a termination meeting. Where there is no immediate need to terminate, it is always advisable to schedule the meeting at a time when two employer-representatives can be present—even if this means delaying the meeting a day or two. (We'll talk more about the timing later in this chapter.)

The first employer-representative (e.g., the supervisor, the human resources manager, or the owner) can speak to the employee about the termination. In other words, this employee conveys the message, "Your employment is ending today." The second employee's function is to witness what was said and by whom. This person should immediately document the details of the meeting so there is a contemporaneous record of what occurred. If the departing employee files an unemployment claim, a Charge of Discrimination, or a lawsuit, having the documentation and two witnesses available to testify about what was said and by whom will be invaluable.

What If There Isn't Time to Plan a Meeting?

Of course, there may be times when it is necessary to exit an employee immediately. For example, if an employee becomes violent, is violating health and safety standards, or is found using illegal drugs, it may be better to escort them from the building for the safety of the other employees. Your company may have other zero-tolerance policies that require an employee's immediate termination, such as violating customers' privacy or falsifying records. In these instances, you can handle the logistics at a later time, via phone.

How Do I Keep My Employees and Myself Safe? (The Security Stuff)

One of the most important parts of determining *how* a termination decision will be communicated involves considering whether the employee might have any propensity toward violence. In my experience, this is extremely rare. However, if there is even a remote possibility that the employee could become violent before, during, or after the termination, it is imperative that you take steps to protect yourself and your other employees.

You might consider some or all of the following tactics:

Hiring an off-duty law enforcement officer or a professional security guard to be present during and after the termination. The law enforcement officer or security guard does not have to be present in the meeting. Instead, the law enforcement officer or guard can be strategically and discreetly placed at or near the location where the meeting is taking place. To protect the dignity of the employee being terminated, to the extent possible, it should not be obvious why the law enforcement officer or guard is present.

If necessary, the law enforcement officer or security guard can be asked to escort the employee to his or her car and/or remain at or near the office for the remainder of the day, week, or even longer.

Having two employer-representatives present. In addition to the legal reasons noted above, this is important because there is safety in numbers. If two employer-representatives are present, there is less likelihood that the departing employee may become violent.

Conducting the meeting in a neutral location with a glass door or window. As noted earlier, three people should ideally be in a termination meeting: the employee conveying the termination message, the employee receiving the termination message, and an employee who is a witness to the event.

Where each person should sit or stand is important. The employee conveying the message should be facing the door or window where others can see his or her face. The witness should sit somewhere close to the door. If the terminated employee becomes physically upset or threatening, it is easy for the witness to signal to the law enforcement officer or security guard, or to other employees if necessary, that help is needed.

For privacy reasons, the employee being terminated should face away from the door or window. If the terminated employee begins to cry or becomes flustered, he or she will not want coworkers to witness his or her tears or facial expression.

Are Remote Terminations Ever Appropriate?

Although terminations should normally be done face-to-face, if an employee works fully remote, or if there is a high likelihood of a safety issue, terminations can be done over the phone or via Zoom or Teams. These terminations, however, tend to lose the human element of compassion.

For more information about preventing workplace violence, see Chapter 2: Show Me You Care by Investing in Security to Keep Me Safe at Work.

How Do I Handle This Situation with Sensitivity? (The Human Stuff)

Now that you have gone through the entire risk analysis and decided to move forward with a termination meeting, the next step is to determine when it will occur.

Many employers prefer to terminate employees on Friday afternoons since it is the end of the workweek for traditional Monday-Friday businesses. I prefer to terminate *during* the workweek. Employees who are terminated on Friday afternoon are limited in the steps they can take to get back on their feet. However, employees who are terminated between Monday and Thursday are generally able to file for unemployment compensation with their state agency, begin a new job search, network with industry colleagues, or register with a staffing agency or search firm the very next day.

As with other important-message meetings, preparing for the termination meeting is of utmost importance. Remember that the employee being terminated is losing much more than salary. The end of employment can result in the loss of group health benefits, disability benefits, life insurance, and retirement savings vehicles for many employees. It can also change an employee's reputation or status in their family or community. Therefore, while you may have many other things on your to-do list that day, the termination meeting must be treated as if it is the most important matter of the day—because to the employee being terminated, it is.

Here are the steps I recommend taking to prepare:

Schedule the meeting at a time when you can really focus on the employee being terminated. You need to be 100 percent present and engaged for that employee. Do not schedule the meeting at a time when you will be hungry, distracted, or worried about another meeting.

Schedule 50 percent more time than you think you will need. If you think the meeting will take 30 minutes, schedule an extra 15 minutes. It may take the employee some time after hearing the news to process what you are saying, to think of questions to ask, and to put themselves (emotionally) back together so they can walk out without looking like a mess. You may have to repeat the message more than once. This is especially true if the employee will be surprised by the news.

Clear your desk (and your mind) of distractions. If your to-do list is right in front of you, you will be tempted to look at it and mentally catalog what comes next for you. There should be no interruptions in the meeting, so turn off your cell phone and office phone. Turn your email notifications off or to silent. If you have an assistant, ensure that he or she does not permit anyone to interrupt you during this time.

Be prepared to explain the "why" of your decision. If you are letting someone go because of a costly error, you may choose to say something like, "I want you to understand the consequences of your behavior so you don't repeat the mistake in your next position. When you failed to perform the task/made the mistake, it cost the company in the following manner." The cost to the company may be stated in terms of dollars, time, lost product, or a lost client. After explaining this to the employee, the employee may understand—and maybe even agree—with your decision. In some cases, understanding the "why" behind their termination might even affect whether an employee decides to seek unemployment compensation or take legal action. For instance, an employee who admits that the termination was justified is less likely to bring a lawsuit against your organization.

Try to anticipate questions the employee may ask. Have as many answers prepared as possible. If the employee asks questions you do not know the answers to, do not put the burden on the employee to email you a list of questions after the meeting. Instead, write each question down, repeat it back to ensure you are communicating clearly with the employee, and then get the answers to the employee as quickly as possible.

If your company offers group health insurance, anticipate and have answers to questions related to the continuation of group health benefits. Common questions include:

- What is COBRA?
- When does my current coverage end and COBRA eligibility begin?
- How long will COBRA last?
- When and how will I receive my COBRA election options?
- Does COBRA cover dental, eye, and other group health benefits?
- Who pays the premiums?
- Are the premiums deducted from my final check?
- How much will the premiums be going forward?
- Will I be expected to pay all of the premiums or only the employee portion of the premiums?
- Where and how frequently will I mail premiums?
- Can I still use my Flexible Spending Account/Health Savings Account?
- If I get a new job that offers group health, can I keep using COBRA or do I have to enroll in the new job's health coverage?
- Does COBRA cover my dependents?

If your company offers other benefit plans, you may be asked:
- Will I lose my long-term/short-term disability coverage?
- Do I roll my 401(k) over to a new employer or can I put it in a private non-employer IRA?
- How do I roll over my 401(k)?
- Will there be a penalty if I roll over my 401(k)?
- Is there a payout of my "banked" sick/vacation/paid time off?
- What if I need to pay expenses using my 401(k)? Is that considered a "hardship" under the 401(k) plan?

Other common questions to anticipate include:
- Can I work two more weeks so I can job hunt before being terminated?
- Can I tell future employers that I quit/resigned, rather than was terminated?
- What can I tell future employers on job applications?
- What will you tell future employers?
- Are you willing to write me a reference?

Can I Serve as a Reference for a Terminated Employee?

Some terminated employees wouldn't dream of asking a former supervisor for a reference. But especially if the termination was (fairly) amicable, if the termination was the result of a reduction in force, or if the employee has no other choice, you might be asked to provide one.

Some companies limit references to information that confirms a person worked for the organization, such as name, job title, dates of employment, and final compensation amount—but nothing more. This is not a bad practice. Their concern, of course, is that if the company says something negative about the employee, the employee will sue for defamation. Therefore, before you agree to provide a reference for a former employee, check your organization's policy. This is another area where consistency is key.

If you choose to provide a reference for a terminated employee, ensure that the reference is truthful. If the person was terminated because they couldn't handle the skills portion of the job but you don't want to say anything overtly negative, the reference can simply say what was true: that they were on time, they were dependable, and they were honest, for example.

- How do I appeal this decision?
- Do I have union or collective bargaining representation, or appeal rights?
- Will I receive severance? If yes, what are the terms?
- How is final pay, "banked" sick/vacation/paid time off, or severance pay paid and taxed?
- How do I receive my personal items in my desk or saved on my computer?
- Do I have a right to a lawyer before this termination becomes effective?
- What can I tell my coworkers (because I don't want them to know I was fired)?
- What will you tell my coworkers?
- If I am able to obtain a job with a competitor, are you going to enforce my non-compete agreement/non-solicitation agreement?
- Can I keep my computer/cell phone/printer, etc.?

Anticipate emotions. Have tissues available. Be kind. Be patient. Even if you are genuinely saddened or moved, do not cry (or, try really, really hard not to!). It should not be incumbent upon the employee to comfort you.

Come to the meeting prepared with the appropriate scripts and documents. I recommend having the following:

- **A script detailing the reason for the termination, answers to questions you anticipate, and information unique to the termination.** In healthcare, for example, this might include a reminder that the employee's confidentiality obligations under the Health Insurance Portability and Accountability Act (HIPAA) continue after employment ends.

   The script will (I promise) help make the termination meeting go more smoothly. It will also ensure that you don't miss key points. Perhaps most importantly from a legal standpoint, it will provide you with proof of what was said at the meeting, should there be any litigation down the road.

Soften the Blow with Yvonne's Script

My friend Yvonne worked in human resources for 30 years and always prepared a script. When she had to terminate an employee for performance reasons, she always made sure to strike the right tone and say, "Even though this was not the job for you, you will be successful elsewhere." This is a great way to soften the blow without missing the message.

And many times, she was right—the person *was* successful at another place.

- **A list of physical items and other information you need to know before the employee exits,** such as:
  - Keys, key/swipe cards, or fobs to the office or building
  - Equipment such as computers, cell phones, printers, or car/truck keys
  - Login information in the employee's possession, including usernames and passwords
  - Sign-on information to any company-provided research or subscription services
  - Any company data maintained on any personal device such as a cell phone or laptop (hopefully there is not any, but it's necessary to ask)
  - Any company data maintained in hard copy in the employee's possession (particularly if the employee works remotely)
- **Any documents the employee needs to take action after leaving**, such as COBRA benefit election forms.
- **A copy of any employment contract/agreement, a non-compete agreement, a non-solicitation agreement, a confidentiality agreement, or any sort of binding agreement you wish to enforce.** Providing a copy of the document to the employee at the meeting allows them to review the terms and conditions you expect them to honor.
- **The name and contact information of any staffing agency with whom you have a relationship and are willing to make a referral.** Providing

such information helps the employee look forward to a positive future.

- **Where appropriate and consistent with company policy, a pre-written letter of recommendation.** For instance, if an employee is being terminated as the result of a reduction in force, a positive recommendation is both a powerful gesture of goodwill and a valuable tool in the coming job search.

Protect the Privacy of the Exiting Employee

Remaining employees often ask their supervisors why a particular coworker is no longer with the company. My standard answer is, "Just as I wouldn't share your personal information with another person, I cannot share another person's personal information with you."

In Conclusion

Despite what reality television may show, terminating an employee is not entertainment. And no matter how many times you've had this type of conversation, it should never be treated as a "normal," routine part of your job. Regardless of the reason for termination, from the first step to the last, remember that terminating the employee will probably radically change their life. Treat the decision, analysis, preparation, and meeting as the serious and important occasions they are. Each individual should be treated kindly, delicately, confidentially, and with grace.

CHAPTER 9

If You Are Curious Why I Quit, Just Ask Me

Molly's Story

Molly has worked as a full-time fitness and nutrition instructor for three years at a locally owned gym, Fitness USA. She loves her job and enjoys the relationships she has built with her coworkers and clients. She and her supervisor have a cordial, professional relationship.

Last week, Molly gave her supervisor notice that she intended to voluntarily resign in two weeks' time. Her supervisor was surprised and disappointed because Molly is a well-liked hard worker who will be difficult to replace. Despite feeling curious about Molly's reasons for leaving, Molly's supervisor wanted to respect her privacy and did not inquire why Molly made the decision.

Had Molly's supervisor asked, she would have learned that Molly did not want to leave; however, her rent had increased. To be able to afford the new payment, Molly needed to seek employment making a higher wage.

Armed with the knowledge that compensation was the only reason Molly voluntarily resigned, it might have been possible for Molly's employer to meet Molly's compensation needs by offering additional tasks, overtime work, or more responsibility. Even if it was not possible to provide Molly the opportunity to earn enough to remain on staff full-time, Molly's supervisor might have been able to retain Molly as a fitness instructor on a part-time, class-by-class, or fill-in basis.

The Takeaway

For most employees, deciding to voluntarily end employment is a very big decision. It has lasting and impactful consequences for the employee and his or her family. The employee may be giving up secure compensation, health benefits, retirement benefits, vested paid time off accrual, and other benefits. It is unlikely that the decision was made lightly.

To improve an organization for the future, learn what changes it can make to encourage other employees not to quit, and potentially retain employees like Molly who are reluctant to depart, it is critical that employers find out why any employee chose to voluntarily leave. Employers may have an idea or assume they know why an employee quit, but until they actually *ask* the employee, they don't *really* know what motivated the person to leave.

You cannot fix things if you don't know they are broken. It won't always be comfortable, but you have to take steps to learn what works in your organization and what doesn't. Therefore, I recommend attempting to schedule an end-of-employment interview for all employees.

Bear in mind that employees do not *have* to participate in exit interviews. To encourage participation, employers can assure employees that the information will be used to evaluate what the organization does well and where it needs improvement.

Consider Giving Employees Who Were Terminated an Exit Interview, Too

Although it can be uncomfortable, determining why these employees were *not* successful at your organization is just as important as determining why other employees chose to leave. It is incumbent on you, the employer, to learn whether there was anything you might have done differently to help make the employee successful—and anything you can do to better support other employees in the future.

In my experience, you'll hear many of the same things from terminated employees that you do from employees who voluntarily leave the organization: "My manager didn't pay attention to me." "I felt like I was being asked to do too much." "The culture here is really negative."

How to Conduct an End-of-Employment Interview

Regardless of the circumstances behind an employee's departure, this is a conversation that should be approached with sensitivity. Handled well, an end-of-employment (or exit) interview can provide eye-opening, actionable information that will help you make positive changes in your organization. Both you and the employee can part on amicable terms, hopefully with a degree of mutual respect.

Handled poorly, though, an exit interview can alienate the employee—who has the power to spread their dissatisfaction with your organization to anyone with a wi-fi signal.

Here are some pointers to help you navigate end-of-employment interviews.

Pick the right person to conduct the end-of-employment interview. Ideally, end-of-employment interviews should be done by someone in the human resources department who:

- has experience in speaking to employees who may or may not be happy to leave an organization
- is trusted by employees to share information only with those in a need to know circle
- has experience evaluating the difference between a personal grievance and a legitimate concern that merits action

A skilled interviewer will ask questions and actively listen to the responses *without* assuming that he or she already knows the employees' opinions.

Determine the best format for the end-of-employment interview. Exit interviews can be done in person, over the phone, via Zoom or Teams, or by submitting written questions to the employee. Ideally, the organization needs to use only one method (to the extent possible), so questions are consistent and results can be measured.

The manner in which exit interviews are conducted depends on the organization. Some organizations are too small to have a human resources department. For those organizations, a casual conversation may be sufficient to gather meaningful information. For organizations with a human resources department, exit interviews may be conducted in person (or via Zoom or Teams for remote employees) if the separation of employment is voluntary. For very large corporations, it may be impossible to interview every single person. Those organizations may find it most efficient to interview by email survey.

If an employee has been fired, the exit interview should not be conducted on site. A conversation via Zoom or Teams, or submitting written questions to the employee, might be better options.

Pay attention to timing. The timing of end-of-employment interviews is important. If the employee has been fired, the interview should be done after the employee has had a few days to process his or her loss. If the departure is voluntary and amicable, it can be done on the last day of employment.

Determine what will be done with the information gathered and with whom it will be shared. Honest feedback is good and important—even if it is uncomfortable to hear. It does not do an organization any good to gather valuable information and then not evaluate and use it. If more than one employee has left for the same reason, has concerns about the same supervisor, is frustrated with a particular internal process, or mentions that a specific policy is unfair, then the organization can learn a great deal from the information and use it to improve in the future.

What Questions Should Be Asked in an Exit Interview?

It's ultimately up to you to determine which questions are relevant to your organization, but important things to ask the departing employee might include:

- Why are you leaving our company?
- Do you feel like you were treated fairly?
- If you were running this business, what would you do differently?
- Are you aware of any concerns management should address?
- Do you feel like you were paid fairly for the work you performed?
- Did you have confidence in your direct supervisor?
- Did you have confidence in management?

- Did you understand steps available to seek advancement or promotion in the organization?
- Do you feel like your advancement or promotion opportunities were fair?
- Do you feel like there is a disparity in the way the company treats different people?
- If you were offered a raise equal to what you will be making in your new position, would you remain with this company?
- Are there more competitive benefits we should be offering?
- Was your supervisor fair to you?
- Does the company live its mission, vision, and values?
- Is there anything you would change about the organization?

There's one important caveat here: You don't *have* to wait until an employee is leaving to ask these questions. In fact, you probably shouldn't! Many of these questions can be posed to current employees during check-ins, evaluations, and surveys. Depending on what you do with the information you gather, you may be able to keep valuable employees on your payroll instead of someone else's.

End-of-Employment Interviews Are Tough for Both Parties

Whether an employee quit voluntarily or was fired, end-of-employment interviews are generally difficult for both the employee and the employer.

Departing employees may be hesitant to participate in exit interviews because:
- They need you as a reference for their next and future jobs.
- They live in a town where they are likely to run into you and do not want to feel uncomfortable, embarrassed, or intimidated.
- They have a severance or separation agreement and fear losing the benefits under the agreement.
- They are concerned about their reputation inside your organization and in the community.

- They do not fully trust your organization to keep the information confidential.
- They have friends at your organization whose employment has not ended, and they wish to maintain those relationships.
- They do not have confidence that their opinion matters.
- Worst of all, they feel "beat up" and just want to end the employment relationship without jumping through any more hoops.

Similarly, as an employer, you may be hesitant to conduct an end-of-employment interview because:
- They are time consuming.
- Employees may say things that are difficult to hear.
- Employees may say things that you do not believe are true or accurate.
- Employees may use exit interviews as a chance to vent grievances (many of which could have been remedied if shared by the employee during employment).

For example, common things employers hear in exit interviews from employees leaving because they are unhappy include:
- "I can earn $1 per hour more doing a different job."
- "My supervisor knew less about the job or organization than I do."
- "I want to work somewhere with better/different values."
- "The organization does not live its mission."
- "My supervisor micromanaged me."
- "I felt ignored at work."
- "My loyalty/production/attitude/quality of work *was never* recognized by management."
- "My supervisor played favorites."
- "I was harassed, discriminated against, or retaliated against."

Even though it can be very uncomfortable, it is critical that employers be willing to hear these things. Remember that although the employer may disagree with the statements, it is the employee's *perception* that these things are true, and in some cases, they are serious enough to justify leaving the organization. Therefore, organizations should honestly evaluate whether information provided by the former employee has credibility and can benefit the organization.

Assuming an employee does not reveal information about illegal activity that requires a response (as in a fraud or harassment report), the key is to look beyond what a single employee reveals. In other words, look for patterns: Is the information isolated to one departing employee, or has the information been said by others about a particular supervisor, department, policy, or practice? If you are hearing the same or similar information from more than one former employee, this is a theme that bears evaluating.

To help you understand and act on what departing employees tell you, let's break down information commonly revealed during exit interviews and identify what you, the employer, should take away from these revelations.

What They Said, What You Should Consider, and What to Do Next

Information provided by the employee in an exit interview: "I can earn $1 per hour more doing a different job."

What the employer should consider: Discovering a pattern that employees are leaving for better wages or benefits signals an opportunity to evaluate these areas. The best employees want to work for organizations with competitive pay and benefit packages. The best employers do not want to lose good employees like Molly if they can afford to keep them. After all, replacing an engaged employee like Molly may be difficult.

What the employer should do next: To determine whether you are paying competitive market rates, evaluate the objective skills required for success in each position, and then determine approximately how much those skills are worth in the open marketplace. This can be done through an in-depth salary survey or compensation study where you evaluate:

- The objective data related to the education or certification requirements for each position (A salary survey will provide a compensation range for specific positions based on educational requirements and job duties.)
- The cost of living where your organization and employees are located
- The market and competition for that job
- Any pay disparities that might exist in the organization (whether caused by wage compression, gender or race discrimination, or historical decision-making)

Not only does a salary survey help an employer determine whether its pay practices are competitive and fair, going through the process of a salary survey and implementing recommended changes can also help organizations defend discrimination lawsuits. The organization will be able to provide objective data to show that its pay practices are based on legitimate, non-discriminatory factors, rather than illegal factors.

Salary surveys are often offered by professional recruiting firms because their goal is to help you find the best person for the position you are filling—and offering a competitive, fair salary can be a key factor in attracting talent. Salary surveys may also be conducted using platforms designed to evaluate jobs based on the job description, geography, size of the company, and other factors.

Information provided by the employee in an exit interview: "My supervisor knew less about the job or organization than I do."

What the employer should consider: Whether a supervisor is a new hire or is promoted from within the organization, it is very frustrating when a subordinate employee perceives that they have to train their supervisor or that they understand the organization better than their supervisor does. Of course, just because an employee perceives this does not make it so.

What If the Employee Really Does Know More About the Job Than the Supervisor?

It is not unusual for employees to be better versed than their supervisors in the technical aspects of their positions; in many industries, this is to be expected. However, organizations should strive to avoid the perception that supervisors "know less" by ensuring that even if a supervisor does not know the details of *how* an employee does their job, the supervisor understands the purpose and importance of the tasks.

What the employer should do next: First, ensure that supervisors (*especially* the supervisor of the employee who made the complaint) are well trained in the technical skills required by the job. If that isn't realistic, as explained above, the supervisor should still understand *why* that position is important and how it should ideally support the organization as a whole. Supervisors should also be well trained in the organization's policies and procedures. Furthermore:

- Ensure that equal promotion opportunities are provided to employees and that employees understand how to take advantage of those opportunities. This empowers employees to act for the benefit of their growth and success. It will also help prevent employees from feeling that they have been unfairly overlooked when a vacant position is filled.

- Companies that promote from within often select candidates for an open position because they know a particular employee is loyal and hardworking. But the best employees may not automatically have management or supervisory skills. The skills it takes to be an effective leader usually differ from the skills that made an employee successful in the role they are exiting.

  To maximize the employee's chance of success and reduce any anxiety he or she may have, the company should offer leadership or supervisory training *before* the employee assumes the new role. Teaching the new leader what is expected is critical to success because the expectations of and processes involved in the new role will likely look very different from the previous role. If the new leader will be supervising employees he or she once worked with, it will be critical to help him or her establish a redefined relationship with the employees he or she is now supervising.

- All supervisors and leaders, whether they are external or internal hires, should have regular check-ins with their own leaders for continued learning and leadership development, to discuss what's going well and what isn't, and to address any barriers or challenges the subordinate leader may be facing. Your organization might even consider pairing each new supervisor with a more experienced one who can act as a mentor.

Information provided by the employee in an exit interview: "I want to work somewhere with better/different values." OR "The organization does not live its mission."

What the employer should consider: Not enough can be said about culture, values, and mission. Many employees seek jobs at organizations *because of* these items. They choose the organization because they want to do whatever it is that the organization says it does. For instance, if you say you value the dignity of all employees, your organization will likely attract employees for whom diversity, equity, and inclusion are important.

Not following through with publicized missions or values can be worse than not having missions or values at all, because it shows your organization to be insincere, dishonest, hypocritical, and in the worst case, mercenary. If your published mission is to provide the best customer service in the industry but leaders do not try to improve long call wait times and frustrating automated systems, employees will quickly become disillusioned. (After all, they're the ones who must interact with irritated customers who finally *do* reach a live agent.) Soon, employees will become distrustful, resentful, and disengaged—and some *will* leave.

What the employer should do next: I'm going to keep my commentary here brief, because in many ways, this whole book is about creating a healthy company culture and living out commonly stated organizational values (all while staying legally compliant). When you treat your employees equitably, respectfully, generously, and with empathy; when you value their efforts and input; when you truly act with their best interests at heart, odds are, they won't view you as only paying lip service to values.

For now, take a fresh look at your organization's mission and values. Are you "walking the talk"? What changes might you need to make to more closely adhere to your mission and values?

Information provided by the employee in an exit interview: "My supervisor micromanaged me."

What the employer should consider: As with all feedback from employees, organizations need to determine whether this information is based on one employee's incorrect perception, reveals a larger systemic problem, or is an accurate one-supervisor problem.

Engaged supervisors who train their employees well and communicate regularly and clearly do not need to micromanage their employees. Employees should be given clear direction, expected timelines for work completion, and broad oversight so the supervisor can spend his or her time doing productive work. If, after providing training and guidance (and retraining and additional guidance, if necessary), an employee cannot or will not do the work they are asked to do, the employee is not the right person for the job.

What the employer should do next: To determine whether this concern needs to be further addressed, the interviewers should follow up and ask for concrete details:

- Are you referring to one particular incident, or was this a pattern?
- Can you give me examples of when you felt you were micromanaged?
- Who micromanaged you (one supervisor or many supervisors)?

If the employee explains that he or she felt micromanaged because the supervisor required that he or she arrive on time, wear a safety uniform, clock in and out, or follow company-wide policies, the employee's complaint may not be valid. If, however, the employee says that his or her supervisor monitored his or her work more closely than was necessary or more frequently than other employees' work, more follow-up may be necessary. The same is true if the employee says that interacting with his or her supervisor and fulfilling the supervisor's requests took up a lot of time and actually made the employee less productive.

Information provided by the employee in an exit interview: "I felt ignored at work."

What the employer should consider: People want to feel like they matter—not just as names on the payroll, but as human beings. They want to feel that they and their efforts are seen, valued, and recognized. People want a meaningful connection to the work they do and to the people with whom they work. This is true of employees *and* employers.

If you are the owner, supervisor, manager, or leader of an organization, your employees will know your name and recognize you. Doing the same for your staff is powerful; it shows them courtesy and respect. It shows them that they matter to you. The positive moments you create for employees become their memories of you and your organization. It is important to create moments that leave employees feeling valued.

What the employer should do next: I once had a supervisor introduce herself and tell me that she made a point to learn the names of all of the employees in the office because she worked at a prior organization *for years* without ever learning her peers' names! After she introduced herself, I noticed that she greeted every employee by name. This fostered a sense of community and belonging among the whole staff.

If you own or lead an organization with hundreds of employees, perhaps spread across multiple sites, it may not be feasible to learn each person's name.

But you should probably be able to identify and greet each employee who works in your location or department. If you see someone on a daily or near-daily basis and *don't* know who they are, this is your cue to learn more about them.

Knowing one fact about every employee creates the authentic connection that employees desire. The fact can be personal ("This is Jorge. Like you, he is a Florida State Seminole fan.") or professional ("This is Jorge. He has been a lead tech for 15 years and was recently certified in safety.").

Tap Into the Power of Nametags!

If you are not naturally talented at remembering faces and names, or if you work in a larger organization where it is not possible to learn the names of every employee, nametags can give you a major assist. If your employees wear name badges or key/swipe cards with photos, have the badges printed with the employees' first names in **BOLD CAPITAL** letters so you can easily read them as employees walk toward you in the hall or sit across from you at a meeting. Then greet them by their names.

In addition to the obvious benefits of calling employees by name, here are two bonuses:

- When you see an employee's name printed in large, bold letters, you'll memorize names and match the names with employees' faces more quickly. Before long, you will know the names of the people you pass in the hall and you won't have to look at the name badge.
- Name badges with photos provide a layer of security because they allow others in the organization to quickly identify who belongs in the building. Some brands of name badges contain timekeeping chips, open doors, identify time and date of access, and perform other nifty tasks with the swipe of a card. As an added bonus, these can provide helpful data in the event of a wage and hour lawsuit because they can help substantiate when an employee was at the work site!

All that said, I'm not trying to imply that knowing names and a random fact or two is enough. Today's generation of talent very much wants to be engaged, valued, and appreciated. They want to give input. They want to feel cared about. If exit interviews consistently show that they don't feel this way, it may be time to revisit how direct supervisors are trained. The ability to build strong, meaningful relationships has become a "non-negotiable" leadership skill.

Information provided by the employee in an exit interview: "My loyalty/production/attitude/quality of work *was never* recognized by management." OR "My loyalty/production/attitude/quality of work *was always* overlooked by management."

What the employer should consider: When you hear the word "never" or "always," ask the employee (and yourself) whether the action or inaction really "never" or "always" occurred. Rarely is "never" or "always" used in a literal sense, but employees may feel that they were not frequently recognized or were frequently overlooked.

What the employer should do next: Vague reports do not provide helpful, actionable information upon which you can base future decisions. Do not accept the convenient answer; peel back the layers to see what an employee really means by asking for more specific examples.

For instance, you might say, "Tell me about a time when you felt overlooked," or, "What made you think your supervisor did not value your work?"

If the employee provides specific information and convinces you that you are not adequately recognizing loyalty, production, attitude, and quality of work, you can take steps to start doing so. Use details from the employee's report to identify opportunities for improvement. Perhaps a specific supervisor needs to be retrained and coached; perhaps it is time for an organizational process or standard to be updated. However, if the employee cannot provide specific examples, their assertion might not have merit.

Information provided by the employee in an exit interview: "My supervisor played favorites."

What the employer should consider: This is challenging because the perception of favoritism may not be accurate. Even if it is accurate, favoritism is often unintentional.

For example, if a supervisor regularly goes to lunch with a particular subordinate employee but does not include other subordinate employees, the employees who are not included might notice and feel slighted. It's natural for those who are not included to wonder what the supervisor and subordinate talk about during lunch.

In a vacuum of information, people tend to make assumptions that have no basis in fact. The employees may become worried and wonder whether the subordinate knows company secrets he or she would otherwise not be aware of. They may worry that the supervisor revealed to the subordinate personal information about other subordinate employees. They may believe that the subordinate employee earns more money, gets better shifts, or receives other benefits because of the friendship. Of course, none of this may be true, but such assumptions can damage morale and trust. For this reason, it is best for employers to avoid the *appearance* of favoritism.

Favoritism (or Even the Appearance of It) Can Lead to Legal Problems

Favoritism can create legal problems when the perceived favoritism excludes a protected class, such as gender or race. For example, if Jason and his subordinate employees Jack and Tony go to lunch frequently, but they never think to invite Jack and Tony's female coworkers, the female coworkers may question the legitimacy of Jack's or Tony's future promotions or raises. They might logically wonder if the friendships that formed gave Jack and Tony a leg up that they themselves were not offered.

Jason may have no ill intent. He may not even discuss work at all with Jack and Tony during their lunches. However, to avoid the appearance or perception of favoritism, Jason and his employer would be better served for Jason to go to lunch with his peers, rather than his subordinate employees.

This would be doubly true if Jason attended after-hours events with Jack and Tony. Spending time together outside of the workday implies a personal friendship rather than a purely professional one—and as we'll discuss in Chapter 16: Do Not Friend Me on Social Media, leader/employee friendships are already tricky enough.

What the employer should do next: When exiting employees provide you with information alleging favoritism, *ask for details*:

- **How, *specifically*, did your supervisor play favorites?** You need to know if a particular supervisor is compensating some employees better than others, providing priority shifts, or transferring profitable clients to only certain employees, for example. You also need to know if a particular supervisor disciplines employees consistently. If you learn the supervisor is not consistent, whether based on simple personal preference or on an illegal discriminatory basis, you must correct the matter as soon as possible.

- **Was one type of employee favored?** If, for example, you learn that the supervisor prefers to assign new clients to employees of one gender or race but not to another, you must take immediate action to avoid a future gender or race discrimination lawsuit. Because the information is based on the employee's perception, there may be very reasonable explanations for a supervisor's decision. The supervisor needs the opportunity to explain his or her rationale. This is an area where an objective, non-biased employment attorney can be a good sounding board, because that person can listen to the supervisor's explanation and evaluate whether the supervisor's decisions create legal exposure for the employer—or whether the supervisor's decisions are supportable.

- **Is there anyone else who can substantiate this information?** If other employees substantiate the claim of favoritism, you must act immediately by doing an investigation to determine if the claim has merit.

- **Is there any data to substantiate this information, such as pay or promotion records?** If an employee can point to pay records or other information to support their concern that a disparity exists, you should act immediately to correct the matter.

If favoritism is substantiated and the matter is simple, bringing it to the attention of the supervisor and training that supervisor to behave differently in the future may suffice. However, if there is evidence that some employees have been adversely affected by the favoritism (perhaps it is determined that non-favored employees have been paid less or offered fewer promotion opportunities) and remedial action is required, a visit with your employment lawyer would be helpful.

Information provided by the employee in an exit interview: "I was harassed, discriminated against, or retaliated against."

What the employer should consider: If you hear this in an exit interview, it does not mean that illegal action necessarily occurred. Employees may use words like "harass," "discriminate," or "retaliate" loosely. Nonetheless, you have a legal obligation to investigate the matter in an impartial manner to determine whether there is truth in the employee's statement.

Title VII of the Civil Rights Act of 1964 and its state counterparts require all employers to *promptly, immediately, and thoroughly* investigate any complaint of discrimination, harassment, or retaliation, and *take steps to prevent and promptly correct* discrimination, harassment, or retaliation in the workplace.[1] Failure to do so may result in strict liability for the organization—even where the reporting employee's employment has already ended.

Legalese Breakdown: Strict Liability and Affirmative Defense

Strict liability means that a court will not consider the merits of a matter (in this case, the organization's attempt to prove that discrimination, harassment, or retaliation did not occur) because liability has already been established (in this case, because the organization did not properly investigate the complaint and/or take steps to correct it). Instead, only money damages are relevant. If the organization *does* take prompt steps to investigate, correct, and/or prevent discrimination, harassment, or retaliation, it might not be held liable by a court. This is called an *affirmative defense.*

Under Title VII, there is no individual liability. Only a company (as opposed to an individual employee in the company) can be held liable for discrimination, harassment, or retaliation. But that doesn't necessarily mean that the employee at fault is "off the hook," so to speak, if a court does not find the company liable. The harasser can be sued individually under a different tort theory (e.g., for battery if touching occurred).

What the employer should do next: Conducting a proper investigation is an art form. Employers with human resources departments likely have professionals trained to conduct investigations in an impartial manner. Depending on the severity, nature, or type of complaint, however, these employers may choose to outsource the investigation.

Employers without a trained investigator on staff would be wise to engage an unbiased professional such as an employment law attorney or an outside human resources consultant to handle the investigation. This person would be responsible for determining what, if any, actions should be taken—including employment consequences for the employees involved.

If the exit interview and subsequent investigation reveal that the employee left because of harassment or discrimination, after consulting with counsel and taking steps to ensure the workplace is a safe and fair environment moving forward, an employer may want to consider offering to return the employee to his or her original job with the same terms and conditions of employment. Doing so limits the monetary damages available to the employee should the employee file a Charge of Discrimination.

In Conclusion

Wait a Month—Then Discuss It Over Lunch

If you *really* want to find out why your employee quit, wait a month and then invite them for lunch, send them an email, or give them a call. A month is long enough for the employee to have begun a new job and determine whether the new organization is a good fit for them. Also, by this point, most people will have become emotionally removed from your company—meaning that they'll be more willing and able to provide you with honest feedback.

While they can be uncomfortable and awkward, exit interviews are a valuable tool that should not be overlooked. They can help you gain context around why an employee chose to move on, which in turn can give you the information you need to improve your organization's culture, processes, and policies. Many employees are at their most honest when they are preparing to leave your organization—so listen carefully to what they're telling you. And, in cases like Molly's, learning the "why" may even offer an opportunity to find an alternate solution allowing the employee to stay with your organization!

Leadership and Administration

CHAPTER 10

Please Think Before You Communicate

Ahmed's Story

Ahmed is the head of a technology-based organization. He expects his team to attend various daily meetings, where he is the key presenter. Due to time constraints and scheduling demands, Ahmed often does not adequately prepare for the meetings. He tends to "wing" it. Rather than use notes or presentation aids, he often speaks to his team in an off-the-cuff manner.

At one all-employee meeting, Ahmed intended to discuss using new technology to become more efficient and achieve company growth. After all 100 employees filed into the conference room, Ahmed began speaking extemporaneously about the benefits of new technology, programs, and processes. He explained how electronic capabilities could streamline the business and generate more sales with significantly fewer employees.

Ahmed's intent was laudable. He wanted to communicate a positive idea: that future technologies could help the company grow and become more efficient, and therefore, more successful. While he knew that this might make employees' jobs look different and require their buy-in to learn new systems, he did not intend to lay anyone off. However, because he was focused on a single topic—efficiencies created by technology—Ahmed inadvertently created a situation where all of the positive parts of his message were forgotten. The only thing his employees heard was that significantly fewer employees would be needed because the technology would streamline the business—meaning that their jobs were possibly at risk.

As Ahmed was describing his broad vision, employees began asking well-reasoned, specific questions about the effect of the technology on their jobs and the timeline for changes in the business. Because Ahmed was speaking without the benefits of an outline, notes, or data, he was unprepared for the employees' questions and became openly frustrated. His irritation and unclear responses made employees feel that Ahmed did not care about their concerns or their futures, compounding their fear.

The Takeaway

It is reasonable for Ahmed, or any employer, to consider technology to make work more efficient and productive. The best employers drive success using technology from production systems to marketing platforms. The mistake Ahmed made was not messaging the *positive information* correctly. **Positive messaging helps create buy-in and enthusiasm from employees.**

Words Are Like Toothpaste

Once toothpaste is out of the tube, it cannot go back in. Words are the same. Employers and other leaders must be very cautious before they speak extemporaneously. Leaders owe it to themselves and to their employees to be thoughtful about word choice. The more people who will hear the message, the more important it is that the message be clear and correct. The more authority a person has in an organization, the more important it is to speak carefully.

Using technology efficiently to modify employees' jobs and replacing employees are two totally different things. The first scenario is hopeful and forward thinking—it can create optimism in employees who may learn new skills. It also sends a message that the company is in growth mode and is strategically planning the future. However, the second scenario is discouraging and frightening. It makes employees feel that their jobs are tenuous.

When employees are fearful for any reason—not just because they think their jobs might be in jeopardy—both the employee and the employer suffer.

Employees who are Pragmatists may immediately begin to look out for their own best interests and job hunt, taking the first better (and/or more secure) job that comes along—even if they previously hadn't intended to leave the company. Peace Makers may become Pragmatists or even Disengaged employees, continuing to work but becoming less and less invested in the success of the organization. Detractors will become more negative.

What Should Ahmed Have Done Differently?

Ahmed made a mistake, which is not surprising; after all, he is a human being navigating a difficult job and many responsibilities in a time when the landscape of work is changing. The important thing is that Ahmed learns from his mistake and establishes better pre-meeting habits. He needs to ensure that employees leave meetings with a clear understanding of the message he intended to convey, rather than leaving meetings feeling fearful.

In this situation, Ahmed should have prepared for the meeting by setting aside time to outline his message. Ahmed's vision for the future of the company is very important and should not be shared with all employees until he is clear on what the vision is, how he plans to lead the company toward the goal, and how the message will be delivered to the employees.

Talking Points Are a Great Tool. Use Them!

Chances are, you've been in Ahmed's shoes before. Whether you were leading a large meeting, delivering a report to shareholders, or simply having a morning huddle with a few team members, a lack of preparation meant that your words did not have the intended impact. We get nervous (yes, it can happen to even the most confident speakers). We forget points we meant to make. Questions might be raised that distract us. Preparation goes a long way in keeping us on track.

Whether you're speaking in front of an audience of two or two hundred, in person or on a Zoom or Teams platform, you should always prepare written talking points. Depending on the size and makeup of the audience, this can be a general outline that includes topics you want to cover, more detailed bullet points, or even a word-for-word script. Your talking points should include questions you anticipate that your audience might have. Most importantly, they should include responses to any weaknesses you recognize.

When You Schedule a Meeting, State Why

If you are scheduling a meeting with an employee or group of employees, state its purpose up front. This can be as simple as *Go over changes to industry guidelines* or *Team update on project progress*. If you are vague, employees will not be able to properly prepare and may needlessly worry about why the meeting is being held.

The exercise of creating written talking points has several benefits before, during, and after the messaging has occurred:

- Creating the talking points helps you flesh out the topics you *do* want to cover and highlights topics that are not necessary, making the conversation more efficient.
- We've all fallen victim to tempting tangents. Talking points keep you on topic when you are delivering the message and ensure that your central theme is accurately conveyed.
- Talking points help your message flow clearly from the introduction, to point one, to point two, to point three, and to the conclusion. They also ensure that you don't miss any key points. This is far more effective than moving from point to point at random, as the topics enter your mind.
- If the topic is a particularly sensitive subject—such as job eliminations or reductions in benefits—or is highly technical, creating the talking points gives you the opportunity to choose precise words that will convey the message clearly.

After the talking points are created, consider running through the message with a trusted colleague who will give you objective feedback. The more important the message is, the more important it is to get this feedback. Sharing the content with a colleague serves several purposes:

- The colleague can help determine if you are hitting the right tone. Are you being sensitive enough? Did you anticipate the right questions?
- Especially if the information is technical, the colleague can provide feedback on the clarity of the message. Is it understandable by people who might not be experts in that particular field? Do you need to tone it down or further explain the technical portions?
- The colleague can also tell you whether the message was memorable and understandable. If the colleague cannot repeat back to you the central theme and key points of your message, then your employees will likely not understand it either.

If Ahmed had followed these guidelines by scripting out his talking points and running through the presentation with a colleague, he probably would not have gotten frustrated and made the statement that created fear.

Creating Talking Points Takes Time I Don't Have!

As a leader, *of course* you're busy. It's practically in the job description. So if your response to the section above was, *I can see the value in creating talking points, but I just don't have time to sit down and write them,* I get it!

However, this is one of those situations where an ounce of prevention is worth a pound of cure. Yes, it will take you some time to prepare talking points, especially if you are not used to speaking with an outline. But in many cases, you will be saving yourself a significant amount of stress, energy, and time in the future. Think back to Ahmed's situation. How long might it have taken him to regulate his own frustration, listen to his employees' concerns, allay their fears, and then redeliver his message in a clearer way? Much longer than it would have taken him to create talking points in the first place, that's for sure!

I'm not suggesting that you carve out hours of your day (that you don't have) to exhaustively outline every message you deliver. For brief everyday meetings, creating talking points can be as simple as jotting down a few important topics on a piece of paper or in your note-taking app. But I *can* promise you that thinking through what you want to say beforehand will ultimately contribute to your organization's productivity, efficiency, and success.

Why Is It So Important to Be Prepared Before You Deliver a Message?

Whether you are speaking with a group or an individual, there are good business reasons to ensure that your words convey only what you specifically mean—and those reasons go beyond preventing your own inconvenience and your employees' confusion. Let's take a closer look at why it's important to accurately and clearly deliver messages to your team—and why all of that preparation is worth the time it takes.

The Legal Reason: Verbal statements can create legal entitlements. Have you ever told an employee something like, "We have big things in store for your future," "You have a bright future here," or, "We would never let you go"? Have you ever asked employees questions such as, "Would you be interested in serving on our leadership team in the future?" In some states, statements like these can create an oral employment contract.

Whether a court would consider these statements binding depends on the law of contracts and promises in that state, but generally, a court considers:
- The circumstances and context of the statement
- Whether the employee reasonably relied on the statement to their detriment
- Whether the employee had a reasonable basis to believe that the statement was a guarantee of a promotion, future continued employment, or some other benefit

This legal theory is generally called promissory estoppel, which means the party making the statement is stopped from breaking their promises.

Legalese Breakdown: Promissory Estoppel

Promissory estoppel is a legal theory whereby one person makes a promise and another person relies on the promise to their detriment.

Here's an example:

A competitor offers June a job earning 10 percent more money than she currently is making. When June tells her supervisor that she has made the decision to leave the company because of the new offer, June's supervisor panics because it will be very difficult to replace June's talent and skills. Therefore, he tells her, "You have a great future here! We look forward to seeing you in leadership soon. Staying on will be worth it—I promise!" June views this as a promise for a promotion, relies on this statement, and does not accept the new job. If a promotion does not occur—with a commensurate increase in compensation—June may bring a cause of action for breach of implied oral contract and promissory estoppel.

In a lawsuit, she would argue:

- The statement about her future was a promise made by her supervisor (which it was),
- She relied on it when she did not take the new job (which she did), and
- She was harmed as a result (which would be true if the promises were not fulfilled).

In other types of cases (e.g., employment discrimination cases where an employee is not selected for a promotion, does not receive a bonus, or is laid off or fired), oral and written statements like the ones made to June are often used as "Exhibit A." These statements may be used to show that the employee's performance was above par and that she should have been selected for promotion.

Walking the Line Between Developing and Promising

Today's employees (especially those from younger generations) want to be coached and developed by their employers. Especially in light of staff shortages and the need to retain employees, leaders are often advised to let new hires know that they have a future at the company. Many hold discussions about skill-building and professional development as part of the onboarding process.

If you're in the habit of having this type of conversation, the good news is that you don't need to stop. I would simply advise that you employ a few strategies to ensure that new recruits don't interpret your words as promises or oral contracts.

First, include verbal caveats when talking about an employee's future, such as, "Of course, at any point, either one of us could realize it's not the right fit..." or, "If both parties agree it's working out..."

For most employers, your employee handbook may include a statement that reads, "All employees are employed at-will, which means that either you or your employer may end your employment for any legal reason, with or without notice. This at-will status may not be changed, except in a written contract signed by both the employer and the employee."

The Personal Reason: Specific words can have long-term impacts on employees' lives. For example, if you are discussing the termination of an employee due to performance issues, your talking points would contain the word "termination" and include objective examples of performance deficiencies. But if you need to discuss a reduction-in-force *not* due to an employee's performance issues, the talking points would contain the phrase "reduction-in-force," which is entirely different from a termination for performance deficiencies.

These words matter. It is more difficult for a person to get a new job if they have been terminated than if they have been reduced-in-force or laid off. Further, if an employee is terminated for performance issues, most state unemployment divisions will not provide unemployment benefits. However, if an employee is reduced-in-force, they will likely be entitled to unemployment benefits from the state.

The Professional Reason: Engaged employees will do exactly what you ask them to do. …Even if you did not realize you were asking something! For example, if you are thinking out loud and say, "I wish we had a different subscription service," your best employees will immediately begin researching different subscription services. If this is not what you intended, the time and effort the employee spends researching will be wasted. That employee could have been spending time doing something more productive.

The Pragmatic Reason: Unclear communication frustrates employees—who will tell others. If you say things you don't mean (whether it is to a group, as in Ahmed's case, or to an individual, as in June's case), employees are likely to get frustrated. Peace Makers and Pragmatists will eventually become Detractors. Many will share their frustrations with others willing to listen. This type of "venting" used to occur around the water cooler or at dinner among friends and family; thus, it was limited to people the employee knew. However, the rise of social media has changed that. And for employers, this is not good news.

Today, employees vent to their coworkers, their family, their neighbors, their friends…*and* to remote acquaintances and complete strangers. Employees post details about their personal and work lives on social media at a staggering rate. (More on this in Chapter 16: Do Not Friend Me on Social Media.) For now, know that anything you say or write to an employee could be repeated to an online audience—and the consequences can be major.

In Conclusion

Most people in leadership positions are decent communicators. They would not have been promoted if they struggled to convey information. That said, the difference between an adequate communicator and a great communicator is significant—and so are the results. Adequate communication usually covers most of the bases, but leaves room for misunderstandings, confusion, and fear. These things hurt engagement, morale, and productivity. Great communication ensures that employees clearly understand the message and are prepared to fully contribute to the company's success.

Especially as a leader or employer, your words matter. It is worth taking the time to ensure that your messages convey exactly what you want to say—no more and no less. Developing this skill, plus consistently preparing for meetings and conversations, will take time, but the dividends are worth it for you, your employees, and your organization's future.

CHAPTER 11

Your Generosity Makes a Lasting Impact

Henry's Story

Years ago, I worked with a business owner who was highly regarded in the community—let's call him Henry. He had a reputation for kindness and was often called upon for advice and mentorship by younger business owners, religious leaders, and individual members of the community. Because of his work ethic and his outstanding reputation in the community, Henry's business was very, very successful. People wanted to work for him, and, once hired, his employees were proud to be part of his organization. They rarely left.

During one of our meetings, Henry told me about a financial decision he needed to make regarding certain earnings. Legally, the earnings did not have to be distributed or shared. Henry could pay these earnings to himself or use them to purchase equipment for the business. No one would have known if he made either of these decisions. However, he told me that neither option would be his preference. Instead, he *wanted* to take care of his employees.

In Henry's mind, there was one simple choice: He could (1) keep the money or (2) share the money. Without hesitation, he said, "It has never hurt me to be generous." This spirit of generosity was the foundation of Henry's outstanding reputation and was a major driver of his organization's success.

Generosity Is a Choice—and It Often Springs from Gratitude

I have thought about that moment many times over the years. I believe Henry was correct: Generosity is a choice, and it comes in many forms. We can be generous with kindness—for example, by giving someone a compliment or asking a sincere question. As volunteers and non-profit organizations know, generosity also exists when people share their time. Another impactful way to be generous is by sharing our talents, whether that is providing free legal advice or distributing home-cooked meals to the homebound. Best-selling author Quint Studer says that generosity is an expression of gratitude. Generosity and gratitude go hand in hand.

In Henry's case, generosity burst into existence the moment he chose to share not just a piece of the pie, but the whole dessert, instead of keeping it all to himself. But it wasn't a spontaneous decision. I'm certain Henry would agree that his generosity was fueled by gratitude for his employees.

The Takeaway

All employers can choose to be generous. They can choose to share profits or keep them. They can choose to invest in their employees' long-term well-being and create opportunities that otherwise would not exist…or they can choose not to.

The benefit of investing in employees can be measured in loyalty and longevity of employment—which often translates to growth and profit. After all, happy employees help create happy clients and customers, and happy clients and customers provide repeat business and excellent referrals.

If you don't believe this is true, reflect on *any* experience you have had with an unhappy employee. Wasn't it obvious the employee did not enjoy his or her job? Now, think back to a time when you were a happy customer. Did you want to frequent that business again? Did you want to refer a friend? And was your experience in some way impacted by an employee's positive attitude? My point is, an employee's demeanor can directly impact customer and client loyalty.

Moreover, employer generosity can ultimately impact the organization's bottom line.

How Can Employers Show Generosity? Let Me Count the Ways.

Fittingly, the opportunities for employers to choose generosity are boundless, and they allow employers to flex their creative muscles. Some opportunities for generosity are free or low cost. Others may have a financial impact in the short-term but yield positive long-term results in the forms of loyalty, low turnover, repeat customer visits, referrals, and an outstanding reputation. Here are some examples of employer generosity.

Compensation and benefits:

1. Offer competitive compensation rather than paying the minimum amount necessary to fill a particular position. Employers who pay top-of-market rates can expect top-of-market performance.
2. Offer full-time employment and pay overtime when necessary, rather than dividing full-time positions into several part-time positions to avoid paying overtime.
3. Provide incentives for employees to earn bonuses or additional compensation.
4. Offer a variety of benefits including:
   a. Flexible work hours
   b. Remote or hybrid work
   c. Competitive group health plans with an employer contribution
   d. A 401(k) with an employer contribution or match
   e. A profit share plan
   f. Supplemental plans such as dental and vision plans, short- and long-term disability plans, and life insurance policies

   These benefits, along with fair treatment and recognition, are often worth more to employees than compensation.
5. Promote healthy lifestyles by offering health and wellness benefits such as Employee Assistance Programs (EAPs), smoking cessation classes, gym membership reimbursements, and annual flu shots.

What Is an EAP?

An Employee Assistance Program, or EAP, is developed for employees who need specialized services. These services may include mental health counseling, family counseling, financial counseling, coaching services, or a combination of these for the employee and/or the employee's family.

EAP-covered services are generally free for a certain amount of time. For example, the plan may provide up to three visits to a counselor in a one-year period. Some plans also provide confidentiality to the employee; the employer may receive a bill from the provider, but the employee's name will not appear on the bill.

Your human resources or benefits department should be able to provide you with details on any EAP that exists. If your employer works with a Professional Employer Organization (PEO), the EAP may be part of a larger suite of benefits available to employees. See the Solutions and Resources bonus material at the end of this book for more information on PEOs.

Personal and professional development:

6. Educate employees about training programs to promote personal growth and learning, such as a financial literacy program designed to educate employees on how to maximize earnings for lower-tax, long-term growth and retirement. Consider offering these programs at work, either during work hours or non-work hours like lunch, to allow more employees to participate.

7. Encourage education and job growth by fully or partially covering the costs of certifications or licenses.

8. Offer full or partial tuition reimbursement programs for employees to increase their job-related skills at a local or online trade school, community college, or university.

9. Create specific promotion opportunities and educate employees on how to achieve those goals. This benefit might include the opportunity to

work with a coach or mentor, either within the organization or the larger industry.

Recognition and appreciation:

10. Publicly recognize employees and teams for jobs well done. This costs nothing but creates a lot of goodwill, and is very meaningful to the person or team being recognized. Recognition can be done in staff meetings, in company newsletters, in an all-employee email, on social media, etc. It has the added benefit of showing all employees which behaviors and achievements you value—and which you would like to see more of.

11. Write thank-you notes to employees to express gratitude for going above and beyond, for doing something exceptional, or to recognize memorable events such as 10-, 20-, and 30-year work anniversaries. Emails are great, but extra points if the note is handwritten. When an employee knows that a leader took the time to write a personalized message of appreciation, the impact is powerful. Many employees keep and treasure these thank-you notes for years.

Put It in the Mail

You might even consider sending thank-you notes through the mail, which often doubles their impact. Not only does the employee receive your appreciation, they are congratulated by their spouse, partner, children, roommates, and others who may see this piece of mail.

12. Order lunch or dinner when employees must work late or during non-regular hours.

13. Recognize positive behavior by giving credit to employees for a job well done. This doesn't have to be formal or elaborate. A simple, "Hey, Bindi, that proposal you put together was awesome! We're fortunate to have such an articulate writer on our team," will be greatly appreciated.

14. Provide small thank-you gifts in the form of movie tickets, coffee gift cards, company "swag," etc.

Work-life balance:

15. Provide paid time off so employees can do the things that are important to them without worrying about losing pay. Many employees choose to work for an organization *because* the organization has a generous paid time off allowance. This is especially true for employees who care for young children or elderly parents, because they may need more flexibility in their schedules.

    To determine how much paid time off is competitive in a particular industry, consult state/national industry organizations, review industry organization materials, peruse competitor websites, and then—if your budget allows it—consider offering a more generous paid time off package. Bear in mind that some states require paid time off. The amount and type (sick, family, etc.) varies by state, so consult state law before establishing the policy.

16. Encourage employees to volunteer in the community for a set number of hours per month or per quarter, and provide paid time off for them to do so. Why does this matter?

    a. Many employees seek employment with organizations whose values are similar to their own values.

    b. Many employees want to have a *purpose* for and a *connection* to their work, other than bringing home a paycheck. Just ask any nurse!

    c. Having employees volunteering in the community is good PR. Community members may be motivated to support a business that is giving back. Some may even want to come work for you!

    d. It contributes to a culture of well-being and psychological safety— if employees know you care about the community, it will be easier for them to believe you care about them and their lives, too.

17. Offer remote or hybrid work if possible. This is a great way to show employees that you care about their well-being. For one thing, remote and hybrid work saves employees money: first and most obviously, in transportation costs. Not having to pay for car maintenance, gas, public transportation, and parking can save employees thousands of dollars per year. Employees may also save by not having to spend as much on dry cleaning and lunches out. Finally, employees who do not have to travel to and from work may save an hour or more each day they work from home. Remote work literally gives them the gift of extra time.

18. Offer flexible work hours if possible. This may be especially appreciated by employees who work in a different time zone from the main office, who desire to work during their children's school hours, or who just happen to be early birds or night owls. The goal is to maximize productivity in a way that works for the business *and* for the employee.

...And more!

19. Participate in hiring programs that benefit certain groups who might otherwise have difficulty finding work, such as those with arrest or conviction records. (Before you think you could never hire someone with an arrest or conviction record, read Chapter 4: My Background Isn't Perfect, But I Will Still Be an Awesome Employee. You might even find that you qualify for a federal tax incentive for doing so!)

All of these offerings create a win-win situation. Happy employees who feel appreciated are more productive and motivated. They benefit because they are able to work in a secure environment, save for retirement, and take care of their health. Meanwhile, generous employers remain competitive in the marketplace and earn a solid reputation for treating employees well. They are able to recruit and retain great talent that might otherwise go elsewhere.

There's one more facet of generosity I want to touch on: employees being "generous" to their leaders and employers. Sure, employers like my friend Henry who are financially generous to their people stand to reap multiple rewards, ranging from a healthy bottom line to a thriving company culture. But the reverse is almost never true. When employees are expected or encouraged to be financially generous toward their leaders, it's a recipe for disgruntlement and resentment. This is abundantly clear when you look at how the infamous Boss's Day—October 16—often plays out.

Boss's Day Is a Scam: Virginia's Story

As I was buying plants to replace the ones in my living room that I kill like clockwork, I bumped into Virginia, an elementary school teacher. She was purchasing plants for her two supervisors in recognition of Boss's Day. It was obvious that she was not happy about taking time at the end of a workday to shop for plants. It was also apparent that she was even less happy about spending her own money on the plants.

I was genuinely curious about her attitude and asked her why she was unhappy. She explained that she HATED Boss's Day. After hearing her reasoning, I totally agree with Virginia: Boss's Day is a scam.

Virginia explained that there are eight different departments in her school. Each department collects money and buys a separate gift for both bosses—the principal and the vice principal. No one is sure how much money to spend on a gift for the principal and vice principal. Do they spend more on the principal than they do on the vice principal since the principal is the "big boss"? If so, how much more? Do they spend more on the vice principal since she presumably earns less than the principal and since they work with her more frequently? Do the teachers spend the same amount per person? What about teachers' assistants, who earn less than the teachers?

The confusion doesn't stop there. Every department feels pressured to somehow make sure its gifts are commensurate with those of the other departments. To come up with an amount close to what they estimate the other departments will spend, each person in Virginia's department contributes a set amount of money that is collected in a pool. The amount each employee contributes is substantial, because there are only a few people in Virginia's department to share in the expense. Members of another department also pool their contributions and collect the same amount of money as Virginia's department, but each of them contributes a lot less than Virginia because there are more employees to share the cost. Virginia explained that there is a third department that has fewer members even than hers, but that department out-collects and out-spends the first two departments, which means those employees each contribute the most.

This occurs in all eight departments because none of them want to be seen as "anti-team-player" by the principal and vice principal (who decide the employees' compensation, set their schedules, assign children to each class, and allocate the school funds the employees need to do their jobs).

Two months after Boss's Day, Christmas and Hanukkah roll around, and the same problem arises. It crops up once more on the principal and vice principals' birthdays, and yet again on the last day of school. This means that the principal and vice principal receive gifts from eight different departments, four times a year. That's at least 32 gifts per school year! (Virginia explained that she said "at least" because sometimes individual teachers purchase gifts for the principal and vice principal *on top of* the contributions given to their departments—usually in an attempt to ingratiate themselves and "stand out from the pack.")

The Takeaway

Boss's Day wasn't created by bosses. Boss's Day was created by companies as a profit-generating phenomenon—and it worked! The fundamental problem with Boss's Day is not the idea that employers should have one day a year where employees say "thank you." Employees who work for caring and generous employers *should* feel thankful and willingly express gratitude. However, Boss's Day—and other "special occasions"—often place unnecessary pressure on employees and makes them feel uncomfortable and/or resentful for several reasons:

Employees often feel they are forced to participate. In some organizations (like Virginia's), there is pressure to participate. Employees worry that their employer knows who participates and who does not. This pressure exists whether employees write something personal on a card, purchase a gift, bring baked goods from home, or participate in some other form of recognition.

It is exacerbated in large organizations or in multi-employee departments of organizations. If every other employee is doing something to recognize Boss's Day or another occasion, it is almost impossible for one person to say, "I'd rather not participate"—even if the person cannot afford to participate, is overwhelmed with responsibilities at home, or simply does not wish to spend their time and money. So, instead, these employees buckle under the pressure and participate in the worst way possible—begrudgingly.

Employees receive the money used to purchase gifts *for* their employers *from* their employers. Employers set employees' compensation and know what they take home at the end of a workweek. Employers likely (really, almost always!) earn more than their employees. Yet on Boss's Day and other holidays, employees feel compelled to spend a portion of the wages employers paid them…for doing a job that benefits the employer…to purchase a gift that benefits the employer.

Face it; that is strange. It's like telling the babysitter that she needs to bring you a gift for the privilege of watching your children while you go to dinner. Your employees are there for the same reason your babysitter is: to earn money for themselves and their families—not to buy employers gifts. When you look at it this way, it's easy to see why employees might (legitimately!) resent allocating part of their paycheck to buy a gift for their boss.

The appropriate amount of money to spend on a gift is challenging to navigate. On the extreme side, groups of employees may pool their money to purchase an expensive piece of jewelry; spa treatments; or other over-the-top, elaborate gifts. Employees who cannot afford to own the gift themselves should not be expected to purchase the gift for a boss who can.

Even if the gift is more modest and purchased individually, many employees will worry about whether they are spending too much or not enough and the message that amount might send to their boss. *I don't want to look like a suck-up… but I don't want my boss to think I'm phoning it in, either…or even worse, that I don't like her or value my job!*

Employees can be pitted against one another. Boss's Day can create an environment where employees spend their work time competing against each other to buy the best gift. Sometimes this adversarial dynamic bleeds into employees' work, too—even in situations when they would be best served by supporting each other.

All of this widens the perceived power gap between leaders and employees, making productive collaboration and bold communication less likely.

How Can Leaders and Employers Alleviate This Pressure?

Easy…communicate to all employees that you do not want or expect gifts from them. *And mean it.*

Explain to your employees that you do not want them to spend their free time and money on you—that you would rather them spend their time and money on their families or themselves. You can address this with new employees during onboarding so they'll clearly understand that you have a no-gifts-for-bosses tradition.

If you have a previous tradition of accepting gifts, you could say something like, "Your generosity in years past has been lovely, but this year for Boss's Day, and for special occasions going forward, I request that you not purchase gifts for anyone. Instead, please spend that time and money doing something meaningful for your own family or for an organization that is important to you."

What About Gifts on Special Occasions?

As with every rule (assuming the organization doesn't have a no-gift policy or that the policy allows for exceptions), an exception may be appropriate if a supervisor has a rare but very significant event: a wedding or the birth or adoption of a child, for example.

That said, some habits are hard to break. (And at first, employees may be skeptical that you *really* mean the no-gifts policy.) If employees tell you that they want to do something special to recognize you, thank them and tell them that you would prefer a handwritten card, a kind word of thanks in the hallway, or a personal email.

If employees really value "doing" something for Boss's Day, you could suggest a casual, low-pressure potluck or brown-bag lunch together.

If they still insist on spending money, suggest that they donate to a favorite local non-profit organization or charity. If your organization directly serves a particular group of people, suggest that they purchase something to benefit that group. For instance, teachers like Virginia might purchase a book for the school library.

Are You Affected by a No-Gifts Policy?

Aside from the HR reasons discussed above, there may be organizational policies governing your acceptance of gifts from employees. All leaders should review the organization's policy handbook to determine whether the receipt of gifts by supervisors is specifically prohibited. Some publicly held companies and municipalities have enacted no-gifts policies across the board to avoid the appearance of favoritism or impropriety.

If a no-gifts policy isn't already in place, owners should consider whether such a policy is necessary for their organization. Policies make it very easy for all supervisors in an organization to politely—and consistently—decline gifts.

When you eliminate the need for employees to purchase "boss gifts," they will thank you for it. And bonus—the thanks will be sincere.

An Extra Bonus

You won't receive 32 candles, houseplants, coffee mugs, or bath products every year!

Bottom line: As a leader, you can—and should!—choose to show generosity toward your employees. You'll be promoting a culture of collaboration, communication, and appreciation between you and your team, and you can look forward to your team's being generous with their effort and loyalty—provided you earn it by treating them with respect and investing in their well-being and success.

CHAPTER 12

Significant Events Are Important to Me—Please Recognize Them

Tom's Story

Tom has worked at the same small company for 15 years and is retiring on Friday. He is very well liked and has a reputation for always going the extra mile to help his fellow employees and his customers. During his tenure, he regularly spoke to and was friendly with the entire management team, including the president and the vice president. Tom is proud of the work he has done for the company and looks forward to retirement.

Everyone in the company knows his last day of work will be Friday; he provided written notice two months before his retirement date, he has announced it at department meetings, and his supervisor has entered it on the company calendar.

On Friday, Tom's department and supervisor throw a potluck lunch, which he enjoys and appreciates. However, neither the president nor the vice president stops by his office to say thank you or goodbye during his final day of work. Tom knows they are busy, but still feels a bit let down.

The Takeaway

Your employees have the option to work at a lot of different places. It is worth considering why they *choose* to work for you. Yes, receiving a paycheck is definitely a big piece of the equation. Having the opportunity to use their talents, skills, and strengths is probably part of it, too. But hopefully, your employees also come to work each day because they enjoy the intellectual or social qualities of their work, and they value your company's mission.

Most employees desire a connection to purpose. They want to feel that their contribution matters to the organization—and that, by extension, *they* matter. This is particularly true for employees like Tom, who dedicated a significant amount of professional time and effort to his organization. These employees deserve to be celebrated when an important event, like a retirement, occurs.

It seems obvious to Tom that his retirement should have been recognized by the leaders of the organization, but there may be legitimate reasons why it was not. Perhaps the president and vice president were not aware that Friday was his last day. It is entirely possible that they missed the announcement. Perhaps the leaders of the organization *did* stop by Tom's office, but he was not in it at that time. Maybe the leaders were out of town, in a meeting that went unexpectedly long, or had a family emergency. Or it could be that the president and vice president simply forgot— they're humans, after all.

Hopefully, Tom understands the demands on the president and vice president and has had enough good experiences with his employer over the past 15 years to assume the best: that there were legitimate reasons for missing his final day of employment.

The good news for his employer is that fixing the mistake is easy. A card in the mail or a phone call after the fact would remedy the error. This simple recognition would go a long way toward letting Tom know that his contributions are valued.

Recognition Lets Employees Know They Matter (Just Ask Uncle George!)

Professional events (like retirement) and personal events (such as the birth or adoption of a child, getting married, and birthdays) should be recognized. Recognitions do not have to be costly or time-consuming.

Be Sure to Recognize "Everyday" Achievements, Too

In addition to recognizing major events and accomplishments, don't forget to be generous with everyday praise, too. If an employee shares a great idea in a meeting, thank them for it. If you were impressed by the way a customer service rep remained calm and empathetic while helping an angry customer, say so. If someone shows up every day with a positive attitude, tell them you've noticed. Interactions like this take only a few seconds, but are very memorable and meaningful (not to mention motivating!).

My husband's Uncle George was a master at small, but meaningful, recognitions. Uncle George was a captain in the Pensacola Police Department. As captain, he was second in charge and responsible for the safety of the entire city—no small task. Despite his enormous professional responsibility, he chose to prioritize employees' birthdays.

Uncle George kept a Rolodex on his desk, organized by date. The Rolodex contained the birthday of *every single employee at the police department.*

Rolodex: The '80s Version of the Smartphone Contact List

Millennial, Gen Z, and younger readers may have never heard of a Rolodex. If you're unfamiliar, a Rolodex is a phone book on a wheel. It is a plastic card holder, organized alphabetically, that houses index cards packed with information. In the '80s, everyone had a Rolodex, and they were absolutely stuffed with handwritten notes, business cards, and contact information. Essentially, the Rolodex was an analog "Contacts" app.

Every morning, before he began his work as an officer, Uncle George walked around the building and said, "happy birthday" to every employee celebrating that day. If the employee was not at work when he made the rounds, he dropped them a quick note or left a voicemail message. When a captain of the Pensacola Police Department cares enough to know his employees' names and to personally wish everyone a happy birthday, his employees know that *they matter*.

There Are Many Ways to Recognize Employees. Find What Works for You.

Saying "happy birthday" to every employee was Uncle George's thing. It does not have to be your thing. There are many ways to recognize employees. They vary with the size and resources of the organization. Many are low or no cost, and many require very little time—but the value they bring can be measured by employee satisfaction and retention.

For example, you could publicly recognize employees at employee or team meetings, or in the company newsletter. You could handwrite a note or send an email when an employee gets married. As Tom's team did, you could organize a potluck lunch (or even cater one if you have the funds) when someone retires. You might even find it helpful to establish a team of employees charged with planning events for personal or professional accomplishments.

What Events Deserve Recognition?

Make an effort to stay aware of upcoming events that deserve recognition so you can plan an appropriate gift, celebration, or acknowledgment. If you have an outstanding assistant, you can request that he or she help you stay on top of this task. Here's a suggested list of events to mark on your calendar.

Professional events that deserve recognition:
- Retirements
- Professional Awards
- Achievement of Professional Licensure or Certifications

- Membership or Leadership on Professional Boards
- Work-Related Educational Achievements
- Promotions
- Achieving Sales/Production Goals
- Annual Work Anniversaries

**Decade Work Anniversaries deserve especially large celebrations!

Significant personal events that deserve recognition:
- Birth or Adoption of Children
- Weddings
- Personal Achievements in the Community
- Educational Achievements

Take Employees' Preferences Into Account

Employees prefer to be recognized in different ways. Some quieter people may not like public shout-outs. Most extroverts love them! Some employees might appreciate tickets to an athletic event, while others would rather receive a gift certificate to a popular restaurant. Still others might value paid time off more than any type of material gift.

The good news is that you do not have to personally remember how employees like to be recognized. Instead, as part of each employee's onboarding, include a fun get-to-know-you questionnaire. You can send it out to current employees too, explaining that while you know many of them well already, you want to make sure you are rewarding and recognizing them in an impactful way. Questions should not address areas that are protected by law, such as marital status, age, religion, and, in many jurisdictions, political preferences. Consider including questions like:

- What is the best way to recognize you for a job well done?
  - Public praise? Private recognition?
- What is your favorite restaurant?
- What is your favorite coffee shop?
- Which college or pro team do you cheer for?

- What is your favorite bookstore?
- What is your favorite snack food?
- What is your favorite type of dessert?
- What type of event would you rather attend: an athletic event or a concert?
- What are your hobbies outside of work?
- Would you rather receive a gift or time off?
- When is your birthday? (The day and month, without the year, are sufficient.)
- When is your work anniversary?

The answers to these questions will allow you to get to know your employees a little and, if you choose to do so, tailor a personal gift when one is deserved.

In Conclusion

Don't overthink this—but do make sure you are sincere. As long as your appreciation is genuine, any form of recognition will be valued and remembered. This is especially true if it comes from a leader in the organization, as was the case with Uncle George, captain of the Pensacola Police Department.

Recognition for Uncle George

In 1978, when a routine traffic stop in Pensacola revealed a car that had been reported stolen, the driver—who resisted arrest—was eventually taken into custody. Uncle George, along with other officers, investigated and learned the identity of the perpetrator: serial killer Ted Bundy.

Before you think, *I am too busy to take the time to recognize employees,* consider the balance Uncle George achieved between his role as an employer and his role as a captain. He was able to connect with his subordinates as a kind and caring employer while still excelling as a tough-as-nails police officer. In fact, part of his success as a police officer was undoubtedly due to the diligence of his team, who were proud to put forth their best efforts on behalf of a leader who had their backs.

Recognizing employees is a win-win-win. In addition to praise and (possibly) a gift, employees gain the deep satisfaction of knowing that they are seen and appreciated—not just as members of your payroll, but as individuals with unique lives, interests, and accomplishments.

When other employees see their coworkers being recognized (for a ten-year anniversary at the organization, for instance, or for breaking a company sales record), many will get an extra shot of motivation to work toward the same goal. They will also feel more secure in their jobs, knowing that their employer values their professional *and* personal milestones.

Finally, you will increase your team's loyalty and engagement—which is great for retention and your bottom line.

CHAPTER 13

Don't Make Me Deal with Your Bad Behavior

Tracy's Story

Tracy's boss, West, holds a certified public accountant (CPA) designation and has a robust book of clients and referrals. His job involves working with high-wealth individuals and local business owners. He also works with government officials on tax legislation and initiatives. Clients love him because he speaks with absolute confidence and is respected by other professionals. By all accounts, he is successful: He is well paid, he is a partner in his firm, and he is a sought-after tax subject matter expert. The problem is that he is kind of a jerk. Okay, he is a full-fledged, card-carrying, loud-mouthed jerk to his staff.

Even though West appears very successful to people outside of his CPA firm, its employees agree that West is a terrible communicator and boss. He has one communication speed, volume, and tone: fast, loud, and aggressive. From day to day, his assistant, Tracy, does not know whether he is upset with something she has done or left undone, whether he is frustrated with a client, whether he might be concerned about something in his personal life, whether he is working through an issue with another colleague or client, or whether there is something else entirely going on.

West also behaves in a physically aggressive manner. He stomps his feet as he walks away, and he frequently slams doors and phones. At one point, instead of signing a document in front of him with the pen Tracy handed him, he picked up the pen and threw it on the floor, and then walked away without explanation. To cope, Tracy has learned to tune West out. She simply ignores his behavior. *The louder he is, the less she hears.*

Tracy knows that all of the employees in her position have observed West's behavior at some point or another. In fact, other staff members and the CPAs with less seniority have nicknames for West—which, of course, are *never* used in front of him. No one confronts West because he is a partner. They recognize that West has enough clout in the industry to assist them—or harm them—in future professional endeavors, both at the firm and in future positions with other employers.

In the past, Tracy has reported West's behavior to human resources, but the human resources manager declined to do anything about West's behavior. Why? Because he is an equal-opportunity jerk to all subordinate employees: He is a jerk to men, women, older employees, and younger employees. Basically, he is a jerk to everybody who does not outrank him. Therefore, the human resources manager said human resources has no power to stop West's behavior and Tracy has no basis to make a claim of harassment.

Upper management has declined to do anything about West's behavior because, even if the human resources manager is wrong on the harassment analysis, he is a high producer and brings in a lot of money to the firm. They believe his contributions are too valuable to risk alienating and losing him.

The Takeaway

Before you say, "This could never happen in my company," realize that many companies have an employee like West (whether in a leadership position or not). Often, management isn't aware of the offensive or aggressive behavior because line-level employees are afraid to report their superior. Also, employees like West tend to be on their best behavior in front of management, clients, and partners who outrank them.

In this case, however, everybody—management, staff, and human resources—is aware of West's behavior. Unfortunately, management and human resources have made the decision to look the other way since West is "valuable."

Let's be clear: West's behavior is that of a petulant teenager. No parent would tolerate their child's behaving in such a manner (I hope!). Throwing items, name-calling, yelling at a sibling or parent, stomping around, intentionally embarrassing others, and failing to communicate or cooperate are all unkind and disrespectful. These behaviors would soon become intolerable in the home. So why would management allow such behavior from a supposedly professional *adult* in the workplace?

Harassment Happens More Often Than You Think (and It Costs More, Too)

Between 2010 and 2022, there were an average of almost 20,000 charges of discrimination alleging harassment *other than sexual harassment* filed each year with the Equal Employment Opportunity Commission. The monetary benefits awarded during this time period range from $68.2 million to $105.8 million each year.[1] This does not include monies paid in litigation settlements, judgments awarded by a court, or awards by a state agency. It also does not include the cost of defense and litigation.

Some companies prioritize and value employees based on whether they are producers or support personnel. Producers are people like West who create direct, traceable revenue for the organization. Support personnel are those like Tracy who support the producers but do not directly generate revenue. Producers may be considered "more valuable" because they are harder to replace. They might have designations of specialties, unique certifications, or higher educational credentials.

- In a dentist's office, the producers are the dentists and the hygienists, and the support personnel are the front desk staff.
- In a real estate office, the producers are the brokers and the agents, and the support personnel are the closing assistants.
- In an organization dependent on sales, the producers are the salespersons who work directly with clients, and the support personnel are those who input the data on the contracts.

Petulant Producers *Shouldn't* Get a Pass

Because of their perceived value to the organization, producers may not be reprimanded or terminated for behaviors that would (and should!) result in discipline or even immediate termination for support personnel (e.g., yelling at others or throwing pens). However, allowing producers to behave in aggressive or offensive manners is extremely shortsighted—even legally risky—for several reasons. We'll use the example of West and Tracy's CPA firm to explore them.

West relies on Tracy to be successful. Whether *he* acknowledges it or not, West could not be as successful as he is without Tracy's support and the support of the less senior professionals in the firm. If West had to do all of Tracy's tasks—formatting spreadsheets; running reports; inputting data; scheduling appointments, flights, and meetings; answering client questions; making copies; and the hundred other tasks she does on a daily basis—he would have no time to do his own job.

This reality is sometimes forgotten by people who have reached the top, particularly by those who begin their careers as producers—think of someone who goes directly from high school to college to a professional position. It is also true for those with a built-in safety net, such as a person whose only work experience has been in a family business.

West's behavior is costing the company money. Tracy tunes West out when he behaves aggressively—meaning that she is not focused and she is less engaged. Tracy may make costly errors because she is stressed out by West's outbursts. Her work is likely not as productive as it could be because she does not feel the desire to go the extra mile. It's probable that she is not very motivated to see the company succeed and is not as loyal to the firm as she might otherwise be. In other words, West's behavior has caused Tracy to become Disengaged (perhaps even a Detractor), meaning that she might be more inclined to leave and work for a competitor. This would result in direct turnover costs for the company.

The company is sending a clear message to all employees: Bad behavior is tolerated. Employees have learned that harassment and aggressive behaviors—up to and including everything West does—are permitted. Since West has not been reprimanded, others may assume it's okay to follow suit. Some employees (especially newly hired producers) may even believe that these behaviors are expected of them.

In fact, the company may be inadvertently conveying that other, even more serious bad behaviors are tolerated. If a partner is allowed to throw pens, is throwing a stapler also allowed? Is hitting another person okay? What about threatening a coworker or subordinate?

"What We Permit, We Promote."

Waffle House Vice Chairman Emeritus Bert Thornton stated, "Passive tolerance of bad behavior serves to encourage others similarly inclined." Leadership expert, best-selling author, sought-out national speaker, and philanthropist Quint Studer agrees and has many times said, "What we permit, we promote. What we allow, we encourage."

This piece of wisdom is true for every organization of every size in every industry. Regardless of the severity of the behavior, by *permitting* the behavior, the organization is *promoting* the behavior. This is especially true when a leader is allowed to behave poorly.

The company is opening itself up to legal risk. West's behavior creates two glaring opportunities for legal action against the firm.

- Suppose another partner, Emily, swears at her assistant and tosses paperwork all over the hallway when other employees or clients are present. Suppose further that Emily's assistant (correctly) reports her to human resources for that behavior. Emily's inappropriate behavior will be measured by the yardstick established by West's well-known behavior. Even if the firm desired to terminate Emily for her outburst, it could not do so because it has *permitted and promoted* such behavior in the past.

  If the company terminated Emily for the outburst but retained West despite his similar (and repeated) behavior, Emily would have a legitimate gender-based discrimination lawsuit. She could make a strong argument that two similarly situated employees engaged in similar inappropriate behaviors, but only the female—Emily—was terminated. Emily's claim would be further substantiated if she were able to show that other men engaged in similar behavior without adverse consequences.

- Tracy has a legitimate claim for workplace harassment, which could be quite costly to the firm. Even though West's harassment is not limited to one person or one group of people, Tracy would likely be successful in a harassment claim because his behavior is severe *and* pervasive. (As we'll cover when discussing other types of harassment later in this book, to be illegal, the behavior has to be severe *or* pervasive. West's behavior is both.) Title VII of the Civil Rights Act, as well as most state counterparts, require that aggrieved employees report inappropriate behavior. Once an employee does so, the employer is required by law to take immediate and thorough corrective action. Because West is a partner who has engaged in repeated harassment, and because management is aware of but chooses to ignore the behavior, punitive damages are possible.

Workplace Bullying May Not Be a Crime, But It Can Still Create Liability

Bullying in the workplace has received increased attention in recent years. At the time of this writing, there is no federal law that makes bullying illegal, and there is no legal definition of bullying. However, persons on the receiving end of bullying behavior certainly recognize it when it happens. The lack of legal clarity does not mean employees or supervisors who bully others are off the hook. Bullying contains the same characteristics as harassment, which *is* defined and actionable under federal law.

Bullying behaviors such as insulting, embarrassing, or yelling at an employee can be considered harassment where the bullying behavior is based on a protected status. For example, if an employee or supervisor of one race yells only at employees of a different race, that behavior can be evidence of harassment on the basis of race. If a male employee or supervisor singles out or intentionally embarrasses female employees, those actions can be evidence of harassment based on gender.

If the bullying behaviors are not based on a protected class, they can still lead to liability in the form of tort claims brought against the bully. These claims might include assault, intentional infliction of emotional distress, or negligent infliction of emotional distress. In an assault claim, an employee would allege that the bully engaged in behavior that caused the employee to fear imminent harm. (Throwing office supplies would certainly suffice!) In claims of negligent or intentional infliction of emotional distress, the employee would argue that the bully intended to cause psychological harm, or knew or should have known that the behavior was likely to cause psychological harm, and engaged in the behavior anyway.

Of course, for employers of all sizes, the best course of action to avoid liability and foster a healthy work environment is not to tolerate *any* such actions in the workplace.

Perhaps most importantly, by allowing a senior employee to treat a subordinate employee disrespectfully, West's firm is sending a message to its employees that *some employees are inherently more important than others.* This message harms the overall morale of the organization and actively works against creating a culture of psychological safety. It also exacerbates the power dynamic that naturally exists between leaders and their subordinates, virtually ensuring that support staff like Tracy will not communicate honestly or boldly with their superiors. (Can you imagine Tracy voluntarily telling West that she— or that he!—made a mistake?)

In some professions, consequences of bad behavior can be even more severe. Imagine that instead of working in an accounting firm, Tracy and West have jobs with life-and-death consequences, such as in the medical profession. Patients' lives could *literally* be changed because of West's behavior and its impact on those around him.

All of these consequences of bad behavior, no matter who commits it or what their position in the organization is, make it difficult to retain current employees and recruit new ones. This is especially true if employees like Tracy decide to share their frustrations on social media or a job-related app or site like Glassdoor.

Good employers know that every single employee matters, that each person on their payroll is a human being with worth, and that every single job is important. It is understandable that West's company wants to retain its most talented producers. However, it is critical that it does so in a manner that respects the dignity of all of its employees *and* protects itself from liability.

Every Job Matters

At a hospital, a custodian knew that many patients were tired, lonely, or in pain, so his practice was to engage patients in gentle, positive conversation. In one particular room, the custodian noticed that the patient did not respond to conversation. After approaching the patient's bed, the custodian determined that the patient did not appear to be breathing. He used the call button to notify a nurse, who immediately arrived in the room.

It turned out the patient had taken her last breath just moments before the custodian arrived. Because the custodian paid attention to the patient and notified the nurse immediately, the nurse was able to greet the patient's family as they exited the elevator and before they entered the room. She was able to notify the family of their loss in a kind and dignified way.

If the custodian hadn't cared enough to look at the patient and notice her condition, the nurse might not have been able to greet the family. Can you imagine their trauma had they walked into the room unprepared?

Certainly, a tremendous amount of credit goes to the custodian. But would he have acted with such kindness and empathy if he felt that his employer, the hospital, did not value and appreciate him and his role? Maybe not. If the hospital did not treat *all* employees as though they were important, the custodian might have gradually become Disengaged...or he may not have been motivated to interact with patients in such a caring way in the first place. (Incidentally, this is a true story—and the custodian in question *was* recognized for his actions by senior management.)

It's so important to make sure everyone in the organization is treating employees at *every* level like they and their work matter...because they do! While your organization may not hold patients' lives in its hands, it *is* responsible for customers' satisfaction, clients' financial well-being, etc. Everyone on your payroll can impact whether that goal is met—or not.

What Should West's Company Do?

At a minimum, West's company should immediately counsel him—on the record—to let him know that his behavior will no longer be tolerated. When counseling an employee for unacceptable behavior, violation of company standards, low performance, or any reason that could be perceived as negative, I suggest following these guidelines:

Always conduct counseling sessions individually... It can be tempting to send a message to an entire group, rather than addressing one person. Announcing that a certain behavior will no longer be tolerated at an interoffice meeting feels less confrontational and is less likely to provoke an aggressive or defensive response from the employee.

However—uncomfortable though it might be—counseling should always be directed toward the employee who is the problem. If it is directed toward an entire group, the employee you are hoping to reach is less likely to hear and internalize the message. Even if they do hear it, that person may assume that some other employee is the intended recipient.

...And in private. As with all sensitive and important conversations, counseling should occur in private—perhaps in an office or conference room, behind closed doors. This is not a casual conversation that is appropriate to have in the breakroom, walking down the hall, or after "sticking your head" into the employee's office without warning.

Refer to the employee's inappropriate behavior with as much specificity as possible. Come to the meeting with documentation of the behaviors you want to address. For instance, you might say:

- On September 1, I overheard you say (insert details of unprofessional words).

- Last Wednesday, you told your assistant (insert details of inappropriate behavior).
- I received a credible report that you (insert specific action that merits counseling).

You should be prepared to explain why each behavior is unacceptable, unprofessional, unethical, against company policy, etc. I recommend thinking through these issues *before* the meeting and writing down the main points you want to address. This will help ensure that you express yourself clearly and thoroughly, even if the conversation becomes uncomfortable or stressful.

Give the employee an opportunity to respond. The employee should be given an opportunity to respond to each and every allegation. By telling their side of the story, they may provide additional details or share a different perspective that changes the outcome of the matter.

If the employee is reluctant to open up, it may help to ask questions like, "Can you help me understand what happened?" "Is there any support you need that you feel you aren't receiving?" "Are there any barriers that are keeping you from reaching this standard?" etc.

When confronted with their poor behavior, many people will attempt to deflect blame; e.g., "It's not my fault!" "She's being too sensitive!" "I'm not the only one who acts this way!" Keep the conversation focused on the employee and their individual actions. Confirm that if others have behaved inappropriately, they will also be held accountable—but don't allow yourself to be drawn into a discussion about a third party who isn't present.

Develop a solution. If it is determined that the employee's behavior, word choice, tone, etc. is unprofessional or inappropriate, develop a plan to help them improve. Make sure the plan includes specific action items, clear expectations, and a timetable for achieving them. If possible, allow the employee to have a say in developing this plan. You might ask for their input on what steps to take first, what goal they would like to work toward initially, what type of support they would prefer, how often they would like to check back in with you, and what a reasonable timetable for achieving the goal might be. Most people—even petulant ones—are more willing to work toward change if they are treated like partners instead of delinquents.

Say This, Not That

For example, West's counseling may require that he participate in harassment and discrimination training, or work with a mentor on communication skills. While it is reasonable for West to make requests of his staff, West can be taught to use a more relaxed tone and to use key phrases that are kinder and more professional to convey the same message, such as:

Instead of saying this:	Say:
Hand me the paper.	Please hand me the paper.
Why didn't you...	Can you help me understand why you didn't...
You need to work overtime this evening.	I'm in a tight spot and am hoping you will be willing to help me by working overtime this evening for an hour. I would really appreciate it. OR I know you probably have things to do this evening, but if it is possible, would you be able to work overtime to finish this? If not, would you be able to come in an hour early tomorrow to finish it?
This is wrong.	I appreciate the effort but a correction needs to be made. OR You are normally really diligent, and I know this was an error. Can you correct it, please? I know you didn't make this mistake on purpose. OR Perhaps I didn't explain this correctly. That's my error. Let me show you so you can do it correctly the next time.

That idea will not work.	I am not sure that idea will work as I currently understand it. Can you explain more?
You're an idiot.	Never. Never. Never name-call. It's not okay in first grade, it's not okay at home, and it's not okay at work.
What the hell were you thinking?	Never. Never. Never use swear words to convey a thought.

Clearly lay out consequences. You *and* the employee should be on the same page about what will happen if goals aren't met within the designated time frame. If your organization has a progressive discipline policy (e.g., verbal warning, written warning, suspension, termination), it will likely guide your actions.

In this example, a performance improvement plan (PIP) or a 30-60-90-day performance review plan should be issued during the written warning phase. If you go this route, be sure to closely monitor the employee's behavior and provide reasonable support to help them correct the issue during the time frame given. Ideally, the PIP should include required periodic meetings to review progress, goals, and behavior during the PIP's time frame, and to give the employee the opportunity to ask any questions they may have.

To ensure that the employee understands that the PIP is *not* a guarantee of continued employment during the PIP's time frame, the PIP should include a clause specifying that although the employee is on a PIP for a designated period of time, the PIP does not alter the employee's at-will status of employment. Employment may be terminated during the PIP period, if merited.

Sometimes, if a serious offense has been committed, it may be necessary to terminate an employee immediately instead of working through a series of consequences. For example, immediate termination would likely be supported if one employee physically harmed another employee or if the organization were convinced an illegal action such as embezzlement occurred. In the event an employee loses licensure or credentialing required by law, immediate termination may also be required. (For more detailed information on best practices to follow when terminating an employee, refer back to Chapter 8: If You Have to Fire Me, Do It With Heart.)

Keep a Record of Counseling Sessions

Whether an employee is being counseled after a first offense or is being escalated up the organization's progressive discipline policy, an employer can reduce liability by memorializing these conversations using the process normally followed to record behavior corrections. The memorialization should:

- include expected future actions and requirements
- be delivered in a manner that allows the employee to provide feedback
- be delivered in a manner that ensures proof of receipt (e.g., via timestamped email or through a required signature)

Remember: If corrective action isn't documented, it didn't happen!

In Conclusion

No matter how successful or important a producer (or other type of employee) is, aggressive, rude, or disrespectful behavior should never be tolerated, whether the employee is "just having a bad day" or the behavior is part of a pattern. Allowing bad behavior to occur without repercussions is harmful to overall morale, engagement, and productivity, and can have costly legal consequences.

Addressing an employee's unacceptable conduct as soon as it occurs will send a clear message that the organization neither permits nor promotes unkind or aggressive behavior in the workplace. When people know that their employer cares about how they are treated (and not just about achievement and metrics), their loyalty and performance will improve.

CHAPTER 14

Don't Ask for My Opinion If You Don't Want to Hear It…Or If You Don't Intend to Take Action

Bob and Barbara's Story

Bob and Barbara run a small manufacturing facility. They do a lot of things well and are proud of the organization they have built over the years. They are good supervisors and business owners and deeply desire to have great relationships with their 25 employees. Their good intentions are reflected in their relatively low turnover rate. Even so, they recognize how expensive *any* turnover is and would love to further reduce theirs to increase profitability.

Recently, Barbara attended a business conference where she heard that conducting a culture study was a great way to measure employee engagement, satisfaction, and happiness. Therefore, Barbara researched culture studies on the internet, wrote 10 survey questions, and emailed them to all 25 employees. The survey included open-ended, fill-in-the-blank questions related to safety, compensation, benefits, and equity in the workplace. Barbara asked the employees to email their responses back to her. She looked forward to getting her employees' input regarding the company culture and better ways to do business.

Both Barbara and Bob were shocked by the results. First, participation in the survey was extraordinarily low. Only eight employees responded. Second, the eight surveys they did receive contained some unpleasant surprises. While the responses revealed that employees did not perceive any discrimination in the workplace and that they found the facility to be a safe place to work (the good news), the employees also felt that there was consistent dissatisfaction on the specific issues of compensation and benefits.

Barbara and Bob felt the survey results related to the first two topics (safety and discrimination) were an accurate reflection of the company. However, they felt blindsided by the negative feedback on compensation and benefits, and were convinced these perceptions were inaccurate. Their thoughts were that they paid their employees what they believed to be a fair market rate and provided health benefits the company could afford.

Moreover, Barbara and Bob took the feedback personally. They felt that *they* had been treated unfairly. Therefore, they chose not to share the results with the staff, and they took no action on the survey results. As a result, all 25 employees became frustrated—even the ones who did not participate in the study—because they felt like their collective voices had not been heard.

The Takeaway

It's true: Culture and employee engagement studies are a great way to evaluate where you are as an organization and what needs to be changed. After all, organizations cannot fix problems they do not know exist. Done properly, such surveys can yield completely honest, meaningful feedback from employees who might otherwise be hesitant to share their true feelings. In this case, Barbara and Bob's instinct to do a study was exactly right—but their methodology was severely lacking. They made mistakes in three major areas:

1. They cobbled together a homemade survey with little thought to structure or goal.
2. They made no attempt to help employees feel "safe" enough to take part or provide honest answers.
3. They didn't act—at all—on the results.

Next, we'll take a quick look at how this whole survey exercise should have been handled.

Make Sure the Survey Itself Is Professionally Constructed

In her survey, Barbara tried to broadly overview many topics that could have (and should have) been their own individual studies. Like Barbara, you may see the value in conducting a culture and employee engagement survey but have no specific goal in mind.

If this is the case, a study can be done to "take the pulse" of the organization and learn what is on the employees' minds. Based on the results, you may choose to conduct additional studies that dive more deeply into certain areas. If you *do* have an area of concern you'd like to target, the initial survey can be focused on that topic. In both cases, the same survey may be conducted annually to measure improvement. Either way, "winging it" with a DIY survey is not a good idea.

Ideally, culture and employee engagement surveys should be created and administered by third-party professionals with knowledge about the organization and its goal in conducting the study. This helps ensure that questions are relevant and results are meaningful.

If, for example, a business owner is concerned about perceptions of safety in the workplace (as Barbara evidently was), the survey should be specifically tailored to that topic and include questions such as:

- Do you know where to find the most recent Safety Data Sheets in the facility?
- Do you feel you have adequate training on warehouse safety?
- Are you provided with adequate safety equipment?
- Is any safety equipment not available that should be provided?
- When was your last OSHA-approved training?
- What is the first thing employees are supposed to do in the event of a workplace accident?
- Do you have any concerns about reporting injuries to your supervisor?

To address the specific topic of discrimination, the survey might ask:

- Were you provided the company's discrimination and harassment policy when you onboarded?
- Do you know where to find the most recent version?
- Do you understand what types of actions violate this policy?
- Do you understand how to report a concern?

Now let's say that an organization desires to learn how management is perceived overall. The survey might be designed around questions such as:

- What could management do during onboarding to help new employees?
- Do you feel free to offer your opinions about process improvement to your manager?
- Is your manager receptive to new ideas or processes?
- Does your manager treat you with dignity and respect?
- Does your manager treat others with dignity and respect?
- Is your manager efficient?
- Does your manager maintain an open-door policy?
- What suggestions do you have that might enable your manager to better support you?
- Do you trust management to do what it says it will do?
- If your manager was not available and you had a concern, how would you handle the matter?

Finally, let's address the subject that seemed to be such a sticking point for Bob and Barbara's employees. If an organization is concerned about the general perception of wages and benefits in the workplace, the study might ask employees:

- Do you believe you are fairly compensated for the work you do?
- Do you understand how production bonuses are calculated?
- If you desired to advance within the organization, do you have a clear understanding of what steps you would need to take to do so?
- Are you able to understand the details of your paystubs/wage statements and what the terms mean?

These questions work for Barbara and Bob's organization, but a professional, third-party firm can assist you in creating specific questions relevant to your organization and your goals.

Help Employees Feel Safe Enough to Answer Truthfully

Barbara's second error was asking employees to provide their replies directly to her via email. No wonder only a tiny percentage bothered to respond at all! Few employees concerned about protecting their privacy on sensitive opinions or issues would risk directly emailing their replies to their boss. To ensure you receive the most honest, meaningful responses from an adequate number of participants, replies should always be gathered in a manner designed to protect the anonymity of the employee.

This is especially true in smaller organizations where it is easy to determine which employee provided specific responses. Employees must be able to trust that supervisors won't try to find a "back door" to determining who provided what feedback. For example, if the boss knows "there are only three people in accounting and only one is female, so this result must have come from Sally," the results are not anonymous.

Once You Get the Responses, Do the Right Thing

As you can see, Barbara made plenty of mistakes from the beginning. But how she and Bob together handled the survey results once they came back may have been the largest error. As a reminder:
- They opined that the employees' collective and consistent voices regarding compensation and benefits were wrong.
- They personalized the employees' responses.
- They did not share the results or take action to respond to them.

First, to deem employees "wrong" in their perceptions is, itself, "wrong" (or at least shortsighted). Rarely are situations "black or white" and answers "wrong or right." When an employer asks a question and employees take the time to answer, a deeper exploration is called for. Rather than taking the survey responses personally and digging in, Bob and Barbara should have taken a more thoughtful approach. At the very least, they should have shared the results with employees.

When employees participate in a culture study, they expect to hear that their employer received both positive and negative results. And the truth is, *well-conducted studies often reveal corporate shortcomings.* There is an expectation that these shortcomings will be acknowledged (at the least) and addressed (if at all possible).

Simply ignoring survey results does more damage than not having done the study in the first place. It signals to employees that the company was really just looking for employees to provide positive feedback, and it may create an impression that the results were overwhelmingly unfavorable (which may not be true), or that the company is hiding the information for some other reason. Further, failing to share and act on survey results sends the message, "We don't really care about your grievances, and we're going to do nothing to alleviate them." This erodes trust, builds resentment, and crushes morale.

In this case, once Barbara and Bob heard the consistent theme that employees were dissatisfied with compensation and benefits, rather than personalize the issue, they should have objectively evaluated whether compensation and benefits *were* fair. They could have researched what competitors in the field are offering, taken into account cost-of-living increases and their own financial soundness, and offered up at least a nominal "good will" increase. If, indeed, employees are being compensated below industry standards, it is probably a good idea to remedy this if possible.

On the other hand, it is quite possible that Bob and Barbara's compensation and benefits were fair and competitive, and that employees simply needed to understand the value of their total compensation package. If that is the case, Bob and Barbara have a unique opportunity to educate employees on how total compensation is calculated, which might clarify and reassure all employees that they are being paid fairly.

A Do-Over for Bob and Barbara: Introduce Employees to Their Total Compensation Package

Total compensation packages give generous employers the opportunity to shine. They signal to employees that their employer values them enough to make additional investments to benefit them *on top of* their wages.

When Bob and Barbara's employees responded to the survey, they may have been thinking, *I earn $X per year.* The employees may not have considered the value of the non-wage portion of their compensation. Providing the dollar value of each item, and noting whether it is tax-free or tax-deferred, will illuminate the total annual compensation—which is likely greater than employees realize.

Total compensation packages will vary from organization to organization, but might include the cumulative value of:
- Regular wages
- Overtime or other supplemental wages
- Bonuses
- Paid time off
- Employer-paid group health benefits
- Employer-paid ancillary benefits (vision, dental, short/long-term disability insurance)
- Employer-paid education or certifications
- Employer-paid short/long-term disability benefits
- 401(k), 403(b), or other investment vehicle matches
- Cell phone, internet, or other technology allowances
- Employer-paid Employee Assistance Program visits

In Conclusion

Employees want good relationships with their leaders and organizations. Likewise, employers want good relationships with their employees. But that can happen only when honesty flows both ways.

In Chapter 1: Surround Yourself with Bold Employees, I talked about the importance of creating a workplace environment where employees are able to communicate freely, boldly, and authentically with their employers. The goal is for employees to proactively come to you with most of their feedback, questions, and ideas for improvement.

Think of culture studies and employee surveys as a "safety net" that underlies your ongoing efforts to create psychological safety. If there *is* a concern or issue that your employees haven't shared (or maybe that they haven't even articulated to themselves yet!), a well-constructed and well-implemented survey can bring it to light.

When you ask for employee perceptions, you're showing caring and respect for them—but *only* if you follow up with sincerity. Your response has the power to build trust and strengthen the culture, which creates the kind of reputation that attracts the best and brightest and keeps great employees from leaving.

CHAPTER 15

Nepotism Sucks; Prove That You Deserve to Lead

David's Story

Before I tell this story, let me put it in perspective: I am very, very familiar with David's particular scenario as a second-generation business owner. I have worked for not one, not two, but *three* second-generation businesses. In all three businesses, the first generation (Gen 1), the father, built the business. Then the son (Gen 2), ran the business after the father retired. (Yes, all three really were father/son combinations! I always found it interesting that none of the mothers and/or daughters worked for the organizations.)

My friend David is a Gen 2 business owner. His father started an exceptionally successful business, which David now runs. Unlike some people in his shoes, David is refreshingly aware of the personal and professional advantages he has by virtue of working for and learning from his father. He summarized all of the advantages he has had in his personal and professional life in a simple statement: "I started on third base; all I had to do was get home. Many people don't even get up to bat. It's up to me to do the very best I can to honor that."

The Takeaway

No doubt about it: Being a Gen 2 business owner has its advantages. The first and most obvious one is the step-up that is simply not available to most people. The second advantage is the almost-absolute job security that comes with it. Throughout their employment at a family-owned business, most Gen 2s enjoy a level of job security that no one else has because:

- Most Gen 1s are hesitant to fire Gen 2s. (To be fair, it would be weird if they weren't!) This is true even when it might be in the best interest of the business for the Gen 1 to do so. Family blood is—and should be—thicker than business connections. Thus, what might be a job-ending mistake for one employee is typically a learning opportunity for a Gen 2. The Gen 2 generally does not have to worry that the financial rug will be pulled out from under them.

- Besides receiving the job itself, most Gen 2s are afforded opportunities not available to non-family-member employees. They can speak more freely to their boss, the Gen 1 business owner. They can propose new ideas, knowing that even if the idea flops, there will not be professional repercussions. They are entrusted with "insider" information not available to non-family-member employees. They might receive plum assignments their coworkers can only dream about.

All of this makes perfect sense, of course. Like all parents, Gen 1 business owners want to help carve out the very best opportunities for their children and are willing to help them accomplish their goals. A Gen 1 leader cannot fairly be faulted for that, and neither can a Gen 2 leader be faulted for wanting to lead the family business. Yet many people *do* fault them—it's hard for some employees to get past the resentment they feel when they compare their own circumstances with those of a fellow leader or coworker who was able to start their career on third base.

The good news is that Gen 2 leaders can do a lot to minimize this resentment and build strong relationships with colleagues and coworkers. The big key is self-awareness.

Unfortunately, some Gen 2s seem blissfully *unaware* of their good familial luck. They seem to wonder why non-family-member employees either don't take them seriously or resent their easy success, or both. Whether these individuals fall into the "lost-cause" category or can work on their self-awareness and redeem themselves is really up to them.

Thankfully, many Gen 2s are like David. They are well aware and fully appreciative of the advantages they have been given. They work especially hard to avoid the appearance that they don't deserve their role or position in the company. And the good news is, there's plenty more that up-and-coming

Gen 2s can do to start overcoming the heir-to-the-throne perception, start building strong relationships, and set themselves and their companies up for success.

First, Get Other Relevant Professional Experience Before Joining Gen 1's Business

Gen 2s should consider working at other organizations and being entirely self-supporting for several years before working for Gen 1. Starting out at another company can give Gen 2 a reality check on the way the real world works: learning how difficult it can be to negotiate compensation, seeing the differences between the family business and other companies, and gaining the confidence that comes from standing entirely on one's own.

The advantages of working at places not owned by Gen 1 are many:

- Having successfully worked in another organization, Gen 2 will arrive at the family-owned business with professional credibility. This will eliminate the perception that "He/she could not get a job elsewhere."
- Gen 2 will have different professional experiences to draw upon, thus being able to contribute fresh ideas and information to the company. This might mean Gen 2 will have different client or vendor relationships than the family-owned business currently has, plus well-thought-out recommendations on new platforms, software, processes, policies, or programs. They will most likely gain unique perspectives based on what they've seen work (and not work) with other organizations.
- Upon return to the family-owned organization, Gen 2 will be able to say with confidence that he/she had other options but *chose* to work with the family-owned business.
- Perhaps most importantly, experience with another organization will help long-term employees visualize Gen 2 as an adult, not a child. Long-term employees who worked for a Gen 1 for any significant length of time may have watched Gen 2 grow up. Those employees know whether Gen 2 was a polite or petulant teenager. Some Gen 2s will have to work especially hard at overcoming perceptions created over the course of many childhood years. Working (and succeeding) elsewhere will help transform long-

term employees' perceptions of Gen 2 as a child to Gen 2 as a credible, professional adult.

Second, Walk Humbly

Because Gen 2 is probably younger in age and may have less professional experience than many employees (especially the long-term employees), Gen 2 must take proactive steps to create and maintain an image of professionalism and maturity. If Gen 2 behaves in an immature manner—for instance, yells during a staff meeting or makes entitled, self-serving statements—then Gen 2 is confirming the impressions of employees.

Gen 2 can demonstrate maturity by using active listening techniques to critically evaluate ideas and suggestions from other employees. Gen 2 might consider declining opportunities that create the appearance of self-promotion, such as using a favored office or parking in the closest space. Gen 2 can also cultivate a reputation as a mature, deserving leader by making an intentional effort to recognize employees' contributions.

Third, Find an Old Gorilla

This advice comes directly from Bert Thornton, vice chairman emeritus of Waffle House Inc., who wrote *Find an Old Gorilla: Pathways Through the Jungle of Business and Life*. In this book, Mr. Thornton encourages employees to seek out mentors. He explains in real-world terms the value the mentor/mentee relationship can bring to the individuals and to the organization.

While this is good advice for all organizational leaders, forming a strong mentor/mentee relationship is especially valuable to Gen 2s. Why? Because the mentor will have a more objective view of the Gen 2 leader than their parent, the business owner, does. The mentor will also be able to be more honest with Gen 2 than their employees are.

It may take some time and perhaps a little trial and error to find the right mentor/mentee match, but the effort is worth it. The long-term value of a mentor cannot be overstated. Good mentors have made mistakes in their careers and are willing to acknowledge and share those experiences in order to teach their mentees how to avoid the same missteps. They can evaluate and critique mentees' decisions without bias. Most important, good mentors are willing to have difficult conversations when necessary, always have their mentees' best interests at heart, and are willing to put in the work to be a part of their mentees' success.

Fourth, Know What You Are Good At—and Where You Need Help

As above, this is true for all organizational leaders, not just Gen 2s. Even though you are the leader of an organization, you do not have to be great at everything.

For example, in a religious setting, it is not reasonable for congregations to expect their priest, rector, or rabbi to be the best preacher; fundraiser; volunteer organizer; facilities maintenance coordinator; bookkeeper; teacher of children, teenagers, and adults; worship leader; scheduler; writer; historian; communications director; outreach coordinator; *and* provider of pastoral care!

It is likely that the priest, rector, or rabbi is great at one or two things, good at a few more things, and not very good at all at some! This is true of all leaders. Knowing what you are good at and what you love to do (and what you are not good at) allows you to focus on those few things and do them well, while delegating the remainder of the tasks. It is much more efficient to delegate jobs to others who are great at those jobs.

Think of your organization as The Beatles: Each member knew what their talent was. Even though each Beatle could play many instruments, each focused on the one instrument they were best at and let the other band members play the instruments they were the best at. John Lennon played rhythm guitar, Paul McCartney played bass guitar, Ringo Starr played the drums, and George Harrison played lead guitar. No one person had to be the best at everything.

Astute leaders understand and are willing to admit what they are good at (and what they are not good at). They actively work to surround themselves with employees talented in those other areas.

Finally, Work Harder Than the Hardest Worker

After a Gen 2 arrives at an organization, it is only natural that non-family-member employees will compare Gen 2 to Gen 1—especially if Gen 1 is or was beloved by employees. Personalities, management styles, education, and good and bad attributes are fair game for employees to subconsciously (or consciously) evaluate.

To overcome the perception that "he/she has this position only because his/her father/mother owns the company," Gen 2s must be willing to work harder than the hardest worker in the organization. Depending on the business, this may mean arriving early, staying late, being prepared for every meeting, knowing the names of non-C-suite employees, hitting every sales quota, participating meaningfully in meetings, listening patiently to ideas shared by others, and willingly sharing credit with others.

In Conclusion

Gen 2 leaders have huge opportunities to succeed and make their organizations even better than they found them in terms of productivity, culture, employee satisfaction, and more. Gen 2 leaders can learn what made the business successful from the person responsible for that success while bringing in fresh perspectives and ideas. When Gen 2s walk humbly and express gratitude for the opportunities they have, more experienced employees will be inclined to welcome the Gen 2 leader, share institutional history, provide input, and root for the Gen 2 to succeed.

Employer-Employee Relationships

CHAPTER 16

Do Not Friend Me on Social Media

Sofia's Story

After starting a new job, Sofia received a Facebook friend request from her supervisor. While she preferred to keep her professional and personal lives separate, she was concerned that ignoring or rejecting the request would cause her boss to dislike her. She also wondered whether connecting on social media was normal and even expected in her new company's culture. Despite feeling uncomfortable, she accepted the request because she did not want to rock the boat immediately after joining the organization.

Soon, Sofia's boss looked through her feed and learned that Sofia and her partner were trying to adopt a child—information he would not have had access to from everyday workplace conversations. He began to offer unsolicited and unwelcome advice he learned from a friend who had cared for several foster children. He also "teased" Sofia about not being able to carry her weight at work once she became a parent.

Sofia felt unfairly targeted by her boss. She worried that if she disagreed with him or asked him to stop discussing that topic with her, their working relationship would deteriorate. As she and her partner moved forward with the adoption, she began to feel so uncomfortable at work that she started looking for other positions.

The Takeaway

Extending workplace relationships into the online realm may seem harmless and even fun, but too often this leads to stress, strain, misunderstandings, and disagreements for one or both parties. Social media connections between leaders and employees rarely provide material benefit, and, as in Sofia's case, can have costly consequences.

Social Media Use by the Numbers

According to Statista, in 2008, only 10 percent of Americans used social media. In 2020, 80 percent of Americans, or 223 million Americans, had a social media profile.[1]

Statista also reports that in 2022, Americans spent an average of two hours and three minutes per day on social media.[2] As of this writing, Americans spent more time on TikTok than any other social media platform: 53.8 minutes a day.[3]

This trend isn't limited to the United States. Demandsage reported that in 2023, 4.9 billion people used social media throughout the world.[4]

Ergo, a large portion of your employees are probably using Facebook, TikTok, Instagram, YouTube, Pinterest, Snapchat, Twitter, or LinkedIn— or all of them! In addition to using these sites for entertainment, this means that your employees have a far-reaching platform to share information unlike any that has ever existed in the past.

When I teach classes on social media usage and how it affects the workplace, the most common questions I get from employers are:

Is it a good idea to use social media to vet candidates?
Should I "friend" my employees on social media so I can see what they are doing?

By employees—many of whom share Sofia's concerns—I am frequently asked:

My employer sent me a friend request. Do I have to accept it?

The answer to all three questions is simple: *No.*

Whether I am speaking to employers or employees, my focus is on the *rights and responsibilities* of both the *employer and the employee*: what an employee may say on social media about their personal life, their job, their boss, or their coworkers, and what an employer may do if they do not like the employee's social media posts.

Social media has many benefits: the ability to remain connected with loved ones who live far away, to join groups of people with whom you have things in common, to learn new skills, and to share personal details about your life with your friends. However, as Sofia learned, those benefits usually *don't* extend to enhancing the employer-employee relationship.

Let's look at several compelling reasons why employers and leaders should refrain from "friending" their employees on social media—and what some of the consequences might be if you choose to do so anyway.

Personal Reasons Not to Be Friends with Employees on Social Media

Personal Reason One: Friendships and workplace relationships are not the same thing.

While you and your employees may have warm, genuine relationships, workplace relationships are different from personal friendships. Employer/employee relationships are predicated on the fundamental fact that your employees work for you. If you have control over someone's financial well-being, there is an inequality in the balance of power that makes it difficult to be friends in the truest sense of the word.

Who Are Your Friends, Really?

If you feel discouraged by the fact that you aren't (and probably shouldn't be) close friends with your employees, recognize that you DO have true friends. Your friends are the people you go to dinner with, the people who come to your house to watch Saturday college football, the people you attend church or temple with, and the people you travel with. They're the people you call if you need to vent in a really open and honest manner because you know they will provide honest feedback and will not disclose confidences. In general, your friends are the people who *choose* to spend their free time with you because they genuinely care about you.

This does not mean you should stop caring about the employees who work for you; after all, they are choosing to work for you when they could work for other employers. But be honest about the dynamics of the relationship. Ask yourself whether both people would want to continue a close relationship if the employment relationship ended. If there's even a small amount of doubt that the answer would be yes, you probably shouldn't be privy to each other's social media posts, because they often reveal intimate information that doesn't really belong in the workplace.

Personal Reason Two: Social media often reveals personal information.

A quick scroll through individual accounts can reveal whether a person is married, what religion they are, how many children or grandchildren they have, what kind of car they drive, where they vacation, what schools their children attend, and whether they support a particular political party or candidate. These are personal details that you may not otherwise share with your employees and your employees may not wish to share with you.

These intimate details are challenging for employers for another reason. Think about your own social media posts. Do they reveal glimpses of your home or the type of place you stay when you take a well-deserved vacation from work? Now, put yourself in the position of the employee who might look at the post. What would that person see and how might they feel? Remember, as we discussed in Chapter 1: Surround Yourself with Bold Employees, leaders and employers should strive to flatten the power dynamic between themselves and employees to create a culture of psychological safety. It's also a good idea to minimize indications that might cause employees to believe you are out of touch with them and their lifestyles.

Legal Reasons Not to Be Friends with Employees on Social Media

Legal Reason One: What you learn about employees on social media might land you in legal hot water.

Social media reveals information about your employees that may place them in federally protected categories. These federal laws set the floor—the minimum—for determining what an employer can consider in hiring, promotion, and retention, and what information cannot be considered.

According to the U.S. Department of Labor, there are approximately 180 federal laws that protect 150 million employees in 10 million workplaces from discrimination, harassment, unsafe environments, or adverse actions based on protected factors.[v] These federal anti-discrimination laws include:

- *Title VII of the Civil Rights Act of 1964* prohibits employers from making any employment decision based on sex, color, race, religion, or national origin.
- The *Pregnancy Discrimination Act* (PDA) makes it illegal for employers to refuse to hire someone because they are or might become pregnant.
- The *Age Discrimination in Employment Act* (ADEA) says employers may not discriminate against people because they are over 40.
- The *Americans with Disabilities Act* (ADA) prohibits employers from making employment decisions solely on the basis of whether someone has or doesn't have a disability, or whether the employer perceives the employee as having a disability.
- The *Genetic Information Nondiscrimination Act* (GINA) prohibits employers from making decisions based on an employee's genetic makeup.
- The *Uniformed Services Employment and Reemployment Rights Act* (USERRA) requires the employment and reemployment of veterans and does not allow an employer to discriminate because of an employee's service obligations.

- The *Pregnant Workers Fairness Act* (PWFA) prohibits employers from discriminating against women who are pregnant, have just been pregnant, or are trying to become pregnant and provide protected leave requirements for women who are pregnant or who are recovering from childbirth. The PWFA, signed into law in 2022, requires employers to provide reasonable accommodations for pregnant employees, unless doing so would create an undue hardship.

These laws mean that an employer may not make any decision based on the factors listed above in *any* employment decision: hiring, promotion, compensation adjustments, terminations, establishing benefits, reprimands, or termination.

Not-So-Fun Fact About Pregnancy Discrimination in Florida

Pregnancy discrimination was not illegal in the state of Florida until 2015. While there were remedies under the federal Pregnancy Discrimination Act for women who worked for employers with 15 or more employees, a woman had no legal remedy in the state of Florida if her employer discriminated against her (including terminating her) because she was pregnant. This means that until 2015, a pregnant woman could not bring a lawsuit in state court against an employer for pregnancy discrimination. Instead, she would be forced to file a lawsuit in federal court, which has different jurisdictional thresholds and procedural requirements. Even today, Florida law does not require employers to offer time off for pregnancy or childbirth.

Because employees often post pictures of and comments about their spouses, children, religion, philanthropies, favorite (or least favorite) politicians or political parties, hobbies, neighborhoods, vacations, and birthdays, if you are friends on social media, you will *(I promise)* discover something about them that you did not know before—and that is completely unrelated to their jobs. In many cases, that personal information will place the employees in protected categories.

Once you know this information, *even if you don't ever use it*, you cannot unknow it…and that knowledge can be used against you in the future should you have to take adverse action against the employee. You may ultimately be put in a position where you have to prove that you did not use your knowledge to discriminate against the employee.

Here's an example of what I mean. Let's say that Samantha works at your restaurant in a state where political affiliation is a protected status. You have a written policy that says you can terminate any employee who fails to call in to report an absence before their shift begins.

Samantha is scheduled to work on Monday at 10:00 a.m. She does not call in or show up at any point during the day. When she arrives at work on Tuesday, you terminate her for violating the policy.

Samantha sues you for discriminating against her because of her political affiliation. She argues that you were aware that she missed Monday to attend a political rally.

When you reply that you had no idea why she missed work or failed to call in, she says, "You are my friend on social media and you saw the pictures of me at the rally. You are really terminating me because you disagree with my political views."

Will Samantha win the lawsuit? Who knows? It does not matter that you may not have even seen the pictures Samantha posted on social media.

What is clear is that if you and Samantha were not friends on social media, you would have a better chance to convince a jury you did not know where she was on Monday or what her political affiliation might have been and that you knew only that she violated a written attendance policy.

The best legal defense is to be able to honestly say, "I had no way of knowing that she was at a rally for (fill in the blank with the name of any political party), so I could not have discriminated against her based on her political affiliation."

Most states and municipalities mirror (or broaden) these federal protections. For example, the federal Americans with Disabilities Act prohibits employers from discriminating against employees who are over 40 years of age. Florida broadens the law to prohibit employers from considering any age in employment (except where there is another law that contains an age requirement, such as a child labor law). In South Carolina, an employer may not inquire as to whether an applicant or employee is a smoker and may not discriminate against an applicant or employee because they are a smoker.

Stay Off Social Media When Hiring, Too

Have you ever encountered the suggestion that hiring managers should check out a candidate's social media as part of the screening process? The idea is that you'll get a fuller picture of who the candidate is, what their habits are, how they might fit into your company's culture, whether they are likely to violate company policy, whether they're telling the truth on their application, etc.

Despite the popularity of this screening tactic, it is my opinion that social media should never be used to vet a candidate who is interviewing for a job. Even a cursory review of most personal social media accounts immediately reveals some combination of the applicant's gender, approximate age, political affiliation, religious preference, marital status, veteran status, sexual orientation, familial status, and whether the person has a disability, appears to have a disability, or is closely associated with somebody who has a disability. Except where one of these factors is a bona fide occupational qualification (BFOQ), these factors are irrelevant to whether an applicant is qualified to perform the functions of the job as described in the job description.

For the same reasons listed above, you don't want to have to prove that you did not discriminate against an applicant based on information gleaned from social media. If you request a connection, comment, like, message, screenshot, or otherwise engage with an applicant on social media, they will be able to prove that you *did* visit their page. Even if you do not engage, be aware that social media sites have ways to archive information about who visits pages. Again, the safest route is to stay away from job candidates' social media in the first place.

Legal Reason Two: Your ability to respond to what you read on social media is very limited.

It makes sense that employees post about their jobs: Employees who work full-time spend at least 2,000 hours per year at work. Even during their off hours, they are often still thinking about work—particularly if they had a bad day, had a negative interaction at work, or have a stressful event scheduled the next day.

Like it or not, many employees use social media to vent or complain about their jobs. This is particularly true for remote employees who do not have the benefit of face-to-face interactions with their coworkers. Unfortunately, it's possible that an employee's heat-of-the-moment post could be seen by other coworkers, clients, customers, patients, vendors, or *prospective* clients, customers, patients, or vendors.

These negative posts may justifiably frustrate you as a leader or employer. You may know that the information in the employee's post is incorrect (or completely fabricated). Perhaps you have more information than the employee does, the employee's post may tell only one side of a multi-faceted story, or the employee's post may cast the employee in the best light while being unfair to other employees or to you. However—regardless of what the true story may be—whether and how you respond to the post could expose your company to liability.

For example, what do you do if your employee posts any of the following on social media?

- "My boss is a jerk! Who agrees?"
- "Today I almost fell in the parking lot at work! We need lights!! #safetyfirst!!"
- "My supervisor gives bonuses only to women! What's up with that?"
- "Joe got the promotion I applied for. Everyone knows that Joe is an idiot. It's unfair."
- "Sitting in a boring training class! #nothingtoseehere"

The permissible response by you, the employer, depends on several factors. But first, a bit of background:

How is social media governed in the workplace? Social media in the workplace is governed by a federal law known as the National Labor Relations Act (the Act). The Act is overseen by the National Labor Relations Board (the Board), a quasi-judicial governmental agency with five members. The majority of the members always belong to the political party of the current administration. The minority of the members always belong to the other political party. The Board has jurisdiction over almost every employer in the United States and oversees many types of workplace issues. In the past, most Americans associated the Act and the Board with unionized workplaces. However, the Act applies to union and non-union workplaces, and the Board has jurisdiction over both union and non-union workplaces.

Around 2010, the Board began examining employers' social media policies to make sure they were fair and equitable. Because the Board is a quasi-political entity, its priorities mirror the initiatives of the sitting president. This means that employers can expect the Board to be very engaged in all employment issues when those issues are the sitting president's priorities. Historically, Democratic administrations and their respective Boards have taken a more active, pro-employee approach, while Republican administrations and Boards have been more hands-off.

What does the Act say about social media? With respect to social media usage by employees, Section 7 of the Act is the most referenced. It guarantees employees certain specific rights and prohibits employers from hindering employees' communications related to terms and conditions of work. The most common terms and conditions of work are, not surprisingly, compensation and benefits. Specifically, Section 7 guarantees employees:

"The right to self-organization, to form, join, or assist labor organizations, to bargain collectively through representatives of their own choosing, and to engage in other concerted activities for the purpose of collective bargaining or other mutual aid or protection," and the right to "refrain from any or all such activities."[vi]

The language of Section 7 means that employees have a right to gather to discuss (in person or online) their compensation or benefit packages, the safety of the workplace, how employees are treated by supervisors, the adequacy of equipment, the policies set by management, or anything else that relates to terms and conditions of employment.

What does Section 7 mean for you as an employer? This important provision means that as an employer, you may not limit your employees' ability to discuss the terms and conditions of their employment.

If you have a statement in your policies and procedures manual or in your employee handbook prohibiting employees from discussing compensation, benefits, or any other term or condition of employment, put this book down right this moment and *go delete that section*! The same is true if the policy is "unwritten but understood." It is important to communicate a correction of such an unwritten policy.

What response options do employers have? The short answer is: Employers' response options are limited, and it is often better not to respond online at all—even when the truth seems very obvious to you. This is particularly true if a response would require you to disclose confidential information about the business or any employee.

Let's use one of the hypothetical posts from above as an example. An employee posts, "My supervisor gives bonuses only to women! What's up with that?" In response, you might be tempted to write, "Actually, you did not get a bonus because you did not meet your goal…for the second quarter in a row!" While that might be a correct answer, you aren't authorized to share that private information. (Yes, you are legally obligated to protect the privacy of the very employee who overshared on social media.)

Or you might be tempted to simply terminate the employee for making wild and inaccurate accusations on a public forum. However, if this aggrieved employee filed a complaint with the National Labor Relations Board, the Board would likely find that the employee's speech is protected under the Act because the employee was discussing compensation—which is probably the most important term and condition of employment.

Finally, no matter how you respond, it is likely that the issue will get more attention than it would if you did not respond at all.

It Doesn't Matter How You Found the Post—Refrain From Responding

Even if you aren't friends with your employees on social media, another employee, vendor, client, or other third party may report a post to you. The advice in this chapter still applies, even though you did not seek out the information.

Instead, the best action for you, the employer, would be to call the employee into your office and simply ask about the post. You could say, "We take claims of pay discrimination very seriously. You indicated that men do not get bonuses from your supervisor. I want to look into that to see if that is correct. What information do you have to support your post that your supervisor gives bonuses only to women?" If the employee is correct, you need to address the matter with the supervisor and ensure that his or her pay practices going forward are non-discriminatory. If the employee is incorrect, you can explain your findings.

Are there any types of posts employers *should* respond to? The following types of comments *do* merit a response if they are brought to the attention of the employer:

- **Threatening comments, even if they are presented as a "joke."** Employers have a right and an obligation to take action in the face of threatening comments. This is true whether the threatening comments appear on social media or in some other medium, including emails, text messages, or verbal threats.

  The Board has specific rules regarding how to determine whether comments are actually threatening. If an employee makes perceived threats in person or online, it is best to contact an employment attorney immediately to assess risk and determine an appropriate response.

- **Comments that are "-ist": racist, sexist, ageist, etc. in violation of your company policy.** Employees often believe that they have a Constitutional right to say whatever they think. However, that right has limits. In the private sector, employees may say whatever they want, BUT there can be consequences for stating their opinions. Depending on your policy, the severity of the matter, whether you are a private company or a government contractor, and whether you have a collective bargaining arrangement, the consequences can range from no allowable action by the employer to an employer's decision to terminate a person's employment.

  Each employer should have a written equal employment opportunity policy that prevents -isms in the workplace. All employees must be trained on this policy and understand what behavior is prohibited. Employees should also be told what the consequences of inappropriate in-person or online behavior will be. It is possible that an employee who makes comments at work or on social media, knowing that the comments violate the organization's policy, may be reprimanded in accordance with the policy.

- **Comments that violate a state or federal law.** State and federal law may prohibit or limit certain speech. For example, if you operate a healthcare organization such as a doctor's office, a dental office, a surgery center, a health clinic, a chiropractic office, or a specialty group, you are probably a covered entity, subject to the Health Insurance Portability and Accountability Act (HIPAA). This federal law requires covered entities to maintain all medical information in a completely confidential manner. Your employees may not share or disclose *any* patient information to *any* outside person without their specific written consent. HIPAA is very broad and means your employees cannot even state whether a particular person is a patient with your organization.

For example, if you operate a dental office, and the very famous, charismatic, multi-talented, and amazing Shaquille O'Neal comes to your office for a checkup, no one in your office may tell any other person that Mr. O'Neal was a patient without his specific written consent.

A Shaquille O'Neal Caveat

The HIPAA privacy rule does not apply *if and only if* Mr. O'Neal gives written consent to be identified....which he probably would...because he is awesome.

In fact, he might even be willing to take a selfie with you...because he is awesome.

- **Comments that "leak" proprietary information.** Depending on the content of the post, if an employee discloses a trade secret or confidential Information on a social media platform, the employer may have a right to reprimand, or even terminate, the employee.

How can employers ensure that they are in compliance with the Act? Every employer, regardless of size and union status, should have a written social media policy of some sort. Luckily, the Board has done the work for you.

In May 2012, the Board approved a sample social media policy. This policy balances employees' rights to engage in activity on social media with employers' rights to protect reputations and secrets. Although the policy is several years old, it is still considered solid. The policy is free and available on the NLRB website.[vii]

To ensure it does not run afoul of the National Labor Relations Act, an employer should consult with their human resource professional or their employment attorney before taking any adverse action against an employee for their private use of social media. This will be money well spent!

What If My Employees Post Misleading Negative Reviews?

Apps, websites, and companies have been specifically developed to allow job seekers to gain insight into the "real" culture of a company. Using these tools, your employees can reach hundreds (maybe thousands) of your potential future employees. Unfortunately, the content in these apps and websites is often one-sided, and the employer has limited opportunities to respond.

To determine what a job seeker might see on one such website, I typed in the name of a random company and looked at the results that instantly popped up. The statements about the company were scathing. Anonymous people who claimed to be former employees wrote that they lived in a state of fear, were surprised to be fired over the weekend, and were more surprised to find out that other employees knew they were fired before they did. Former coworkers were described as "dishonest," and management was described as "uneducated" by one anonymous poster.

Ouch! Even though these reviews are one-sided and may have been written by Detractors, they may still discourage job seekers from applying for jobs with this company.

What can you do if similar reviews are written about your organization? Know up front that there is no PR or marketing firm that can entirely combat, eliminate, or respond to negative reviews on websites not hosted by your company. Therefore, it is better to create a fair and equitable culture to begin with than to spend time, money, and resources in an attempt to recapture a positive reputation.

This is a good time to take a break and do a quick search to see whether there are any positive or negative reviews about your company. If there are reviews that concern you, work with your legal and marketing teams to determine whether and how to respond to the reviews.

Remember: Not every shot fired requires a response! Often, responding to negative comments adds fuel to the fire and creates the impression that the information in the post is credible.

Legal Reason Three: You must treat all employees equally.

The timestamp of a social media post by an employee reveals whether the employee uses social media during work hours. Wouldn't keeping tabs on employees' use of work time be a *good* reason to "friend" your employees on social media? Well…probably not.

While it is very frustrating for an employer to realize that an employee is wasting company time by scrolling and posting on social media during the workday, taking action requires a thoughtful response. For this reason, proceed carefully.

- First, determine whether the employee's action violates a written policy. If there is no written policy prohibiting the employee from using social media during the workday, you have no legal leg to stand on.

Consider Prioritizing Productivity Over Prohibitions

Many companies *do* have policies that prohibit employees from using personal social media during work time. This would seem to be an easy solution, but I'm not sure how realistic it is. Instead, a better approach might be for employers to focus on objective productivity.

In today's world, software programs make it easy for employers to monitor employees' work and productivity. (If you choose to go this route, make sure you have a written policy that specifically says employees have no expectation of privacy in their electronic communications.) Some employers monitor keystrokes to assess productivity; others monitor website usage. If your organization uses programs like Teams or Slack, remind employees that these are work-related tools that are subject to the organization's monitoring rights. They are *not* personal communication channels.

If an employee is spending excessive time on social media sites, watching Netflix, or gossiping with coworkers on Slack, that can affect productivity—and you are within your rights as an employer to address the distraction.

Incidentally…employers also monitor websites to ensure that there is no illegal or illicit activity occurring on their equipment or systems. For example, employers have a legitimate reason to ensure that employees aren't visiting gambling or pornographic websites. It's safe to say that if employees are doing these things on company time, they're probably not maximizing their productivity!

- Second, determine whether the employee was scrolling and posting during work time. There is a difference between working hours and working time, and the distinction can be crucial. Working hours are the hours someone is scheduled to be at work (e.g., 8:00 a.m. to 5:00 p.m.). Working time is the time during the working hours when someone is fulfilling the terms and tasks of their job description. For example, if an employee takes a lunch break from 12:00 p.m. to 1:00 p.m., that isn't working time because they are not expected to perform any work tasks. They may engage in any personal task, including posting on social media, during that time.
- Third, if an employee has violated a policy by using social media during work time and an employer legitimately desires to reprimand the employee, that employer must be willing to reprimand *all* employees who do the same. If your largest Detractor is using social media during work time and you want to reprimand her, you must equally reprimand your best employee if she is found to be doing the same thing. Treating these two employees differently may subject you to a claim of discrimination or a complaint of favoritism.

I'm a Leader, and I Do Want to Use Social Media!

Now that you've read through the reasons why you may not want to "friend" your employees, the decision whether or not to do so is yours. While there are legitimate risks, you have the legal right to connect with employees, colleagues, and even your own leaders on social media. Should you choose to go this route, here are a few words of caution:

Create two profiles. If you use social media as a way to connect with your employees, consider having two profiles: one personal page for close friends and family, and one professional page for colleagues and employees. The personal page allows you to post the vacation highlights, family pictures, and news you want to share with friends who know you well. The professional page allows you to post pictures and information that are related to work, or that may allow your employees to see you as a real person (but *always* in a professional light).

To discourage employees from stumbling upon the personal page, some employers create it using a slightly different name. The personal page might use your maiden name if you have one, a nickname your close friends and family use, or your middle name—and the professional page might use your full business name.

Think about how your posts might appear to others who lack context. Molly's boss, Emily, decided to friend her employees on social media. Scrolling through Emily's social media account, Molly is under the impression that during the past year Emily took her family on three vacations, bought her daughter a brand-new Jeep for her 16th birthday, and that Emily's son is an honor student at his school.

Why does Molly believe these things? Because she saw it on social media. And so did Every. Employee. In. The. Company.

While it is tempting (and very common) to share details of one's life in social media posts, leaders of organizations must be especially mindful about oversharing personal information with employees on social media. Why?

- **They can exacerbate the power gradient between employers and employees.** Personal posts can appear to reveal an extravagant lifestyle to employees—even if the posts aren't intended to do so, and even if the content of the posts is not necessarily different from the content of posts created by employees. Remember that most employees in an organization earn less money than leaders of the organization and may not be able to afford what the leaders can: a new car, for example. Posts like this can chip away at your efforts to build a culture of psychological safety, and can spark envy and resentment.

- **Posts on social media rarely tell the whole story.** Incorrect assumptions are often based on the limited information shown on social media. In this case, what Molly may not know is that Emily did not take any time off the year before because she was working so hard to keep the business running. Molly may not be aware that Emily's daughter saved the money she earned at part-time jobs for several years to pay for the Jeep. Molly may not be aware that Emily's son spent nights, days, and weekends studying to earn a spot as an honor student at his school.

Do *not* brag on social media. The *worst* type of post on social media is the falsely humble "look-at-me" post, as in:

"I am so humbled to receive this award." (photo attached)
"I am so blessed to have been promoted to (whatever)."
"I am so grateful that my child was admitted to (whatever dream school)."

Real humility, blessings, and gratitude are often quiet and personal. If you put yourself in the shoes of your employees, you will develop empathy for them and see issues from their vantage point.

Instead, brag on others. With all social media usage (personal and professional), the better practice is to brag on other people's accomplishments… and let others brag on you.

On your company page, post meaningful comments about your employees' successes. Providing public recognition of a job well done, of a goal achieved, of work anniversaries, or of a recent promotion sends the message to your employees and clients (and competitors!) that you are appreciative of your employees and that you support and recognize their accomplishments.

On your personal page, post pictures of your friends' successes. Share information about things of community-wide interest. Post videos of animals frolicking in the sun! But before you start to post something that could be perceived as bragging, think twice.

In Conclusion

Social media is a multiplier and an accelerator. Sometimes that's a good thing—many individuals and organizations owe their incredible success to social media's accessibility, reach, and popularity. But when it comes to the relationship between employers and employees, social media often has a negative impact. It can violate privacy, create or exacerbate resentment, spread misinformation, and much more. And as we have discussed, you as an employer are very limited in how you are able to respond.

When engaging with employees on social media, if you choose to do so at all, think very carefully about the optics of your content, the responses you create, and what impact you hope to have by connecting and posting. If a clear positive outcome is in doubt, hands off your keyboard!

CHAPTER 17

Don't Make Assumptions About Me—They May Be Microaggressions

Dr. Prakash's Story

George Smith is a leader in a science lab. He has worked with his colleagues Mandy Prakash and Paul Jones, who are fellow scientists, for several years. George, Mandy, and Paul are scheduled to attend a university conference that requires registration. George's assistant, Ben, handled this task. When asked to input how the attendees' names should appear on their name tags, Ben registered George and Paul using their titles and surnames, and Mandy using only her first name.

At the conference, attendees addressed George and Paul using the names that appeared on their badges: Dr. Smith and Dr. Jones. The use of their titles communicated to other attendees the men's academic and professional achievements. On the other hand, conference attendees addressed Mandy using only her first name and no title designation, which failed to recognize her academic and professional accomplishments.

When Mandy realized there was a difference between her badge and her colleagues' badges, she felt demeaned, undervalued, and overlooked by Ben. She also knew that the networking connections she made at the conference could affect her career in the future. She felt that she had been placed at a disadvantage because unlike her male colleagues, she had to proactively explain her credentials in every new interaction. Mandy worried that others would remember her as simply "Mandy," not "Dr. Prakash."

Ben did not have any negative intent, nor did he consciously desire to diminish Mandy's professional status. In fact, he did not even realize that he registered her differently from how he had registered George and Paul. As it happened, he had a closer friendship with Mandy than with the other two, and naturally thought of her on a first-name basis—and it was this circumstance that resulted in the "accidental microaggression."

Perhaps you're thinking, *This is a fairly obvious misstep, and I don't believe I am in danger of making it.* And perhaps you're right. But this is only one example of the many types of microaggressions it's possible to commit. Before we delve more deeply into this topic, I'd like you to take the following quiz.

Are You Guilty of Any of These Microaggressions?

Answer the following questions based on your first reaction. In quizzes like these, it's usually possible to figure out the "correct" answer (or at least the incorrect answer) with a little thought. Here, I challenge you to be honest about your initial gut reaction *before* your upper brain weighs in. After all, we are able to grow only after we have clearly identified areas that need improvement.

You hire an engineering company to provide expert advice on a pre-construction project on vacant land. A young-looking, 5-foot-tall woman carrying a clipboard walks onto the job site wearing a hardhat. She is:
    a. The owner of the engineering company
    b. Lost
    c. The owner's assistant

You work in the clerk's office at the county courthouse. Policy dictates that members of the public may request that the clerk make copies of files, but lawyers may check out files and make their own copies at the law library inside the courthouse. A professionally dressed young man of color enters the office, introduces himself as an employee of Lawfirm, LLC, and asks to check out a particular file. You:
    a. Ask which lawyer he works for and explain that only the lawyer may check out the file
    b. Ask for his state bar credentials
    c. Direct him to complete the "member of the public" form to request that the clerk make copies
    d. Hand him the requested file

You are a receptionist at a professional office. A female calls and requests to speak with a partner at the office. After asking her name, you:
   a. Ask whom she is calling on behalf of before transferring the call to the partner
   b. Transfer the call to the partner
   c. Tell her that you will pass along the message as soon as possible

You are with your child, who is a patient at a new pediatrician's office. A male and a female, both wearing scrubs, enter the exam room. You:
   a. Introduce yourself and wait for the doctor (or the assistant) to make introductions
   b. Introduce yourself to the male because he is probably the doctor

You want to hire a receptionist to greet your clients. Close your eyes. What does that receptionist look like?
   a. A young, white female
   b. Anything other than a young, white female

You are a waiter or waitress at the local country club. After lunch, the bill for a man and woman dining together is ready to present to the club member. You:
   a. Automatically hand it to the male
   b. Automatically hand it to the female
   c. Ask which person would like to handle the bill

The Takeaway

Most people do not intend to cause harm through their everyday words and actions. Most would not openly or intentionally discriminate against another person. Yet, harm and discrimination occur more often than many of us realize through unintentional actions called "microaggressions."

There has been a lot of talk in recent years about microaggressions—but they're more than a trending buzzword, and they have been happening throughout human history. Microaggressions occur when people make automatic, often incorrect, assumptions about other people based solely on stereotypes or appearances, and without any factual basis. Another way to think of them is "macroassumptions."

While the person making the unfounded assumption may not realize their behavior is having a negative impact, the person about whom the assumption is made might feel embarrassed, patronized, insulted, overlooked, invalidated, harassed, discriminated against, etc. Microaggressions can result in a breakdown of trust, lost opportunities, increased stress, poor mental and physical health outcomes, lowered morale, the perpetuation of harmful stereotypes, and more.

Who Experiences Microaggressions?

Experiencing microaggressions is not owned by any one group of people. Every person who is "other" has experienced microaggressions:

- The person using a wheelchair who is yelled at—as if the wheelchair somehow makes him hard of hearing
- The Hispanic-American who is asked for proof of citizenship—even though she is a United States federal employee with national security clearance
- The black male who is asked to provide proof that he "belongs" in a certain neighborhood while he is parked in front of his own house
- The young professional who is referred to as a "diversity hire" but graduated at the top of his business school class
- The man who is routinely asked at work functions if he has a wife or girlfriend, even though he and his husband have been married for over a decade
- The woman who is teased about not working on the Sabbath

In each of these cases, the person is forced to choose between ignoring the microaggression—which requires them to bury or betray a part of their identity in order to "belong"—or explaining their situation to the other person, who often isn't entitled to the information in the first place.

The root cause of microaggressions is often not malice; usually, it is simply a lack of awareness or the failure to thoughtfully reflect before reacting. As a leader, it is your responsibility to root out ingrained prejudices or misconceptions so you can treat employees equitably. Not only is this good management, it will help avoid bad publicity, costly turnover, claims of discrimination, and lawsuits. Ignorance of the law and a lack of bad intentions are *not* defenses to claims of discrimination.

The good news is that once a person gets in the habit of pausing and examining ingrained assumptions about other people, real changes in perception occur. Your mind can develop a new "muscle memory" in regard to how you approach and treat others.

Quiz Answers

Now that we've discussed the basics of what microaggressions are and what some of the consequences might be, let's take a closer look at the quiz questions I asked you to answer earlier. As you'll see, they are not hypothetical scenarios—they are all drawn from my personal experiences or from those of people I know well. Perhaps some of them will seem familiar to you, too.

Question 1

You hire an engineering company to provide expert advice on a pre-construction project on vacant land. A young-looking, 5-foot-tall woman carrying a clipboard walks onto the job site wearing a hardhat. She is:
Correct answer: The owner of the engineering company

My friend Erica owns an engineering company. She is a tiny woman in stature but a giant in her industry—well respected and hardworking. She has a reputation for excellence. Yet she regularly encounters surprised reactions when meeting clients, vendors, construction crews, or code enforcement officials for the first time. These people openly and frequently tell her that they expected a man to meet them at a job site. Some even refuse to work with her *because she is a female.* As a consequence of her small stature and her gender, she has lost bids—and income.

Erica is not a woman of color, but it's easy to imagine how many more obstacles and incorrect assumptions she might face if she were Black, Latina,

Indigenous, etc. This is a reality that many women of color (and men of color, too) face every day, especially in industries where leaders are traditionally white and male.

Women in STEM

The U.S. Census Bureau reports that women make up 48 percent of the U.S. workforce but only 27 percent of STEM workers. The STEM fields include technology/computers, mathematics, engineering, and the sciences. Within the largest STEM fields (computers and engineering), women represent only about 25 percent of computer workers and 15 percent of engineering workers. The Census Bureau also reports that women who are in STEM professions consistently earn less than their male colleagues.[1]

Microaggressions are not harmless. They are not something that women (or other groups) should brush off, ignore, or "get over." They directly contribute to the perpetuation of statistics like these, because they prevent marginalized people from accessing opportunities, being evaluated based on their demonstrated skills and experience, and being treated with equity.

Employers in the STEM arena have the ability to take proactive and positive steps to end the pay gap in the STEM field using culture studies, evaluating pay practices, creating anti- discrimination policies, and establishing mentoring programs for young STEM professionals, especially those from marginalized groups.

Question 2

You work in the clerk's office at the county courthouse. Policy dictates that members of the public may request that the clerk make copies of files, but lawyers may check out files and make their own copies at the law library inside the courthouse. A professionally dressed young man of color enters the office, introduces himself as an employee of Lawfirm, LLC, and asks to check out a particular file. You:

Correct answer: Hand him the requested file

A slightly different version of this scenario happened to me when I was a young lawyer. Rather than being the target of a macroassumption based on race, I was stereotyped based on my gender. When I asked to check out files from the local courthouse, the desk clerk insisted that I provide proof of membership in the local or state bar association. In other words, she required proof that I was a lawyer and not a paralegal. Once I provided a business card that read "Attorney at Law," she stammered an apology and admitted that she did not question the men who asked to check out files (the vast majority of whom were white). Because I was a young female, she had assumed I was either an assistant or a paralegal.

Curious, I discussed this with many of my male and female lawyer friends and found that, almost without exception, the women were asked to verify their credentials and the men were not. Lawyers who were not white, both males and females, also reported that they were asked to verify their credentials.

According to the U.S. Census Bureau, in 2018 almost 40 percent of the lawyers in the United States (more than 400,000) were women.[2] Therefore, it should not shock a clerk of court to learn that the person requesting the file is a female *and* a lawyer.

In 2020, the American Bar Association estimated that 14.1 percent of lawyers in the United States were not white.[3] Again, the clerk shouldn't be skeptical that a person of color is also an attorney.

A better policy for the clerk's office would be to ask every single person for proof of credentials. To make decisions based on race, gender, or age (or any other protected category) is not only embarrassing for all involved, it is clearly discriminatory.

Question 3

You are a receptionist at a professional office. A female calls and requests to speak with a partner at the office. After asking her name, you:

Correct answer: Transfer the call to the partner

When I began practicing law and called other lawyers, the call was frequently answered by the lawyer's assistant. I always said, "Hi. This is Amie Remington with Lawfirm, LLC. May I speak to John Doe?"

Many, many, *many* times, the assistant would say, "Who are you calling on behalf of?"

I responded that I was calling on my own behalf. The assistant would inevitably respond, "I mean, which lawyer are you calling for?"

I would then say something to the effect of, "I'm calling for myself."

They would then say, "No, who is your lawyer?"

At that point, I would have to explain that I was the lawyer and that I was calling to speak with the other lawyer. Finally, the call would be transferred.

This dance continued for years.

When I asked my male colleagues if they were questioned in the same manner, none recalled being asked whom they were calling on behalf of. Instead, because their voices and names were male, it was assumed that they were lawyers—not assistants—and their calls were transferred immediately.

Question 4

You are with your child, who is a patient at a new pediatrician's office. A male and a female, both wearing scrubs, enter the exam room. You:

Correct answer: Introduce yourself and wait for the doctor (or the assistant) to make introductions

My female friend is a pediatrician. Her registered nurse is a male. Both wear scrubs and have stethoscopes around their necks. When they walk into a room together, parents of new patients frequently assume that my friend's nurse is the doctor and that she is the nurse.

Becker's Hospital Review reported that as of February 13, 2020, there were more than 359,000 female doctors currently practicing. That's a 1:1.8 women-to-men ratio.[4] *The Washington Post* reported that as of December 23, 2019, women outnumbered men in medical school, 50.5 percent to 49.4 percent.[5] Therefore, employers hiring physicians—and patients seeking physicians—should expect a male about half of the time and a female about half of the time.

Question 5

You want to hire a receptionist to greet your clients. Close your eyes. What does that receptionist look like?

Correct answer: This is a trick question.

The appearance of the receptionist does not matter. What matters is his/her ability to remember clients and callers, exhibit grace under pressure, communicate with various members of the public, organize materials in a cohesive manner, and represent the company well.

Outside of maintaining a professional appearance or conforming to a dress code, the receptionist's appearance, gender, race, and age have nothing to do with their skill and suitability for the job. Instead, hiring decisions should be made based on the legitimate, objective criteria of the job, as stated in the written job description provided to each interviewee.

The legitimate, objective criteria might include prior experience in similar positions, the ability to operate a multi-line phone and/or text and transfer system, the ability to greet and properly direct clients and vendors, the ability to maintain a multi-user calendaring program, and the ability to keep track of the whereabouts of many employees in the office. These job responsibilities are entirely unrelated to the ideal receptionist's appearance, gender, race, and age.

Question 6

You are a waiter or waitress at the local country club. After lunch, the bill for a man and woman dining together is ready to present to the club member. You:

Correct answer: Ask which person would like to handle the bill

This happens at restaurants *all. the. time.* when men and women dine together.

For the past twenty years, my dad and I have had lunch together every Tuesday at different local restaurants. Almost every week, the waiter or waitress hands my dad the bill and is surprised when I take it.

It happens in other businesses, too. When my husband and I were looking for places to hold our wedding reception, we visited a local venue. After speaking to both of us about the details, the wedding coordinator handed the cost estimate to my husband. My husband looked at the wedding coordinator and said, "I don't know why you are handing this to me. I don't have any money. She is paying." The wedding coordinator sheepishly handed me the estimate. Not surprisingly, the venue lost our business.

This type of situation can be embarrassing for everyone involved. To avoid confusion, the waiter, waitress, or other employee (whether that person is a doctor, dentist, salesperson, lawyer, etc.) should simply ask which party will handle the bill.

The Bottom Line

Microaggressions happen all the time, to more people than you might realize—and they are perpetuated by individuals who don't perceive themselves as being sexist, racist, ageist, or otherwise prejudiced. But as we've discussed, the consequences of microaggressions are real and can be very serious for both parties.

The good news is that by recognizing microaggressions, all people—employers and employees—can choose to change their automatic reactions for the better.

CHAPTER 18

If You Compliment Me, Make Sure You're Sincere

Joe's Story

Joe owns an automotive store. When his longtime assistant, Marjorie, arrives every morning, he greets her with what he intends to be a positive remark. Here's a weeklong sample of how their interactions usually go:

Monday
Joe says to Marjorie, "Hey, you look great!" She hears him pass another person and say, "Lookin' good this morning!"

Tuesday
Joe passes Marjorie in the hallway and remarks, "Your hair looks great! Are you doing something different to it?" He continues walking without waiting for an answer.

Wednesday
Without glancing up from the paper he is holding, Joe asks Marjorie, "Hey! New dress today?" He walks by without stopping to see if she replies.

Thursday
Joe passes Marjorie at the copy machine and says, "Hey, great work on that… what was it you were working on?" He continues to saunter on before she answers.

Friday

Joe greets Marjorie with a, "Hey! Big plans this weekend?" and keeps walking. She hears him say, "Hey! Big plans this weekend?" to the next person in the hall. That person does not answer either.

What Joe doesn't know is that these daily interactions leave Marjorie feeling irritated, overlooked, and patronized. She is particularly uncomfortable with the frequent compliments related to her appearance. However, because Joe is the owner of the store, neither Marjorie nor her coworkers feel comfortable telling him that his daily "conversations" come across as insincere.

I Know How Marjorie Feels

This happened to me Every. Single. Day. for more than a year. The stray comments from my boss ended after he said to me, "Hey, you look great! You losing weight?"

Instead of allowing him to walk on by, this time I stood in front of him and looked him directly in the eye. "No, I hope not," I replied. "I'm five months pregnant!"

My response was probably rude (okay, *definitely* rude), but in my defense, I actually was five months pregnant. My snarky comment caused my boss to stop and notice, for the first time, that I was obviously going to have a baby.

The Takeaway

Joe's interactions with Marjorie were an attempt to connect with her. However, to be seen as sincere, connections require the active participation of two people. Both parties must be interested in sharing information with each other—and that information must be true and meaningful.

In this case, Joe *acted* as if he cared about Marjorie and the other people to whom he spoke. He may have even believed that by offering a different observation, compliment, or question each day, he was showing extra consideration. But because Joe failed to stop, look his employees in the eye, and wait for them to answer, they perceived him as insincere and disinterested—exactly the opposite of what he intended.

Your employees are smart. They recognize when you are simply going through the motions. They can tell when you don't really mean what you say, or when you aren't truly interested in hearing their feedback. Most would rather not interact with you at all than be unwilling participants in insincere conversations.

What your employees *do* want is to be recognized for good work performance. This type of compliment is powerful because it shows that you have been paying attention, that you notice each person's individual contributions, and that it is important to you to recognize those efforts. (Look back at Chapter 11: Your Generosity Makes a Lasting Impact and Chapter 12: Significant Events Are Important to Me—Please Recognize Them for meaningful ways to generously recognize and reward employees.) Employees would rather have one authentic compliment or conversation focused on performance than five disingenuous interactions.

A Meaningful Compliment

For years, I had a boss who was always pleasant, provided constructive advice, and was a great mentor—but he did not freely offer compliments. Because his praise was limited, I knew that when it *was* offered, it was completely sincere.

One day several years into my employment, I walked into my office and saw that a project had been returned to me with a yellow sticky note on it. The note simply read, "Good Job, Amie!" Because compliments were the exception and not the rule, I knew I had done a really good job. I kept that note for a long time; it motivated me to do my best work on every project in the future.

More Than Words: Thoughtless Compliments and Comments Can Have Legal Ramifications

Giving compliments that are not earned based on accomplishments or that are based on appearance can have consequences beyond eroding your connection with employees. Using Joe and Marjorie as an example, let's look at three different types of legal ramifications:

A sexual harassment claim. Joe's near-daily comments about Marjorie's appearance can create a legally actionable hostile work environment. Behaviors that are *severe* **or** *pervasive* can give rise to valid claims if the behaviors interfere with an employee's work performance. In this case, the daily compliments are not severe; however, their frequency could lead to a finding that they are pervasive.

In sexual harassment law, the relevant perception is the one of the person who is the subject of the action: in this case, Marjorie. Therefore, even though Joe never overtly asked her on a date, threatened her job, or took any other quid pro quo action against her, Marjorie may meet the threshold for a sexual harassment claim under Title VII because Joe's constant comments about her appearance are unwelcome and make her uncomfortable.

As a reminder, Title VII of the Civil Rights Act of 1964 is a federal law that prohibits employers from making employment decisions or taking employment actions based on or because of a person's sex, color, race, religion, or national origin. Sexual harassment is a form of sex discrimination and is therefore prohibited by Title VII. (If you'd like more detail on the complex topic of sexual harassment in the workplace, see Chapter 19: Do Everything You Can to Prevent Sexual Harassment.)

When Complimenting Employees, Look *Beyond* Looks

Giving thoughtful compliments about employees' performance is particularly important in the #metoo age. Few employees want to be noticed and recognized for their appearance or clothing. In a professional setting, being attractive or well-dressed does not feel like much of an accomplishment, but completing a big project does.

Further, Joe is setting the standard for his subordinate employees' allowable behaviors. If he is engaging in behavior that makes Marjorie uncomfortable, his subordinates may follow his example—opening the organization up to additional legal actions (not to mention contributing to a dysfunctional and toxic culture).

The Importance of Reporting Mechanisms

If Joe has a written and well-disseminated anti-hostile work environment policy with a reporting mechanism, it is incumbent upon Marjorie to use the reporting remedies set forth in the policy. If she does not do so, she may unintentionally waive her rights under the policy.

Employers of all sizes should have a written and well-disseminated reporting mechanism. Employers with human resources departments may select department leaders to receive complaints and concerns. Employers without human resources departments may select an appropriate person to receive complaints, such as an office manager or an administrator. Another option available to employers of any size is to subscribe to a third-party service that takes complaints from its clients' employees and reports them back to the clients.

Regardless of the method chosen, the key to success is to ensure that all employees understand how to share a concern, to take every complaint seriously, and to investigate each matter to determine the appropriate response. When in doubt, call your employment lawyer, who will be happy to help you determine how best to resolve the issue.

A charge of discrimination *or* a lawsuit for wrongfully taking adverse action. Suppose that instead of complimenting Marjorie on her appearance, Joe routinely complimented her on the quality of her work—even though it was mediocre. In this case, Joe is inadvertently resetting the standard for what he considers acceptable work. Mediocre work is now good enough work for Marjorie—and for all of Joe's employees.

If Joe has to take an adverse action against his assistant (such as a demotion or termination) due to the quality of her work, she will be able to argue that Joe repeatedly complimented her and told her that her work product was acceptable—and she will be right. Marjorie could argue that Joe's stated reason for terminating her (poor performance) was a pretext (a false reason), and that there must be another reason for her termination, such as her sex, color, race, religion, or national origin. Given Joe's compliments about her work, Joe would have a difficult time defending a charge of discrimination filed with the Equal Employment Opportunity Commission or a state agency, or worse, a lawsuit.

Legalese Breakdown: Adverse Action

"Adverse action" is a legal term used to describe any employment action that is adverse to an employee and that negatively alters the terms or conditions of their employment. Adverse actions come in many forms and may be direct (actions that impact the employee's terms and conditions of employment) or indirect (actions that change others' perceptions of an employee or that ultimately result in lower pay or status).

Examples of direct adverse actions include:
- Reduction in pay
- Reduction in benefits
- Demotion
- Reprimand
- Termination of employment

Examples of indirect adverse actions include:
- A change of sales territory to one that is less desirable or less profitable, and that results in lower pay or commissions
- A change in job title to one that is lateral but seen as "lower," which can diminish the level of authority an employee has
- Removal from a team, department, or leadership position
- Moving an employee from a corner office to a smaller office, or from an office to a cubicle

- Taking away equipment that is necessary to be successful in a position
- Resetting goals, quotas, or job duties to an impossible standard

A cause of action for breach of implied oral contract and promissory estoppel. Now, suppose Joe made vague comments to Marjorie like, "We have big things planned for you," when, in fact, there were no "big things" on the horizon. Joe has created an expectation, and Marjorie very reasonably believes there are "big things" on her horizon—raises or promotions, for example. If Joe does not deliver on his vague promise, Marjorie will be justifiably confused and frustrated, and may become Disengaged.

As we discussed in Chapter 10: Please Think Before You Communicate, depending on her state's laws, Marjorie might even be justified in bringing a cause of action against Joe for breach of implied oral contract and promissory estoppel (the legal theory whereby one person makes a promise and another person relies on that promise to their detriment), *especially* if Marjorie has turned down other employment opportunities because she believes she will be receiving a raise or promotion from Joe.

Furthermore, if an employee with more merit is the recipient of the perceived promise and that employee differs from Marjorie, Marjorie may argue that she was not promoted because of a protected status (her sex, color, race, religion, or national origin, for example).

The Better Practice: Be Sincere and Specific

If an employee is doing a great job, tell them so and show them you appreciate it. The more specificity you can provide on why you believe the employee did a great job, the better. For example, saying, "You did a great job on the Quarter 4 reports. They were very clear and comprehensive, and in keeping with the long-term goal of prioritizing sales in the Southeast," is much more powerful than, "You did a great job this year."

If an employee is doing a mediocre job, tell them so with the same level of specificity so they know exactly what areas need improvement. For example, saying, "Your Quarter 4 report was two days late and did not contain column 4, which meant the summary data was incomplete," is much clearer than saying, "Your Quarter 4 report did not meet expectations." Once you have communicated the specific deficiencies you have observed, you can work with the employee to correct whatever deficiencies exist.

If an employee is close to an adverse action or being terminated, let them know in no uncertain terms, and explain precisely what needs to be done for them to remain employed at the organization. Rather than saying, "Your performance is not meeting our standards," say, "Your performance is not meeting our standards. In the past month, you have been late twice and you missed the department meeting last Wednesday. You also failed to copy me on the final report, even though you have been trained to do so. As a consequence, I did not have adequate time to prepare for the company meeting. These repeated behaviors are inefficient and are likely to lead to termination."

Saying what you mean and meaning what you say can sometimes be uncomfortable, but in the long run, truthfulness will set your employees up for success because they will understand your expectations—and they will not be operating under false assumptions. Truthfulness will also set you up for success if you have to terminate an employee at a later date.

Remember, there is no such thing as a "white lie" when it comes to employee feedback. As we discussed in Chapter 10: Please Think Before You Communicate, your words matter because they directly influence your employees' beliefs, expectations, morale, and actions—and *those* things directly impact your organization's productivity and bottom line.

CHAPTER 19

Do Everything You Can to Prevent Sexual Harassment

"Sexual harassment" is a broad term that can encompass many different behaviors and situations—and that can have a variety of legal, professional, and personal consequences. Because this *is* such a complex topic, I am going to open this chapter with three different stories to illustrate how sexual harassment can play out in the workplace. As you'll see, Scenarios 1 and 2 are perhaps more common than Scenario 3—but all three have important lessons for employers.

Scenario 1: Caroline's Story

Caroline has worked in the office of a construction company for several years. When she applied for and accepted the job, she was aware that her coworkers and supervisors would likely be men. So far, her fellow employees have treated her respectfully. She has always felt like a member of the team.

Recently, a male employee named Jim was hired. His is an outdoor job, but he usually visits the office several times per day. This isn't unusual; many of Caroline's coworkers frequently come inside and use the office break room to rest, eat lunch, or just cool off. Jim, however, has not confined his visits to the break room. Instead, he frequently pulls a chair next to Caroline's desk to talk to her.

Within the first week, Caroline noticed that Jim's visits hindered her productivity because she could not focus on her tasks. Worrying about the quality of her work, Caroline gently suggested that Jim use the break room when he was in the office. When her suggestion did not change Jim's behavior, Caroline was direct and told him that she was unable to visit during work hours because she needed to focus on her assigned tasks.

The next day, Jim waited for Caroline to exit the office after work and suggested that since she couldn't visit during the workday, perhaps they could visit in the evening over dinner. Caroline thanked him for the offer but said that she did not think that was a good idea.

A few days later, Jim texted Caroline and renewed his offer to take her to dinner. Caroline did not know how Jim got her cell phone number; she again stated that she did not think dinner was a good idea. She asked him not to text her cell phone again. Nevertheless, Jim sent another message to apologize for contacting her on her personal phone. He wished her a good night and used a heart emoji.

At the end of the next workweek, Jim waited for Caroline in the parking lot and suggested that they go to a local music festival that weekend. Caroline declined. On Sunday morning, Caroline was surprised to see Jim at her church, as she had never seen him there before. Jim asked Caroline whether she would like to join him for lunch after the service. Caroline declined the invitation.

On Monday, Caroline talked with the owner of the business and told him the sequence of events. The owner asked whether Jim had been aggressive or violent, and whether he had ever touched Caroline. She replied that none of those things occurred. She emphasized that she had declined all of Jim's invitations but that he didn't seem dissuaded. The owner told Caroline that Jim sounded infatuated but harmless. He also said that because some of Jim's actions occurred offsite, those were not related to work. He advised Caroline to report back to him if Jim's behavior was threatening in any manner.

Caroline shared the sequence of events with her college roommate, Anna, who is a human resources professional specializing in the area of compliance. Anna advised Caroline to review the company's sexual harassment policy and follow the reporting procedure in the policy. Anna further advised Caroline to seek counsel from an employment law attorney to determine how to end Jim's pursuit without negatively impacting her job.

The Takeaway

Although the company's owner seems not to realize it, Jim's behavior could subject the organization to liability. For sexual harassment to be actionable, it must be severe or pervasive. Severe behavior is behavior that is threatening or involves unwanted touching. Pervasive behavior is unwelcome behavior that is ongoing.

Asking an employee to go on a date one time is an isolated event that likely would not rise to the level of sexual harassment. However, in this case, Jim's behavior is pervasive because it occurred multiple times—even after Caroline declined his invitations. When the behavior was reported, the company owner should not have dismissed it as an innocent infatuation, especially since Jim's behavior escalated over time.

The better option would be for the company owner to take immediate and appropriate action, which would include speaking to Jim about the company's policy regarding sexual harassment and outlining the consequences if the behavior did not end. To ensure Jim understands why his continued behavior was not appropriate, training on the sexual harassment policy might also be in order.

Don't Let Stereotypes Blind You—Anyone Can Be a Harasser

Although the harasser in this scenario is male, it could just as easily be a female. Any person who engages in unwelcome behavior in a workplace—regardless of their gender, age, race, sexual orientation, etc. (and regardless of the gender, age, race, sexual orientation, etc. of the behavior's target)—can be the harasser.

Scenario 2: Martina's Story

Martina is a service advisor at a car dealership. She has been in the service industry for 30 years and is one of the few female service advisors at her organization. She is well-respected and always takes the initiative to teach skills to coworkers and new hires. After her boss retired, Martina was assigned to work for Peter, a younger manager at the dealership.

Peter and Martina generally work very well together. However, there is one major issue (at least from Martina's perspective): Peter regularly calls her "dear" or "darling." Just yesterday, at the end of a telephone call, Peter said, "Thank you, dear," and hung up. He also refers to Martina as "my girl" when talking about her to others. For example, Martina has overheard him telling a salesperson that "my girl will handle that portion of the transaction."

Martina is becoming increasingly annoyed that Peter calls her "dear," "darling," etc. She finds the use of these pet names condescending and overly personal, and she feels singled out because she does not hear Peter referring to her male coworkers in a similar fashion. However, since Peter is Martina's new boss, she is hesitant to let him know how she feels.

No One in Your Organization Is a "Girl"

I have often heard my male colleagues say, "I'll have my girl reach out to you to schedule a call," or, "The girls are planning the event."

Let me be clear: *Unless you employ 12-year-olds, the females who work with and for you Are. Not. Girls.*

They are women with professional degrees, women with families at home, women with financial obligations, and women who have overcome obstacles to accomplish goals. Calling these women "girls" creates the impression that you don't take them seriously and makes you look like you are stuck in the 1950s.

The Takeaway

Why might Martina be annoyed by Peter's comments? There are three main reasons I would like to highlight.

First, terms of affection are meant to be used for just that purpose: showing affection. Martina is not Peter's "dear" (or, for that matter, his "darling," "honey," "babe," or "sweetheart"). These terms are rightfully used by those with closer, more intimate relationships. Occasional use of affectionate pet names may not rise to the level of gender-based discrimination or sexual harassment, but persistent use of these terms can be evidence of both. Persistent use, while not severe behavior, could certainly be considered pervasive—particularly where the name is gender or sexually based.

Second, using terms of affection with subordinate employees is condescending because it is reminiscent of decades such as the 1950s when women in the workforce had fewer options than they do today, and were often treated as objects of beauty to be admired (as long as they were pretty) rather than as people who could make meaningful contributions to the workplace.

Third, using terms of affection with subordinate employees destroys the professional credibility of the employee. Because our society *has* conditioned us to see the use of pet names for female employees as (somewhat) normal, let's reverse the roles. Imagine that Peter is in a high-level meeting surrounded by senior leadership and board members. Martina walks in and says to him, "Hello, sugar." How would the other people in the boardroom react? They would likely assume there was some closer, less-professional relationship between Martina and Peter, which would destroy his professional credibility.

When I ask whether pet names and terms of affection are appropriate for bosses to use with subordinates, the response is divided almost 50/50, in exact proportion to gender. What I mean is that almost 100 percent of men do not see a problem with using terms of affection toward women, and almost 100 percent of women see a problem with their supervisors using terms of affection toward them. So why does this issue perpetuate?

Consider this: In the scenario I just shared, Martina has been employed by the dealership longer than Peter and has more years of experience in the field than him. *However, as a subordinate employee, she may not feel that she has the power to tell Peter—the person who is responsible for evaluating, disciplining, and promoting her—that she is annoyed by his behavior without fear of retribution.*

A better approach is to simply call people by their names and/or titles, if appropriate.

Scenario 3: Susan's Story

Susan is one of four partners in a law firm. She has a vote in establishing the general terms and conditions of her subordinates' employment, including setting compensation and benefits for all employees. In particular, she is also the direct supervisor of the office's bookkeeper, Joe. Susan is in charge of setting Joe's hours of work, determining how and when his work should be done, and handling his annual performance evaluations.

Susan is married and has been dating Joe for two years. Susan's three partners do not know about the relationship. Her husband certainly does not know about it!

During the most recent annual budget meeting, the partners noticed that the profit/loss numbers simply didn't add up. They individually audited their billings and receivables. The individual audits revealed substantial discrepancies that could not be reconciled. As a result, all four partners agreed to hire an accounting firm to do a thorough forensic audit.

The forensic accounting firm determined that Joe had transferred money between multiple accounts, opened credit cards in the firm's name, and used those cards to withdraw cash and pay personal expenses. He had also written firm checks payable to "cash" but recorded them in the ledger as legitimate expenses. In sum, the forensic accounting audit revealed that Joe had slowly and methodically stolen a total of $80,000 from the firm in the past two years.

All three of Susan's partners want to immediately fire Joe, report him to law enforcement for embezzlement, and make a claim on their fidelity bond insurance policy. Meanwhile, Susan is grappling with the realization that Joe has been stealing while he has been dating her.

Susan is stunned, furious, and hurt. She feels deceived. She tells Joe that her partners are going to report him to law enforcement for embezzlement to seek reimbursement of the money. This means he will likely be arrested for a felony.

Joe tells Susan that if his actions are reported to law enforcement or if the partners seek reimbursement, he will reveal to Susan's partners *and to her husband* that they have been in a relationship for two years. He also informs her that he will tell her partners and her husband that the money was not stolen because *she* authorized *him* to take the money. Joe will claim that some of the money was spent on things they did together, such as dining out. Joe concludes by telling Susan that he now believes the entire two-year relationship was not consensual, and that he dated her only because he was in constant fear of losing his job.

Susan is caught between the proverbial rock and hard place. She is concerned because she knows that:

- Her husband will learn she has been cheating on him.
- The firm's fidelity bond contains a clause stipulating that a claim will be denied if a business owner (like Susan) is complicit in the loss. She realizes

that her relationship with Joe likely makes her complicit and that it is probable the insurance claim will be denied.

- If the insurance claim is denied and Joe is unable or unwilling to repay the money, her partners will expect *her* to repay them their share of the stolen money.

What Is a Fidelity Bond?

A fidelity bond is an optional insurance policy held by business owners. It generally provides reimbursement of monies lost due to theft by an employee.

To obtain the benefit of the policy, there are often many conditions. The first and most important condition is that the policyholder must have clean hands. If the carrier of the insurance policy determines the policyholder is complicit in any way, the carrier can usually (and probably will) deny the entire claim. Next, most fidelity policies have deductibles paid by the policyholder. Finally, they require the policyholder to report the loss to law enforcement and cooperate fully in any investigation and prosecution.

Fidelity bonds are quite common in some industries, such as those that frequently deal in cash and those with high-value transactions. To determine if you should purchase a fidelity bond, speak with your industry colleagues and your insurance agent to assess your risk.

- Once the relationship is revealed, Susan's partners will question her integrity and may believe that she authorized Joe to embezzle the money, or that she directly benefited from the theft.
- Her partners and other staff may also question whether Joe's wages were part of a quid pro quo arrangement between him and Susan.
- Once the relationship is revealed, her clients, friends, and neighbors may learn of her behavior.

- Joe may file a sexual harassment claim with the Equal Employment Opportunity Commission and/or a state agency, naming Susan's firm as a party. This would put her partners at further financial risk and open the door to a full investigation of the intimate details of their relationship to determine whether it was consensual.
- Since some of the stolen money was spent with Susan on dining out and the like, if her partners or Joe can prove that Susan benefitted from Joe's theft, Susan's license to practice law might be in jeopardy.

The Takeaway

Dating a subordinate employee in the workplace has only two possible outcomes:
 1. Marriage/long-term commitment
 OR
 2. Breaking up

There is no third option.

When a workplace relationship ends, the potential for a sexual harassment claim exists—particularly if there is an imbalance of power or if the relationship was not completely consensual. In other words, the employee without the power (most often a subordinate) may argue that they entered or continued the relationship involuntarily. This is very difficult for an organization to defend, especially if the parties took steps to keep the relationship private.

A Long List of Consequences

As demonstrated by Susan's long list of worries, the potential consequences of dating in the workplace are not limited to sexual harassment claims. Depending on the circumstances, one's personal and professional reputation, relationships, finances, employment, and future prospects might also be on the line.

For this reason, unless it is absolutely clear that a relationship is consensual, that there is no imbalance of power, and that both parties would be comfortable if the relationship became known by the public, it is better to avoid dating in the workplace. (Later in the chapter, we'll look at some best practices to follow if employees *do* choose to date one another.)

Now that we've looked at three (of the many!) different scenarios of what sexual harassment can look like in the workplace, let's get into the nuts and bolts of how sexual harassment charges affect organizations, and what employers can do to prevent them.

What Are the Costs of a Sexual Harassment Charge?

Filing a charge of discrimination with the Equal Employment Opportunity Commission is the first step an employee must take to bring legal action for sexual harassment against a company. The Equal Employment Opportunity Commission reports that it receives thousands and thousands of charges of discrimination each year from employees who believe they have been sexually harassed. Sexual harassment claims are extremely costly to American businesses. Consider the following from the Equal Employment Opportunity Commission:[1]

Sexual Harassment Claims in the United States		
Year	Number of Charges of Discrimination Filed	Monetary Benefits
2010	7,944	$41,200,000
2011	7,809	$45,100,000
2012	7,571	$43,000,000
2013	7,256	$44,600,000
2014	6,862	$35,000,000
2015	6,822	$46,000,000
2016	6,758	$40,700,000
2017	6,696	$46,300,000
2018	7,609	$56,600,000

2019	7,514	$68,200,000
2020	6,587	$65,300,000*
2021	5,581	$61,600,000
2022	6,201	$59,000,000

*The 2020-2022 numbers are the lowest in more than 10 years, but that does not indicate a positive change in behavior. COVID-19 shut down many workplaces beginning in March 2020, which meant employees were working at home, rather than in a traditional office environment. Interestingly, the dollar value of claims increased during that time.

These numbers are significant—but they are only the tip of the iceberg.

The second column, "Number of Charges of Discrimination Filed," does not include claims that are handled by internal human resources departments before formal action is taken. It also does not include charges filed exclusively with state equal employment agencies, such as the Florida Commission on Human Relations.

The third column, "Monetary Benefits," shows that American businesses paid more than **$68 million** in monetary damages in 2019 *alone*! Again, this does not include monies paid by companies to employees who reported sexual harassment and agreed not to file a charge of discrimination. It does not include monies obtained through post-charge settlements or litigation settlements. Also not included are judgments entered against a company after a trial. Finally, these numbers do not show the cost of defense (monies paid to defense attorneys to defend the charges or lawsuits) or the corresponding increases in insurance costs.

Finally, there is a fourth, more theoretical, column that cannot be included on this chart because it cannot be quantified: the costs that result from damaged reputations. This applies to individuals, such as Susan, and to businesses, such as Susan's firm. It is very possible that Susan and her firm may lose clients if her behavior becomes public, if she is disciplined by the state bar association, or if she loses her license to practice law.

How Can Your Organization Avoid Being Sued for Sexual Harassment?

Sexual harassment is not a new problem. However, it *is* a problem that has received more attention since the #metoo movement empowered women to say, "That happened to me, too!" (Of course, women are not the only gender identity to experience sexual harassment, and the #metoo movement has provided space for these individuals to speak up, too.) The good news is that it is possible to prevent sexual harassment, save your company thousands of dollars and hours, and preserve its reputation.

The best strategy is to seek to prevent the possibility of sexual harassment in the workplace. Let's look at some proactive measures organizations can take.

Have an anti-harassment policy. First, all organizations must have an easy-to-understand policy prohibiting all forms of discrimination or harassment, specifically including sexual harassment.

As with all policies, this policy should be in writing and shared with all employees.

When It Comes to Sharing Your Anti-Harassment Policy, There Is No Such Thing as Overkill

Organizations cannot overshare their anti-harassment and anti-discrimination messages. A defense lawyer's nightmare is hearing a charging party and other employee-witnesses say, "I did not know there was a policy," or, "I had no idea to whom I should make a report." Having employees acknowledge receipt of the written policy via a signature in their onboarding or new hire paperwork is a good idea. Placing the policy on your company's intranet or in some other location that is easy to access is also a good idea. Conducting periodic training and maintaining attendance records also provides proof of a company's intent to eliminate sexual harassment. Doing all three is the best idea: Employees should be able to easily locate and read the policy at any time, and be familiar with its contents.

Your employment lawyer can write a policy that fits your culture and is compliant with federal law, as well as the law or codes of your state and municipality. The policy should prohibit all forms of harassment—not just sexual harassment. At a minimum, the Equal Employment Opportunity Commission requires that your policy:

1. **Clearly and unequivocally state that harassment based on sex, color, race, religion or national origin, disability, age, or genetic information is illegal and won't be tolerated.** [2]

   For years, federal courts grappled with what was protected in the "sex" category. Gender-based discrimination and sexual harassment were clearly intended to be prohibited. What was less clear among the federal courts was whether Title VII of the Civil Rights Act of 1964 included employment protections for the LGBTQ+ community. The Biden Administration, via an Executive Order signed on Inauguration Day, made the answer crystal clear: Title VII protections prohibit employment discrimination on the basis of gender identity or sexual orientation.

2. **Provide examples of prohibited conduct, as needed.** [3]

   The examples can be tailored to what is relevant in your industry and your organization. Prohibited conduct includes offensive or degrading speech, non-consensual touching, or conditioning employment opportunities on sexual favors (quid pro quo). It can also include the posting of questionable materials in the workplace, such as calendars with bikini-clad women or beach-ready men, and the sharing of inappropriate materials such as sexual photos or jokes via email.

3. **Explain how employees can report harassment.** [4]

   One of the most important elements of the policy is the reporting mechanism. Reporting harassment should be easy for an employee. After all, you cannot fix a problem if an employee does not report it. To ensure employees feel comfortable reporting harassment, if possible, designate both a male and a female to receive harassment complaints. Also, if possible, make your selections so that at least one of the designees is likely to be outside of a reporting employee's chain of command. If all managers are well trained in how to respond to a complaint, and the company has confidence that its managers will take appropriate action, you might consider permitting employees to report harassment to any manager.

4. **Specifically state that you will protect the confidentiality of employees who report harassment or participate in a harassment investigation, to the greatest possible extent.**[5]

   Employees generally should not be told that a report or complaint of sexual harassment (or any form of harassment) will be treated confidentially—even if they ask. If an employee says, "I want to make a report but I do not want you to tell anyone," the best response to the employee is, "I want you to report whatever is on your mind, but I cannot guarantee confidentiality because depending on what you tell me, I may be required by law and/or by our company policy to take action. This action may require me to share the information with someone else and conduct an investigation."

   Complete confidentiality generally cannot be guaranteed because the person who is the subject of the sexual harassment investigation has the right to know what they are being accused of so they may respond to the allegations. Also, doing a thorough investigation likely requires interviewing others who have firsthand knowledge of the matter. Therefore, while you cannot guarantee complete confidentiality, you *can* commit to protecting all information to the greatest extent possible.

5. **Inform employees that they will not be punished for reporting legitimate harassment or participating in a harassment investigation or lawsuit.**[6]

   As an employer, you *want* employees to feel comfortable coming forward with meritorious information that requires action. Therefore, your policy should make employees feel empowered, not intimidated. It must contain a statement that specifically prohibits a manager from retaliating against any person for reporting sexual harassment (or other forms of harassment or discrimination).

6. **Require managers and employees with human resources responsibilities to respond appropriately to harassment or to report it to individuals who are authorized to respond.**[7]

   The policy should state that managers may not ignore harassment complaints; they MUST report them to the correct entity for immediate investigation.

7. **Provide for prompt, thorough, and impartial investigation of harassment complaints.**[8]

Handling investigations is an art form. Experienced, unbiased internal human resources professionals or outside third-party consultants can conduct interviews, evaluate the merit of the claims and defenses, and make recommendations on appropriate remedial actions.

8. **Provide for prompt and effective corrective and preventative action when necessary.**[9]

This may include periodic training on what behaviors are acceptable and what behaviors cross the line. Training should also include a review of the policy and reporting steps.

Conduct appropriate follow-up on all complaints. While not explicitly covered in the EEOC's guidance, I strongly suggest the following:

1. **Ensure that your organization notifies employees who make complaints about the status of their complaint, the results of the investigation, and, where appropriate, any corrective and preventative action taken.** Without follow-up, the employee is left wondering whether the matter was fully investigated and whether the organization took action to prevent the behavior from happening again.

2. **Involve the harassed employee in determining consequences.** If it is determined that one employee did harass another employee, it is important to seek the harassed employee's input regarding what he or she would like to see happen. Sometimes, it may be as simple as an apology. However, the harassed employee should understand that although he or she may have a strong opinion on the matter, deciding on an appropriate consequence is the *employer's* responsibility.

What Are Some Potential Consequences an Employer Might Impose on an Employee for Sexual Harassment?

Consequences should vary according to the pervasiveness or severity of the offense. Note that the consequences listed here are examples of those that might be imposed by an employer. They do not include consequences that might result from any legal action taken by the victim.

- An informal explanation of why certain behavior is not acceptable
- A private or public verbal or written apology
- Mandatory in-house training on company policies and expectations
- Mandatory training by an outside professional
- Mandatory counseling by an outside professional
- Formal write-up to be maintained in a personnel file
- Removal of supervisory duties
- Demotion
- Change of geography/territory/office location
- Change of shift hours
- Voluntary dismissal from employment
- Termination

Provide anti-sexual harassment training. In an effort to protect employees, many states, such as California, Connecticut, Delaware, Illinois, Maine, New York, Washington, and the District of Columbia, require periodic training on sexual harassment for employers of certain sizes. Even if your state does not have this requirement, in-person training is the most effective means of communication, because it gives employees an opportunity to review the policy and ask questions. Good trainers should convey to all employees—at all levels and in a language employees understand—that like all forms of harassment or discrimination, sexual harassment will not be tolerated.

In person training should be memorialized by having the attendees sign an acknowledgment that they understand the policy, had an opportunity to ask questions, understand reporting procedures, and agree to utilize the tools in the policy whenever necessary.

Create an organizational dating policy. In addition to the sexual harassment policy, you may consider creating a policy outlining what behaviors are permitted and what behaviors are not. The goal is not to limit friendly relationships. The goal is to encourage *professional*, friendly relationships. Dating policies can help accomplish this goal.

Some dating policies say that if a supervisor and subordinate enter into a dating relationship, the supervisor will be moved to a position where he or she isn't supervising the other person. If another position isn't immediately available, the supervisor will be asked to resign or will be terminated. This type of policy is effective because it discourages supervisors from beginning dating relationships with subordinates in the first place, and sets the standard for appropriate behavior in the workplace.

Other dating policies allow supervisors and subordinates to date but require both parties to sign an acknowledgment that the relationship is consensual, that neither party will provide nor receive any employment benefit from the relationship, and that if one party wants to end the relationship, the other party will not take any action that could be perceived as retaliatory or harassing. This type of policy is good for preventing relationships that are potentially harmful to the organization, such as where one party is married. However, it works only if both parties disclose the relationship. Because romantic relationships have the potential to create liability for the organization, the policy should also provide the consequence for failing to make a disclosure.

Ensure that leaders lead by example. Leading by example includes not engaging in behavior that could be considered inappropriate or that could create the appearance of impropriety. This includes fairly obvious things like not dating subordinate employees in the workplace or not allowing your employees to date their subordinate employees.

It can also include less-obvious things, like avoiding the appearance of impropriety by not having frequent one-on-one lunches outside the office with subordinates, not giving subordinates personal gifts, or not continually commenting on an employee's personal appearance.

"What We Permit, We Promote"

This goes right back to Quint Studer's famous quote, "What we permit, we promote." If a manager is stealing, it sends a message that stealing is permitted. If a leader is taking excessive time off, then all employees will feel entitled to do so. If a manager is violating the anti-harassment/

discrimination policy, it sends a message that any employee may violate any policy.

The good news is that the converse is true, too. If an employee sees Quint Studer picking up stray pieces of trash he happens to notice in a hospital waiting room, employees will do the same. If an employee sees retired Waffle House President/COO Bert Thornton refilling empty water glasses because the waitstaff is slammed, they will do the same. If employees see *you* treating everyone at the organization with respect and consideration, they will do the same.

In Conclusion

Like all claims of harassment, sexual harassment claims have the ability to derail an organization's productivity in many ways:

- Employees who believe they have been harassed—and employees who witness other employees being harassed—may feel unsafe at work, making them less productive and less engaged. They may even become Detractors.
- Failing to respond properly to concerns likely sends a message to the employee that the organization did not take their complaint seriously.
- If an employee files a charge of discrimination, the organization will spend a significant amount of time, money, and resources responding to it.
- If the allegation of harassment becomes public, the organization's reputation may be in peril.

Taking proactive steps to avoid claims of harassment will reap great rewards: When employees feel satisfied, safe, and taken care of, they are more engaged and productive, which results in less turnover. Moreover, creating an environment free of harassment is just the right thing for great organizations to do!

If you are interested in learning more about women in the workplace and gender discrimination, please refer to Amie's Required Reading at the end of this book.

CHAPTER 20

Do Not Assume Your Causes Are the Same as My Causes

Sarah's Story

Sarah works at a mid-sized company in the technology industry. Because the industry is highly regulated by state law and federal administrative agencies, the decisions of state legislators and Congress often impact the industry as a whole. Sarah's boss is understandably interested in the legislative process, the decisions of state and federal lawmakers, and how those decisions will affect the company.

Sarah is well-known in her community and industry, and by virtue of her education and prior work experience, is versed in the legislative process. However, her job has nothing to do with lobbying, legislation, or industry regulation. Nonetheless, Sarah's boss often asks her to explain pending legislation to company leaders, attend political fundraisers, and donate to certain lawmakers who are influential in the technology industry.

To complicate the situation further, Sarah's boss drives a car with political bumper stickers, posts about politics on social media, and keeps the break room and lobby televisions on a one-sided news station. It is abundantly clear to all of his employees that he supports certain candidates and one particular party.

The problem is that Sarah's personal convictions differ greatly from her boss's. She does not support his political party or the individual lawmakers he backs. She would love to put a political bumper sticker on her car but she worries that it would be frowned upon, based on past comments she has heard her boss make about those with opposing views.

Sarah does not want to attend fundraisers for or donate to the lawmakers her boss supports. However, because of her subordinate position, she feels like she has no choice. She wants to keep her boss happy, but she resents being asked to take a position she does not believe in, particularly when these activities are completely unrelated to her job. She certainly does not feel comfortable telling her boss that his requests conflict with her personal beliefs.

The Takeaway

Sarah's boss has made the error of assuming she supports the same party and candidates he does. Not only are his actions and requests detrimental to Sarah's satisfaction and engagement, they could potentially lead to legal trouble.

Although Sarah understands the lawmaking process and is well-known in her community, her boss is abusing his position by asking her to do things completely unrelated to her job, such as attend fundraisers. If he expects her to perform these tasks on behalf of the company, her job description and compensation should reflect that. Further, if Sarah is a non-exempt employee, the company is likely violating the Fair Labor Standards Act, as well as state wage and hour laws, unless Sarah is tracking and being paid for the time spent at the fundraising events as a company representative. (Refer back to Chapter 6: Pay Me Now or Pay Me Later: Wage and Hour Basics for a refresher on wage and hour basics.)

Asking Sarah to donate to particular candidates is not okay either because directing how an employee spends their wages violates the Fair Labor Standards Act. (Also, donors often end up on mailing lists, which means that Sarah's boss's political positions will, literally, be delivered to her home mailbox for years to come. That's intrusive and annoying!)

Refresher: The Fair Labor Standards Act

The Fair Labor Standards Act is a federal law that applies to (almost) every employee in the United States. It requires employers to pay its non-exempt employees for all time worked. It also requires non-exempt employees to be paid one and a half times the regular rate for all hours worked over 40 in a given 168-hour workweek.[1]

"Time worked" is broadly defined. If the task benefits the employer, it is considered time worked. Employers who violate the Fair Labor Standards Act can be sued by employees or by the United States Department of Labor.

Every state has some counterpart to the Fair Labor Standards Act. Often, employers are sued under the federal law and the state law in one lawsuit.

Rather than relying on Sarah's personal social connections and prior education and work, the better practice would be for her boss to attend the fundraisers himself, hire someone to monitor industry regulations, or hire a registered lobbyist to lobby. If Sarah's job requires her to perform these tasks, her boss should add the duties to her job description and compensate her for the additional tasks and expertise.

As matters stand now, Sarah's boss has crossed a line and invaded her personal space by assuming she shares his political convictions. By asking her to support a specific party, cause, or candidate, he has put her in a no-win position. Her options are limited: She can fulfill his requests despite her personal convictions, or she can tell him no and hope he will understand (and, by extension, not overtly or subtly retaliate).

Can Employers Act Based on an Employee's Politics?

You might be wondering whether it would even be legal for Sarah's boss to retaliate should she make her political beliefs known. The answer is: It depends on where their organization is located.

Being a member of a political party is *not* a protected class under any federal law. This means that unlike sex, color, race, religion, or national origin, which are protected by Title VII of the Civil Rights Act, under federal law a private sector business *is* free to consider an applicant's or employee's politics when making employment-related decisions.

However, most states and many municipalities have laws that protect private sector employees from adverse actions based on political affiliation and/or political activities. These laws prohibit a variety of activities, including voting intimidation, interference with an employee's exercise of their political rights, or taking an adverse action against an employee because of their political opinion.

Broadly speaking, in these states, an employer cannot consider an applicant's or an employee's political affiliation when making employment-related decisions. Employers also cannot prohibit employees from engaging in political activity and cannot require that employees engage in political activity.

Remember Samantha, the hypothetical employee from Chapter 16: Do Not Friend Me on Social Media who was terminated after failing to call in her absence from work? Because Samantha missed work to attend a political rally and lives in a state where political affiliation is a protected category, she was able to sue her employer for discrimination. This legal tactic would not have been possible in a state where political affiliation is *not* a protected category.

I'll Say It Again: Stay Away From Your Employees' Social Media Accounts

You might also recall that Samantha claimed her employer knew she was at the political rally because of photos posted on social media. Political affiliation can often be determined by a quick glance at an individual's social media page—particularly during election season.

For this reason, employers who are *not* friends with their employees on social media will be in a better position to defend a claim of discrimination based on political affiliation than employers who *are* friends with their employees on social media.

And because nothing on the Internet ever really disappears, employers should not even look at publicly available social media profiles to surreptitiously determine an applicant's or employee's political status.

Even if your organization is located in a state where political affiliation is not a protected category, employers should be very cautious about making employment decisions based on an employee's presumed political views. Let's revisit the premise that your employees are not your friends in the purest sense of the word. This means that unless you know an employee extremely well, you cannot assume you know which political party or candidate (if any) they support.

Even if an employee has clearly communicated which party they generally support, you cannot know where they fall on specific issues. It seems easy to throw all Democrats in one bucket and all Republicans in another, divide the social and political issues evenly among buckets, and say, "All Republicans support (whatever); all Democrats are against (whatever)," or vice versa.

However, that worldview is overly simplistic and often unrepresentative of the way human beings really think. Most people (and therefore most of your employees) are more nuanced and do not support every single initiative of a single party or candidate.

The Better Practice: Try to Leave Politics Out of the Office Whenever Possible

Especially in today's complex and often-contentious environment, it is critical that employers understand how to navigate politics and political issues in the workplace. Whether we're talking about #metoo, social justice issues, the pros and cons of labor unions, or elections and their outcomes, politics in the workplace has been elevated to the number-one employment law challenge for some organizations.

Generally speaking, unless you work in politics, your work is directly tied to politics (such as a lobbying firm), or your work is indirectly tied to politics (such as print or media organizations), the office is no place for politics. The goal is to create a workplace where all employees (and clients, customers, patients, and vendors) feel welcome and safe, and are treated with dignity. To that end:

Don't tune in to potentially contentious channels. The break room television should not be tuned to one particular news channel if that outlet overtly supports one party. Instead, choose a neutral news source. Better yet, choose a home and garden improvement station that is relaxing, entertaining, and cannot offend anyone (except, perhaps, employees who are averse to neutral color schemes…but that's a different story!). This is true for customer-facing televisions, too—more on that later.

Create a company-wide dress code. Employees should be discouraged from wearing political items such as buttons, hats, or t-shirts. You may also choose to prohibit employees from wearing clothing that addresses social issues, as well. You can deal with this in your dress code as long as the rule is consistently applied to all employees.

Think Twice Before Banning Union Apparel

An exception to this rule applies to clothing that contains union insignia. In August 2022, the National Labor Relations Board found that an employer violated Section 8(a)(1) of the National Labor Relations Act when it prohibited union insignias on clothing. The board ruled that the employer must show "special circumstances" to support the prohibition.[2] Therefore, if you are considering prohibiting union-specific clothing or buttons, double check the National Labor Relations Act cases to ensure you are not running afoul of a rule.

After confirming that your state law allows it, an easy way to address prohibited clothing is via a dress code requiring either shirts with a company logo or solid, unadorned shirts (i.e., no graphic t-shirts, political or otherwise).

Be clear about what topics are off-limits for discussion... Private sector employees have different First Amendment free speech rights in the workplace from public sector employees. Specifically, public sector employees' First Amendment free speech rights are much broader than the rights of private sector employees. Private sector employers may set more specific rules on what sort of speech and expression is allowed at the worksite.

While the National Labor Relations Act does not allow an employer to limit speech regarding the terms and conditions of employment (see Chapter 16: Do Not Friend Me on Social Media for a more detailed explanation of this portion of the National Labor Relations Act), private sector employers *can* limit political speech in the workplace by having consistent rules that apply across the board. For example, an employer may not prohibit discussions that favor one side of a particular topic, but an employer may prohibit political discourse as a whole.

Before implementing such a rule, however, the rule should be reviewed by an employment attorney to ensure it does not inadvertently violate the National Labor Relations Act and that it is narrowly tailored and drafted in a non-discriminatory manner. Then, the rule should be set forth in writing (e.g., in the employee handbook). Again, the key for private sector employers is to apply the rule *consistently* and to *all employees*.

…Or for displaying. Along the same lines, employees should be discouraged from posting political items or items with divisive statements in their workspaces. To ensure all employees are aware of this requirement, this rule should be part of the employee handbook.

Give employees time off for voting—but refrain from commentary. Leaders may encourage employees to vote and provide paid time off to do so, but should refrain from making politically charged statements related to a particular candidate or party.

You May Be Required to Provide Time Off for Voting

In some jurisdictions, employers are required to provide a certain amount of time off for employees to vote on election days. This list includes: Alabama, Alaska, Arizona, Arkansas, California, Colorado, Georgia, Hawaii, Illinois, Iowa, Kansas, Kentucky, Maryland, Massachusetts, Minnesota, Missouri, Nebraska, Nevada, New Mexico, North Dakota, Ohio, Oklahoma, South Dakota, Tennessee, Texas, and Utah.

The amount of time off varies in these jurisdictions. Some, like Utah, require that an employer provide at least two hours at the beginning or the end of an employee's shift. Others, like Texas, do not specify how much time employers must give employees. Still others, like Tennessee, require a "reasonable" amount of time to be given. About half of the states listed here require *paid* time off to be given. The other half provides unpaid time off.

To ensure compliance with state law, be sure to look at your state's individual requirement well before any election. If you have employees in many states, be sure to look at each state's requirements.

Create an organizational "political expression" policy. Creating a policy regarding political expression in the workplace may be helpful in setting the tone and culture of your workplace. Such a policy might contain language regarding creating a peaceful and welcoming environment for employees and customers, respecting the dignity of all people, embracing all types of employees and customers, and ensuring that speech or images that are likely to offend others are not acceptable. If you create such a policy, it might be a good place under which to nest the guidelines and rules we've already covered, such as prohibiting political apparel and signage.

Make Your Organization a Politics-Free Space for Customers, Too

Unless your organization is directly or indirectly political in nature, you may want to take steps to ensure that you aren't inadvertently alienating customers. To that end, make sure company facilities and equipment do not contain any material, signs, logos, or stickers that would potentially offend any of your clients or customers. For example:

- Political bumper stickers or endorsements on a company vehicle might send some of your clients right into the arms of your competitor.
- Having a one-sided political news show on in your waiting room is sure to annoy some of the people waiting to pay you for your services.
- Email signature lines or mottos on invoices that contain information unrelated to the business (such as quotes, memes, or religious verses) might upset recipients, which could include prospects or clients.

Finally, unless you know a customer on a very personal level, don't discuss politics, political candidates, voting positions, or anything that occurs in Washington, D.C. Based on outward appearances, you may assume someone shares your opinions, but if you are wrong, you may lose their business. The better tactic is to remain neutral and keep conversations professional.

A Few Alternatives to Political Small Talk

If you must make small talk as part of your business, take the lead from your customers and discuss instead:

- Pets (an easy, favorite topic for all pet owners)
- Kids (a favorite topic for all parents)
- Grandchildren (the most important topic for grandparents)
- New movies/television shows
- College or professional sports
- Upcoming or prior holidays ("What did you do this summer?")
- The customer's hobbies
- Community events
- Weather (if you can't think of anything else to discuss)

Wrapping It Up: Politics and the Workplace

Today's 24/7 news cycle makes it possible for politics to be a part of our lives all day, every day. On the plus side, this allows us to stay informed and to make educated decisions. On the con side, politics and specific political topics can quickly become divisive.

For an organization to be successful, its employees must respect the opinions of coworkers, even when those opinions differ from their own. Topics of conversation that are likely to create division are not consistent with a healthy workplace. For this reason, employers should consider whether they are inadvertently introducing division into the workplace by allowing political speech, providing content-specific media, or outwardly supporting specific groups or causes.

If so, the remedy may be as simple as creating neutral policies to limit political speech and encouraging employees to bond over fun (and politically neutral) topics.

Politics Aren't the Only "Cause" to Avoid

We all know that politics can easily become a hot-button issue—and for that reason, it probably doesn't surprise you that I included it in this book. But before we move on, I want to look at a related topic: supporting charities.

Committing your organization to support certain charities or asking your employees to do the same might not initially seem anywhere near as problematic as involving your organization or employees in political efforts. But for many of the same reasons, I advise approaching philanthropy with care and consideration. Let's look at why.

Ralph's Story

Ralph owns a mid-sized company with one primary location and a few smaller out-of-state offices. One of the company's core values is volunteerism.

Ralph's personal passion is a local faith-based denominational charity that works with homeless teens. There is no dispute that the charity's work is valuable to the teens and the community. Ralph and his wife, who is not an employee, both volunteer for the charity on a regular basis. They often include short stories about and pictures of their volunteer work in the company newsletter, which is distributed to employees, clients, and prospects.

To help raise funds for the charity, Ralph often offers opportunities for his staff to contribute. He encourages his employees to take up to eight paid work hours a year to volunteer with the organization. He holds "Wear a T-Shirt to Work" days, during which employees can dress casually for a $10 donation. He also encourages some employees to bring homemade chili for an annual office chili cook-off. Non-cooks can donate money to sample all of the chilis and vote for their favorite one. To make it as easy as possible for the employees, Ralph has even set up a payroll deduction system that allows employees to have their donations automatically deducted from their paychecks.

Last year, Ralph's wife was selected as Volunteer of the Year by the organization, so the company purchased a table at the organization's annual fundraising event and invited employees to attend.

The Takeaway

Generosity to "good causes" comes in many forms. Financial pledges, donations, and contributions are key to the success of any non-profit organization. While financial gifts are the most obvious form of generosity, non-profits also rely on people to generously donate their time and talent. All should be equally valued.

Perhaps at this point you're wondering, *So what's the problem? If generosity is such a good thing, why are you singling Ralph out?*

In this case, it is wonderful that Ralph and his wife choose to participate in a meaningful way with an organization they are passionate about. Their mistake, though, is linking that passion with their company in a way that may feel coercive to Ralph's employees. Specifically:

Ralph's employees may not feel as passionate about the organization as he does. They may not like or agree with the organization, or may not want to financially support the organization. Yet because they work for Ralph, they may feel compelled to donate to and participate in the organization's events—especially when not doing so would be obvious to Ralph and to other employees (e.g., not wearing a t-shirt on Wear a T-Shirt to Work day or not making or tasting chili in the cook-off).

Involvement with a religious organization might make some people uncomfortable. Because the organization is faith-based, Ralph may have unintentionally created the opportunity for an employee to claim discrimination based on religion because the employee felt coerced into participating in or supporting a faith-based organization. While the organization's work with homeless teens may be a worthwhile cause, Ralph should consider that his employees may feel just as passionate about sharing their time, talent, and treasure with their own church, synagogue, or mosque, rather than the faith represented by Ralph's organization. It's also possible that some of Ralph's employees may be non-religious and do not wish to support a faith-based organization of any kind.

Employees may prefer different ways of giving. They may prefer anonymous gifting to organizations. They may prefer to share their talents with a non-faith-based organization that works with children, the elderly, disabled people, or incarcerated people. Employees may prefer hands-on activities such as reading or mentoring at a public school. They may prefer to support their local animal shelter or wildlife refuge. Or perhaps they donate their skill as a lawyer, IT professional, electrician, tutor, teacher, or accountant to help people who otherwise could not afford those services. All of these are valuable ways for employees to help their communities. And—let's not forget!—there are also many reasons why a person might not want to donate time or resources at all, such as financial constraints or needing to focus on personal challenges. Regardless of an employee's motivations, it should ultimately be their decision—not the employer's—whether or not to contribute to a charitable cause.

What Should Ralph (and Other Employers) Do Instead?

Ralph's overarching goal of allowing employees to use company resources to provide much-needed help and assistance to a non-profit organization in the community is laudable. Such activities create opportunities for connectedness among employees and company leaders. It also connects employees to their community. For these reasons, Ralph *should* continue the practice of encouraging volunteerism and giving.

To ensure employees have a choice in their philanthropic efforts, rather than being given a single faith-based organization to support, better ideas for Ralph to consider include:

- Creating a diverse employee committee to nominate and vote on charities or non-profit organizations to support, dividing any proceeds among the ones selected by the committee
- Polling employees to learn about their volunteerism ideas
- Allowing employees to take a certain amount of paid time off to donate time and talent at the non-profit organization or charity of their choice
- Rotating charities by month or quarter so many different non-profit organizations and charities are represented throughout the year

The key to building a successful philanthropy program at your organization is simple: Put employees at the center. Ask them what causes and organizations they want to support, and what form they would like that support to take. When you support your employees in making a positive impact on their community, *in a way that is meaningful to them and that aligns with their values*, their engagement and enthusiasm at work will grow.

CHAPTER 21

Please Respect My Religion—But Don't Force Yours on Me

Josie's Story

Josie applied to be a cashier at the Burger House, a local fast food restaurant. During the interview, the manager explained to Josie that the Burger House was open seven days a week. Based on her interview, she was offered a job.

On her first day of work, the manager gave Josie her schedule for the following two weeks. She was scheduled to work five days per week, including Wednesday afternoons from 12:00 p.m. to 6:00 p.m. and Sunday afternoons from 12:00 p.m. to 5:00 p.m. Josie explained to the manager that she could not work Wednesday between 5:00 p.m. and 8:00 p.m. or Sunday between 8:00 a.m. and 1:00 p.m. because she had religious obligations during that time.

The manager told Josie that as an employee of a seven-day-a-week-restaurant, she would be expected to work any scheduled shift unless she had preapproved time off. Josie reiterated her religious obligations and asked whether she could be exempt from working during those specific times. She said she would be willing to work any other shift any other day, but that she could not work during the three-hour block on Wednesday evenings or on Sundays until 1:00 p.m. The manager declined her request.

On Wednesday, Josie arrived at 12:00 p.m. as scheduled and reminded the manager that even though she was scheduled to work until 6:00 p.m., she had to leave at 5:00 p.m. When Josie clocked out at 5:00 p.m., she was written up for leaving her shift early without permission.

On Sunday, Josie arrived a few minutes after 1:00 p.m. Josie's manager reminded her that she was scheduled to begin working at 12:00 p.m. and wrote her up for being over an hour late.

The following Wednesday, Josie took the same steps as the prior Wednesday: She arrived at 12:00 p.m. and reminded her manager that she had to leave at 5:00 p.m., even though she was scheduled to work until 6:00 p.m. At 5:00 p.m., Josie told her manager that she was clocking out. He terminated her employment.

The Takeaway

If the Burger House has enough employees to be covered by Title VII of the Civil Rights Act, it is likely that Josie could prevail in a claim of religious discrimination. Religion is very broadly defined under Title VII. If an employee espouses a sincerely held religious belief, it is generally protected by the law. This is especially true if, as in Josie's case, the religious behavior is consistent and seemingly reasonable.

Josie's request was limited to two short periods of the work week. It is unlikely that allowing Josie to leave at 5:00 p.m. on Wednesdays and to begin working at 1:00 p.m. on Sundays would have created an undue hardship for the Burger House. The better practice would have been for the manager of the Burger House to revise Josie's schedule so she could attend religious services. He could have likely accommodated her request by allowing Josie to leave one hour early on Wednesday and come in one hour late on Sunday. He could have also tried to schedule her for shifts that did not conflict with her religious obligations, which could have included making Wednesdays and Sundays her regular days off.

The result might be different if Josie applied and was hired for a management position that required her to open or close the restaurant, and the hours she requested overlapped with those tasks. In that case, the accommodation might create an undue hardship because there are likely only a few employees with the authority to perform those tasks.

An Ounce of Prevention

Every employer's situation—and every employee's request—is different. There is no single "blueprint" for determining whether an accommodation request is reasonable. A reasonable accommodation request for one employer may constitute an undue hardship for another. Therefore, employers are well-advised to review accommodation requests with their employment lawyer, who can look at the undue hardship analysis objectively and consider cases in the employer's jurisdiction to determine what a court is likely to find with respect to a given accommodation request. As is the case with most matters concerning employment law, an ounce of prevention—consulting your attorney—is worth a pound of cure.

What Does the Law Say About Religious Discrimination?

Title VII of the Civil Rights Act of 1964 protects applicants and employees from being subjected to discrimination in the workplace when their employers have 15 or more employees in 20 or more calendar weeks in the current or preceding year.[1]

Employee Headcount Matters

Interestingly, the "15 or more" rule applies to discrimination claims brought under Title VII based on sex, color, race, religion, and national origin, as well as to discrimination claims brought under the Americans with Disabilities Act or the Genetic Information Nondiscrimination Act. However, the "15 or more" rule does not apply to age-based discrimination claims brought under federal law. The jurisdictional basis for an age discrimination claim is 20 or more employees.

That said, even if they cannot be sued under federal law, organizations smaller than 15 may be subject to discrimination, harassment, and retaliation claims brought under other laws or regulations, such as state laws or municipal regulations.

Discrimination claims based on religion differ from other sorts of discrimination claims because some faith-based organizations *may* legally discriminate in limited circumstances on the basis of religion. That said, unless your organization is a bona fide faith-based organization with an allowable exemption under federal law (such as a church, temple, or faith-based school), discriminating against or taking any adverse employment action against applicants or employees because of or on the basis of their religion is illegal. As noted above, religion is broadly defined and includes an employee's sincerely held religious belief.

This means that an employer cannot refuse to hire a person, refuse to promote a person, prefer one qualified person over another qualified person, offer different benefits, demote, terminate, or make any employment-related decision because of or on the basis of that person's religion. All of this makes sense when you stop to consider that except in the cases of bona fide religious organizations or where a religious accommodation creates an undue hardship, a person's religion is completely unrelated to their skill set and ability to perform the tasks of a job.

Bona fide religious exemptions are granted where religion is *central to* the job—like a teacher at a Catholic school or a Christian ed leader at a church. However, that same church would have a difficult time saying the janitor had to be of a certain religion.

Remember Ralph? He Could Be in Violation of the Law.

Think back to Ralph, the employer in Chapter 20: Do Not Assume Your Causes Are the Same as My Causes who strongly encouraged his employees to donate their time and money to his favorite faith-based charity. Ralph did not explicitly hire, fire, promote, or punish anyone based on their religion…but his actions made some employees fear that they *might* be viewed less favorably or even become targets for retaliation if they did not participate in Ralph's charitable endeavors.

Except for organizations whose primary mission and business is religion (churches, synagogues, parochial schools, etc.), employers should be cognizant that asking employees to participate in any faith-based activity can be perceived as potentially coercive and can unwittingly expose the employer to a claim of religious discrimination.

How Common Is This Type of Claim?

As with other types of harassment, discrimination, and retaliation claims, employees must first file a charge of discrimination with the Equal Employment Opportunity Commission *before* proceeding with a lawsuit in federal court. The number of charges received by the Equal Employment Opportunity Commission and the monetary value of those benefits show a steady concern about religious discrimination in the workplace in the United States.[2]

Religious Discrimination Claims in the United States		
Year	Number of Charges of Discrimination Filed	Monetary Benefits
2010	3,790	$10,000,000
2011	4,151	$12,600,000
2012	3,811	$9,900,000
2013	3,721	$11,200,000
2014	3,549	$8,700,000
2015	3,502	$10,800,000
2016	3,825	$10,100,000
2017	3,436	$11,200,000
2018	2,859	$9,200,000

2019	2,725	$9,900,000
2020	2,404	$6,100,000
2021	2,111	$9,500,000
2022	13,814	$12,800,000*

*Between 2021 and 2022, the number of religion-based discrimination claims jumped from a little over 2,000 charges to 13,814 claims! The EEOC explains, "In FY 2022, there was a significant increase in vaccine-related charges filed on the basis of religion. As a result, FY 2022 data may vary compared to previous years."[3]

As startling as these numbers are, they include ONLY charges filed and monetary benefits obtained through the Equal Employment Opportunity Commission. They do not include charges filed exclusively with state equal employment agencies, such as the Florida Commission on Human Relations.

Additionally, these numbers do not include monies obtained through pre-charge settlements, litigation settlements, or judgments entered by a court after trial. They do not take into consideration the financial damage to an organization's reputation should news of alleged religious discrimination become public. Finally, these numbers do not show the monies paid to defense attorneys to defend the charges or lawsuits, or the corresponding increases in insurance costs.

These monetary benefits paid by employers support the argument that **it is better to avoid any appearance of pre-employment or post-employment discrimination based on religion than it is to try to defend a claim.**

While there are numerous actions an employer might take that could be considered religious discrimination, there are two specific categories I would like to look at in this chapter: religious discrimination in hiring and handling an employee's request for a religious accommodation. Many employers will find themselves in these situations at some point, and it's important to know how to navigate them.

What Can Employers Do to Avoid Claims of Religious Discrimination in Hiring?

First things first: As is the case for information that falls into any federally protected category, employers should not try to determine the religion of an applicant or an employee using social media (even though in ten seconds or less, you can probably determine the faith of some people by scrolling through any one of their social media accounts!).

Further, unless your organization is a faith-based organization that qualifies for a bona fide religious exemption, employers should avoid questions related to religion when they are interviewing an applicant. For example, it is not okay to ask:

"Why are you wearing that headscarf/turban/burqa/yarmulke?"

"What religion do you practice?"

"Where do you go to church?"

"Do you go to a church, synagogue, mosque, or somewhere else?"

"Do you agree to participate in morning prayer with us before beginning the workday?"

"Do you go to Sunday school or other Sunday worship?"

"Do you practice any religious observations that would limit your ability to work on Saturday evenings or Sunday mornings?"

"What are your faith beliefs?"

"Why do you have a tattoo of a religious symbol?"

"Do you have to wear that cross/Star of David necklace?"

"Will you agree to use an email signature line that contains specific religious language?"

It *is* okay to ask generic questions of every candidate, such as:

"Here is our dress code. Can you comply with this dress code?"

If the answer is no, you may follow that question with, "Why are you unable to comply with the dress code?"

The reason the applicant cannot comply with the dress code is directly relevant to whether they are entitled to an accommodation. If the applicant's answer is that they cannot comply with the dress code because of sincerely held religious beliefs, unless the accommodation would pose an undue hardship on your organization, you will probably need to accommodate it. An undue hardship would exist, for example, where failing to follow the dress code could result in safety violations or harm to the employee or coworkers.

"Are there any days or times you are unavailable to work?"

If the answer is yes, you may follow that question with, "Why are you unavailable at that time?"

As above, the reason the applicant is not available is relevant to whether they are entitled to an accommodation. If the applicant's answer is that they are unavailable because they have a standing paintball appointment or because they love to brunch with friends, they are not entitled to an accommodation. But if the applicant's answer is that they observe religious practices in furtherance of their sincerely held beliefs, an accommodation is required unless it would pose an undue hardship to the organization.

Accommodations may extend to providing certain shifts or days off each week, allowing breaks in the workday for prayer, or ensuring the employee is not scheduled during required religious events or holidays. (More on this later.)

"Here is the job description. Are you able to perform these tasks?"

If the applicant tells you that he or she cannot perform some of the tasks because of his or her religion, you may have to provide an accommodation, unless doing so would create an undue hardship for the organization.

"Tell me specific tasks you have accomplished in the past related to the position for which you are applying."

Asking what specific job-related tasks an applicant has accomplished in prior positions is better than asking what a candidate is capable of doing, especially when the implication is that a candidate's religion would prohibit him or her from completing certain tasks. This question allows the candidate to speak freely about their successes that are relevant to the job.

How Can Employers Work with Employees to Craft Fair Accommodations?

As with accommodation requests for a qualified person with a disability, employers are required to reasonably accommodate an employee's religious beliefs or practices unless the accommodation would pose an undue hardship to the organization. An undue hardship exists where the cost to the employer is too high or there is a valid safety concern based on the possibility that an employee may suffer harm or be injured. This may be the case in manufacturing facilities, for example, where hair, headscarves, or clothing may get caught in machinery.

Guidance for Employers: Is This an Undue Hardship?

The Occupational Safety and Health Administration (OSHA) provides guidance on safety in the workplace and can help employers determine if a legitimate safety concern exists that is sufficient to deny the employee's request for accommodation.

To determine if an undue hardship exists based on safety, review the requested job accommodation, the job description for the position, and any Safety Data Sheet with your employment lawyer.

If a religious accommodation is appropriate, it is best to understand an applicant's needs *before* an offer is extended so both parties have a clear understanding of what they can expect during employment. However, if that does not happen, employees may make faith-based accommodation requests after they are hired. Thus, post-hire accommodation requests need to be treated as if they were made during the interview.

In other words, an employer may not say, "If I had known this, I would not have hired you." Such a statement would be direct evidence of discrimination. Instead, the employer should listen to the employee's request for an accommodation and determine whether it is possible to provide such an accommodation, or whether the accommodation would create an undue hardship. If the request does not create an undue hardship, the accommodation must be granted.

Employers are not expected to be mind readers. Employees who require religious accommodations (or any protected accommodation, for that matter) have an obligation to work with their employer to help their employer determine what accommodation is reasonable under the law. This communication is referred to as the *interactive process* because both parties are expected to actively engage in conversation about what the employee needs and what the employer can reasonably be expected to provide.

Although an employee may prefer one accommodation over another, at the end of the day, it is the employer's right to determine what accommodation it will provide. The key is for both the employer and the employee to be open, honest, and flexible. Here are a few examples of accommodations an employer might make:

- For an employee who has faith-based obligations on a particular day of the week, an employer might modify the employee's schedule.
- For an employee whose religion requires certain clothing, such as a Jewish yarmulke or a Muslim hijab, modifying the dress code may be necessary if it can be done safely. Safety concerns are often a legitimate reason to deny a religious-based clothing accommodation request.
- Religions might prohibit wearing certain items. For example, if you own a restaurant and require the female servers to wear shorts or short skirts, an adjustment to the dress code may be a suitable accommodation for a female employee whose religion prohibits those items.
- An employer with a strict no-visible-tattoos policy might need to make an accommodation for employees whose tattoos are religious in nature. Tattoos are an important part of religious expression in many religions around the world, including Buddhism and Hinduism, and are often akin to religious jewelry. For this reason, employees generally cannot be compelled to cover tattoos that are religious in nature.
- Policies that address facial hair may require modifications as well. For example, unless there is an objective, supportable safety reason that beards are not allowed for any employee in a particular position, an organization with a no-facial-hair policy may not require an Orthodox Jewish man to shave his beard.

In Conclusion

I'll close this chapter by pointing out that employers do not have an "accommodations crystal ball." In other words, you will not know that an employee needs an accommodation *unless that employee makes the request*. So, how can you ensure that you are providing any necessary accommodations based on religion—or any other protected category? Communication is key.

As I've described throughout this book, it is imperative to focus on employees' satisfaction, psychological safety, morale, and well-being from the interview forward. If a job applicant feels that they have been treated with consideration, and if they see that your organization is respectful and generous to its employees, they will be more likely to share information relevant to accommodations *before* accepting a job offer.

If an existing employee has not shared this information before being hired, try to create an atmosphere going forward where both parties are looking for a win-win, rather than an adversarial winner-takes-all situation (in which no one *really* wins!).

CHAPTER 22

Keep Your Personal Life and Tasks to Yourself

As a leader, you should take pains to keep your personal life out of the workplace. But as you may already know, this can be easier said than done. In this chapter, I'd like to share two stories that illustrate how a leader's personal life can damage the employer-employee relationship if it is allowed to seep into the workplace.

Matt's Story

Matt has spent 30 years building a window manufacturing company. Due to his decades-long dedication to his business and his outstanding work ethic, he has become a respected community figure and has made many strong networking connections, both inside and outside of his industry. Because of these connections, Matt was able to introduce his 20-something daughter to a friend, who ended up hiring her.

Matt's daughter has developed her father's excellent work ethic and now holds a prominent position with another company. Matt understandably loves to tell his friends about his daughter's professional accomplishments. He drops the names of influential people with whom she rubs elbows. He shares details of her travels. He regularly holds his phone out for any friend who might have a moment to scroll through pictures with him.

The problem is that Matt shares the same unfiltered information with his employees.

The Takeaway

Being a proud parent is awesome. Bragging about your children to your employees is not.

In this case, Matt's pride is causing him to overshare information with his employees. They are probably happy to know a little about Matt's daughter's success. But his constant oversharing may indicate a lack of self-awareness in front of this particular audience.

Matt may not have considered that many of his employees, who may be decades older than his daughter, never had the opportunity to achieve what she has at such a young age, simply because they started in a very different place. Also, they may not have the resources to create similar opportunities for their own children. Perhaps they don't have long-term community connectedness. Perhaps they do not have friends who own businesses. Perhaps they did not have the opportunity to obtain the education that Matt's daughter received, which prepared her for the job she now holds.

Knowing your audience is critical to connecting in a meaningful way. In this case, Matt's pride is well-founded; his daughter has built an amazing professional life at a young age. However, speaking frequently of her success to an audience who may never have the same opportunities— regardless of merit or ability— may be perceived as insensitive. It could even generate resentment.

The Better Practice

The better practice for employers is to share personal information with employees sparingly…and share it with friends and family generously. Since we covered a very similar topic in Chapter 16: Do Not Friend Me on Social Media, I'll keep my remarks here brief and reiterate a few key points:

- Your employees are *not* your friends in the truest sense of the word. While workplace relationships can be warm and genuine, there is always an imbalance of power between leaders and subordinates.
- Before sharing personal information with employees, think about how your stories, photos, etc. might appear to someone who lacks detailed context about your life. Ask yourself if the information you want to share is likely

to boost your employees' morale and engagement, or if it could potentially widen the power gradient between you and them.

- When you feel the urge to share (or overshare) personal information with your employees, challenge yourself to say something meaningful *about an employee* instead. While bragging on your family can create resentment, bragging on an employee increases their satisfaction, loyalty, and even productivity.

Jim's Story

Jim is a new junior financial advisor in the investment management department at a bank. Rob, a senior financial advisor, is Jim's direct supervisor. Rob often asks Jim to complete tasks unrelated to his job description, including responding to Rob's personal emails, paying a few personal bills using Rob's online banking account, picking up Rob's dry cleaning, and making copies of his children's homework packets. Rob's rationale is that the less time he has to spend on personal tasks, the more efficient he is at work.

Meanwhile, Jim is frustrated. He applied for a position as a junior financial advisor because he is licensed and credentialed as such. He did not apply to be a personal assistant or to perform personal errands. Completing these tasks does not further Jim's professional goals, teach him the skills he needs to progress in the organization, or put him in contact with clients or the community. In fact, doing these personal tasks diminishes his credibility among other financial advisors in the firm because he is not able to contribute in the same manner others are. Finally, these tasks also give Jim a glimpse into Rob's personal life and finances, which makes him uncomfortable.

The Takeaway

Rob's personal requests do not help create a healthy and professional supervisor-employee relationship for several reasons.

Jim can't comfortably refuse Rob's requests. As a new employee in a junior position, Jim has very little ability to refuse Rob's requests, even though they are wholly unrelated to the job and they are preventing him from progressing as quickly as many of his peers.

Rob's requests can be construed as theft from the organization. Unless specifically allowed by an organization and stated in the job description, asking a subordinate employee to perform personal tasks is akin to theft. The organization presumably is not paying Jim to perform Rob's personal tasks; it hired Jim to provide financial advice to its clients. The expectation is that Jim will contribute to the organization's overall financial success. In asking Jim to complete personal tasks, Rob is using company resources (Jim's time and talent) to accomplish non-productive, personal errands—*and* he is causing the organization to lose revenue Jim might otherwise have brought in by doing banking work. Unless using company resources for personal benefit is allowed, Rob could find himself subject to disciplinary action. Depending on the severity of the behavior, such disciplinary action could very well include termination.

Rob's requests create potential liability for Jim. Should Rob experience any fraud or mistakes related to his personal finances, Jim will be in a precarious position because he had access to these accounts. Even if he is not responsible for the fraud or mistakes, and even if he did not want to perform these non-work-related tasks, he might still have to prove to an insurance company, bank, or even a court of law that he was not responsible for the fraud or mistake. This could be costly to Jim not only financially, but in terms of his reputation and future prospects.

Jim's perception in the office is affected. Asking Jim to perform family-related tasks diminishes his credibility in the workplace. Being seen copying Rob's children's homework, for instance, creates the impression among coworkers that Jim is less of a financial expert and more of an administrative assistant. Once established, these perceptions are very difficult to change, especially for employees who are new, young, or have not had the opportunity to shine as a professional in their field.

Jim just doesn't want to know! Finally, Rob's requests related to his finances put Jim in an uncomfortable position. Most subordinate employees do not want to see how much they earn in comparison to their bosses, and do not want to know how their bosses spend their money.

The Better Practice

If a company determines that it is inappropriate for leaders to ask other employees to conduct personal business, it can handle this via a well-written and publicized policy that specifically addresses expectations of employees. The employee handbook is a great place to put such a policy because it is shared with all employees at all levels—meaning that Jim and Rob both understand the company's position on this issue.

At most organizations, for all of the reasons listed above, performing personal errands for supervisors should be off-limits. The better practice for supervisors is to either carve out a few hours a week to handle personal tasks, or hire someone—*on their own dime and time*—who has the desire and skill set to be a standout personal assistant at a location away from the office.

That said, some companies allow employees to ask subordinates to handle personal tasks. This is okay as long as these tasks are defined in the job description, the company pays employees to perform the personal tasks, and employees understand they are part of their workplace responsibilities.

If a company *does* hire an employee for the specific purpose of being a personal assistant, organizational policy and all relevant job descriptions should define which categories of tasks are allowable (e.g., picking up lunch for a supervisor) and which are not allowable (e.g., reconciling personal bank accounts, making children's doctor's appointments, etc.).

Definitely Don't Allow Your Partner or Child to Ask *Me* to Run *Their* Personal Errands

If you are a supervisor, and your wife, husband, girlfriend, boyfriend, or child wants to ask your employees to run their personal errands or complete their personal tasks, STOP and see above. You may think this piece of advice should go without saying. If so, you would be very surprised to hear how often I have encountered this situation in my career!

In Conclusion

Great leaders are self-aware. They generally know what information makes employees comfortable and what information makes employees uncomfortable. Great leaders are also intentionally modest about their success. While it is human nature for people to talk about themselves, when communicating with employees about personal matters, take a moment and ask whether the information you are going to share presents you in the best light in the eyes of the employee. If the information could make the employee uncomfortable, place the employee in a potentially risky position, or make the employee feel "less-than," consider not sharing that information at all.

Things are even simpler when assigning tasks to an employee. Ask yourself if the task is work-related and in their job description. If the answer is no, don't assign it.

CHAPTER 23

Apologies Create Goodwill and Give You Credibility

Younger Amie's Story

Years ago, I was working with a subordinate employee who was one of the nicest guys in my company. While we were speaking with a client on a telephone call, I made an off-hand comment about my coworker. The comment was intended to be funny, but it was not. It was not true, nice, OR amusing. Immediately after the words left my mouth, I knew that I had made a mistake. I felt terrible. I could not put the toothpaste back in the tube, so to speak—the words had been spoken aloud—but I could attempt to clean up the mess I made.

Immediately after the call ended, I looked the employee in the eye and profusely apologized. I told him that I was sorry for three things: I made a stupid comment, the comment was at his expense, and the comment was in front of someone else.

Luckily, the employee gracefully accepted my apology. We moved past it and worked together successfully for several years after that. But that memory has continued to have a significant impact on my life. When I think back on it, I am reminded to be much more circumspect about the words I use—particularly in front of others or when a comment is at another person's expense. I am also reminded of how powerful and important a heartfelt apology can be when I *do* make a mistake or an error in judgment.

The Takeaway

Apologies should not be difficult. We learn to apologize as children when we intentionally or unintentionally hurt another person. But too often, after we grow up, pride takes over, and it becomes more difficult to say, "I was wrong, and I am really sorry."

The reality is that we all make mistakes, and we are often wrong. As adults and as business leaders, it is critical that we re-learn to admit when we are wrong, and that we gracefully accept a sincere apology when one is offered. My own experience taught me several things.

First, I learned how to own a mistake in a professional setting. In this case, I was the leader and in the wrong. As embarrassed as I was by my behavior, I could have finished the call and moved on to something else to pretend my "joke" did not happen or that it was not offensive or hurtful. That course of action would have been a lot easier for me *in that moment*. However, it would also have meant that there was an elephant in the room each time I worked with that employee in the future.

More importantly, that course of action would have conveyed the message that my coworker's feelings were not important, or worse, that *he* was not important. Neither of those things was true. His feelings *did* matter, and he was an important person who deserved to be treated with dignity. By apologizing sincerely and immediately, I conveyed that message to him.

Second, I learned the value of gracefully accepting an apology. After I apologized, the employee could have held a grudge or lashed out, which would have made me feel worse than I already did—but which might have made him feel better in that moment. Or he could have gossiped to other employees about what a jerk I was, which might have hurt my professional reputation. But instead, he chose to accept my apology and gave me the benefit of the doubt.

Some time later, I was in a meeting, and a coworker made an unkind joke about me in front of an entire group of colleagues. I was embarrassed by the comment. Later, in private, I told the coworker that I thought his comment was disrespectful. I did not know what to expect from this coworker because I did not know him well.

His response told me a lot about his character: He immediately and sincerely apologized. In that moment, I reflected on how my previous employee had reacted to my apology, and I chose to follow his example: I accepted the apology from my coworker, and we moved on to have a respectful, productive, professional relationship.

Third, I was reminded to always think before speaking. Acknowledging my mistake and apologizing to my colleague motivated me to guard against the bad habit of speaking without forethought, and to work on the good habit of pausing to think before speaking. Like a lot of extroverts, I get energized by being with and speaking with other people. The result is that I have to be intentional about listening instead of speaking and about pausing for a moment before responding to others.

As a leader, I should have exercised better control over what I said. Had I taken one second to consider the comment before I uttered it, the words would never have left my mouth. In years to come, I learned to intentionally pause for just a second before speaking. While I still actively work on this, I'm sure those one-second reflections saved me from many more embarrassing moments and, even better, spared the feelings of others.

Bonus Reason to Admit Your Mistakes

If you are in the wrong, chances are everyone else will know it. If you don't admit it, your credibility among your employees will be diminished.

Apologies Can Be One of a Leader's Most Valuable Tools

I chose to close this book with a chapter on apologies for a reason. That reason is simple: At some point (probably at numerous points), you *will* need to apologize to your employees, peers, clients, vendors, etc. As the preceding chapters have shown, there are many decisions, actions, statements, policies, etc. that can have a detrimental impact on other people and on your business. Maybe, like me, you said something offensive to an employee. Maybe you failed to give an employee credit when you should have done so. Or maybe you just flaked out and forgot to do something you said you would.

My hope is that this book will give you the tools to avoid a lot of these pitfalls, but no matter how careful and considerate you are, we are all human, and we all make mistakes. By choosing to acknowledge and own your mistakes, you will:

Enhance your credibility. I've met a lot of people who believe that if they admit to being wrong, their reputations will be damaged. I have consistently found that the opposite is true. When you react with humility after making an error, others will appreciate your self-awareness and honesty. When they see you holding yourself accountable, learning from your mistakes, and acting differently in the future, they will hold you in even greater respect.

Create goodwill with your employees. When leaders make a mistake and don't acknowledge it (or worse, try to hide it, or *even worse*, try to blame someone else), employees are likely to believe that these leaders 1) don't believe the rules apply to them, 2) hold themselves to a different standard, 3) are dishonest, or 4) all of the above. But when leaders hold themselves accountable, it increases employee trust. That leads directly to greater employee satisfaction, loyalty, and goodwill.

Set an example for how you expect employees to behave when *they* make a mistake. Employees pay attention to how their leaders navigate various situations—especially the tough ones. If they see you acknowledging your mistakes with integrity, they will be more likely to do the same. It's also likely that they will have less trepidation about coming forward with their errors in the first place. After all, a leader who is open about his or her own missteps is unlikely to respond to an employee's by blaming, berating, or retaliating.

Giving employees the freedom and security to admit mistakes can pay significant dividends. You want employees to report matters, which, left unreported, would result in a damaged product, a broken delivery, an erroneous client communication, or worse, an injury to an employee.

Potentially stave off legal trouble. Words have power and can convey a sincere desire to remedy a situation before it escalates. By gracefully admitting mistakes, you will be encouraging all leaders to do the same—which may reduce the likelihood of small problems becoming large legal problems. In litigation, I've often asked disgruntled employees what result they wanted prior to bringing a lawsuit. The answer, often, has not been money. Instead, the answer has often been an apology.

In Conclusion

The best employers are the ones who can admit their mistakes. Saying, "I was wrong," is difficult for many people—personally and professionally. The interesting thing is that the more often one apologizes, the easier it is to do. Making sincere apologies helps cement trust and credibility, which in turn begets loyalty and a healthy workplace.

Bonus Material

AI and the Future of HR

As I was writing this book, OpenAI's chatbot, ChatGPT, became available for public use—and almost immediately went viral. ChatGPT has very quickly become a widespread tool for generating ideas, creating content, streamlining work, automating tasks, and more. School systems, universities, businesses, and even governments have had to rapidly decide how (or if) it should be used in their operations.

Unless you've been living under a rock, you know that opinions about ChatGPT (and other types of AI) range from "love" to "loathe." Depending on who you ask, AI could be a revolutionary and valuable tool to transform our world…or a major threat to independent thought, the labor market, academic integrity, digital security, and more. Whatever your personal feelings might be, one thing is for sure: AI is here to stay—and it will continue to evolve.

I've found myself wondering how AI might impact the field of human resources going forward. I have seen AI successfully used to formulate corporate policies. I've also seen it used—unsuccessfully—to research legal issues.

Instead of speculating about this myself, I decided to ask AI for its "thoughts." *After all*, I mused, *I, a human, have already written an entire book about the HUMAN side of HR. I'll let AI share its own perspective about what its role might be going forward.*

So, I gave ChatGPT a prompt for a story: "Write a story as if you are a professional in the field of human resources and you are wondering how AI will affect your job over the next decade."

Then, I asked for a scholarly response: "Write a scholarly analysis addressing how AI will affect the day-to-day jobs of professionals in human resources over the next decade."

Here are the results.

AI Disclaimer: I Wrote the Rest of This Book Myself!

Artificial intelligence was not used to write any portion of this book—except for this bonus material. Rest assured that all of what you've read up to this point was written by me, hunched over my laptop, feverishly writing, editing, deleting, and editing again.

Artificial intelligence is a tool that enables human resource professionals to become more efficient, but there is no substitute for the "human" portion of human resources.

The Human Touch in an AI Era

In the bustling heart of downtown, amidst towering skyscrapers that kissed the clouds, lay the headquarters of Delphi Dynamics—a titan in the corporate world. At the heart of its operations stood Olivia Grant, the esteemed human resources director. With her keen eye for talent and compassionate approach, Olivia had steered the company through countless challenges, always relying on her intuition and empathy to connect with employees.

Yet, as the world hurtled toward an AI-driven future, Olivia found herself pondering the implications of technology on her role. It wasn't that she feared being replaced by machines; rather, she wondered how she could adapt her human touch to complement the advancements of artificial intelligence.

One crisp autumn morning, Olivia settled into her office, surrounded by towering stacks of résumés and employee files. The soft hum of her computer filled the air as she began sifting through the day's tasks. But her thoughts kept drifting to the looming presence of AI.

As she delved deeper into her work, a notification popped up on her screen—a seminar on "AI and the Future of HR." Intrigued, Olivia decided to attend, hoping to gain insights into how technology could enhance her role rather than diminish it.

The seminar hall buzzed with anticipation as experts from various fields took the stage, discussing the transformative power of AI. Olivia listened intently, her mind racing with possibilities. She realized that AI could streamline mundane tasks, allowing her more time to focus on the human aspect of HR—nurturing talent, fostering a positive work culture, and resolving conflicts with empathy and understanding.

Armed with newfound inspiration, Olivia returned to her office, determined to embrace the future while staying true to her core values. She immersed herself in learning about AI algorithms and predictive analytics, eager to leverage these tools to enhance her department's efficiency.

Months passed, and Delphi Dynamics thrived under Olivia's leadership. AI-powered recruitment software sifted through résumés with lightning speed, identifying top candidates based on skill sets and cultural fit. Performance evaluation systems analyzed employee data to provide personalized feedback and development plans. But amidst the sea of technology, Olivia remained the guiding force—a beacon of empathy and compassion in a digital world.

One day, as Olivia was reviewing quarterly reports, a knock echoed through her door. It was Marcus, a seasoned employee who had been with the company for over a decade. His face was etched with worry as he took a seat opposite Olivia.

"Is everything alright, Marcus?" Olivia asked, her voice laced with concern.

Marcus hesitated before speaking, his words tumbling out in a rush. "I've been feeling overwhelmed lately, Olivia. The workload keeps piling up, and I'm struggling to keep up. I don't know what to do."

Olivia leaned forward, her eyes reflecting genuine empathy. Despite the advancements in AI, she knew that nothing could replace the human connection forged through understanding and support.

"Marcus, I'm here for you," Olivia said softly. "Let's work together to find a solution. Whether it's adjusting your workload or providing additional support, we'll figure it out."

Tears welled up in Marcus's eyes as he nodded, relieved to have someone to confide in. In that moment, Olivia realized the true essence of her role—to be a source of comfort and guidance in times of need, transcending the boundaries of technology.

As the years went by, AI continued to evolve, revolutionizing every aspect of the corporate world. But amidst the whirlwind of change, Olivia remained a steadfast presence—a beacon of humanity in an increasingly automated landscape.

On her retirement day, colleagues gathered to bid Olivia farewell, expressing gratitude for her unwavering dedication and compassion. Amidst the heartfelt speeches and well-wishes, Olivia reflected on her journey—a testament to the enduring power of the human touch in an AI era.

As she stepped out of the office for the last time, Olivia felt a sense of fulfillment knowing that, no matter how advanced technology became, the essence of HR would always lie in the warmth of human connection. And with a smile on her face, she embraced the future, knowing that the legacy of empathy she had built would endure for generations to come.

The Impact of Artificial Intelligence on Jobs in Human Resources: A Scholarly Analysis

Abstract:

The integration of artificial intelligence (AI) into various industries has sparked debates regarding its potential to revolutionize job markets. In the realm of human resources (HR), concerns have arisen regarding the displacement of traditional roles by AI technologies. This scholarly article seeks to examine the multifaceted impacts of AI on jobs in HR, exploring both the potential threats and opportunities it presents. By analyzing current trends, research findings, and expert opinions, this article aims to provide a comprehensive understanding of the evolving relationship between AI and HR employment.

Introduction:

The emergence of artificial intelligence (AI) technologies has brought about significant transformations across diverse sectors, promising increased efficiency, productivity, and innovation. However, as AI continues to advance, questions arise regarding its implications for the future of work. In the field of human resources (HR), where interpersonal skills and human judgment are paramount, the integration of AI raises concerns about job displacement and the changing nature of employment.

AI in Human Resources:

Artificial intelligence encompasses a range of technologies, including machine learning, natural language processing, and data analytics, all of which have the potential to reshape HR practices. AI-driven tools can streamline recruitment processes by analyzing vast amounts of data to identify top candidates, assess their fit within organizational culture, and predict future performance. Additionally, AI-powered chatbots and virtual assistants can enhance employee engagement, providing round-the-clock support for inquiries and feedback.

Potential Impacts on HR Jobs:

Despite the benefits of AI in HR, concerns persist regarding its impact on employment. One of the primary fears is the automation of routine tasks, such as résumé screening, interview scheduling, and performance evaluations, which could lead to the displacement of traditional HR roles. Moreover, the implementation of AI may require upskilling or reskilling for HR professionals to adapt to new technologies and remain competitive in the job market.

Challenges and Considerations:

While AI has the potential to streamline HR processes and improve decision-making, its adoption also presents challenges and ethical considerations. Bias in algorithms, data privacy concerns, and the depersonalization of employee interactions are among the key challenges that organizations must address when integrating AI into HR practices. Moreover, the displacement of human workers by AI could exacerbate socioeconomic inequalities and contribute to job insecurity if not managed effectively.

Opportunities for HR Professionals:

Despite the challenges posed by AI, there are also significant opportunities for HR professionals to leverage technology to enhance their roles. By embracing AI-driven tools, HR professionals can focus on strategic initiatives, such as talent development, diversity and inclusion, and organizational culture-building. Moreover, AI can augment human capabilities, enabling HR professionals to make more informed decisions based on data-driven insights and predictive analytics.

Conclusion:

In conclusion, the integration of artificial intelligence into human resources has the potential to transform the way organizations manage their workforce. While AI technologies offer opportunities to enhance efficiency and decision-making, they also raise concerns about job displacement and ethical implications. To navigate these challenges and harness the full potential of AI in HR, organizations must prioritize ethical AI practices, invest in employee training and development, and foster a culture of innovation and adaptability. Ultimately, the future of HR lies in striking a balance between human expertise and technological advancements, ensuring that AI complements rather than replaces the invaluable contributions of HR professionals.

Solutions and Resources

After reading this book, you might find yourself thinking, *How will I ever manage to remember and implement these rules, policies, and best practices? Staying in compliance seems like a never-ending, Herculean task that I don't have the bandwidth for...after all, I have a business to run!*

Legal and human resource compliance *can* seem overwhelming for many employers. This is particularly true for smaller employers that do not have on-staff human resources professionals or in-house attorneys. Luckily, there are several business resources that can provide affordable and effective solutions.

Professional Employer Organizations

A professional employer organization (PEO) is a business designed to help other businesses succeed. Under this model, the PEO takes a business's existing employees and, via a written contract, co-employs them.

In the Spirit of Full Disclosure...

...I must reveal that I've spent almost two decades working in the PEO space, for two very good but very different companies. Both companies offer amazing services to their clients and alleviate administrative burdens, which helps the clients focus on their core businesses.

PEOs are *not* joint employers. PEOs are service providers with a written co-employment relationship. Each PEO contract varies, but generally, the original business (i.e., the PEO's client) retains all day-to-day control and decision-making authority, and the PEO assumes responsibility for compliance matters such as:

- paying employees for all work performed for the client (again, the original business) at client worksites
- gathering and remitting state and federal taxes
- providing Form W-2s
- providing workers' compensation coverage

In short, PEOs are great solutions for employers who want to retain control over day-to-day workplace choices such as which employees are hired, what types of work they perform, and how they perform their job tasks—while seeking long-term payrolling and employment assistance.

PEOs operate pursuant to written services agreements. These agreements define the duties of the PEO and the duties of the business (the PEO's client), and provide the terms of payment for the PEO's services. In most states, PEOs are regulated by state law and must comply with very strict licensing requirements. Some PEOs are certified and regulated by the Internal Revenue Service as well, giving them the designation "CPEO."

A wide variety of organizations, including dry cleaners, builders, physicians, law firms, non-profit organizations, construction and hospitality businesses, and industry-specific businesses like transportation companies, can all benefit from contracting with a strong, reputable PEO. The key is finding the right PEO for your business. Considerations for finding the right fit include:

Geography: Some PEOs are national and provide services in all 50 states. Others are regional or licensed in only a single state. Because state licensing requirements are complex, some PEOs may limit the number of states in which they provide services. If your business has employees in more than one state, a multi-state PEO may be a good choice. If your business is large or has a remote workforce working in many states, a national PEO may be a better choice.

Services offered: Some PEOs offer a full suite of services, which may include on-site reviews for OSHA compliance, human resources services or advice, access to research tools, or the provision of forms or policies used in day-to-day business. Other PEOs may add those services on to a base contract for a separate fee.

Expertise in specific areas: PEOs may specialize in one area, such as transportation, retail services, hospitality, white-collar professional businesses, or non-profit organizations. Visiting a PEO's website will provide insight into whether it specializes in a particular area.

Benefits: For many employers, especially smaller organizations, one of the most valuable services a PEO can provide is its ability to negotiate health and wellness benefits on a large scale. If a PEO has thousands of co-employees in a particular state, it will generally have much greater negotiating power than a single business. As a consequence, the PEO may have a larger menu of health and wellness benefits for you to offer your employees.

Financial services: There are a lot of good 401(k) providers in the PEO space. Most PEOs have a relationship with one. This allows smaller businesses to provide a retirement plan to their employees at a reasonable price.

Access to additional insurance: Some PEOs have insurance policies that provide coverage for their clients' businesses. Often, these policies would be too expensive for the clients to purchase on their own. For example, a PEO might have employment practices liability (EPL) coverage, which provides coverage in the event of a claim alleging a wrongful act by a business. Especially for smaller organizations, EPL coverage can be prohibitively expensive. This makes it a valuable benefit of contracting with a PEO.

Technology: Because of their sizes, PEOs may offer superior technology for employee onboarding and records retention than a smaller business would otherwise have.

For a list of PEO services and member PEOs, visit www.napeo.org.

Staffing Companies

For shorter-term payrolling and employment solutions, a staffing company may be appropriate. Staffing companies supplement a workforce on a temporary or a longer-term basis. While they function differently from PEOs, they can be just as valuable to a business.

One primary benefit of a staffing relationship is that at all times, the employee "belongs" to the staffing company—not to the business to which they are assigned. This means that the staffing company onboards the employee and performs any screening that needs to be done, such as background checks or drug tests.

Once an employee is placed at the client's work location, the staffing company provides workers' compensation coverage and is responsible for all workers' compensation claims. The staffing company also provides Form W-2s to its employees and handles all tax matters associated with FICA, FUTA, and SUTA. The staffing company is responsible for all human resources and compliance matters associated with the employee.

As with PEOs, there are many staffing models. Some staffing companies search for specific candidates for their business clients. Other staffing companies have a database of persons ready to go to work. Staffing companies may also allow their clients to send selected candidates to them to roll onto the staffing company's payroll and then work at the client's site.

Generally, the fee associated with this arrangement is a negotiated percentage of the employee's hourly wage.

To learn more about staffing companies, visit the American Staffing Association's website at www.americanstaffing.net.

Amie's Required Reading

Throughout this book, I've touched on important topics that some readers may want to know more about. Below, you'll find my reading (and viewing) recommendations on crime and justice in America, race in America, fair wages, and women in the workplace and gender discrimination.

I have found all of these resources to be interesting and informative. Regardless of your industry, I believe this required (okay, *recommended*) reading will give you insights, tools, and knowledge that will enable you to become an even better leader.

Amie's Required Reading on Crime and Justice in America

Enforcement Guidance on the Consideration of Arrest and Conviction Records in Employment Decisions Under Title VII of the Civil Rights Act, available at www.EEOC.gov.

Believe it or not, this 2012 employment guidance written by the Equal Employment Opportunity Commission is a great read. It is packed with statistics on the impact of race on employment.

Just Mercy: A Story of Justice and Redemption—**Bryan Stevenson**

Lawyer/writer Bryan Stevenson tells the story of his decades-long defense of Walter McMillian, who is wrongfully arrested and convicted of the murder of a young woman. If reading isn't your thing, you're in luck—the movie is just as brilliant as the book.

The Sun Does Shine: How I Found Life, Freedom, and Justice—**Anthony Ray Hinton**

Defended by Bryan Stevenson, Anthony Ray Hinton spent decades incarcerated on death row before ultimately being exonerated.

The Nickel Boys—**Colson Whitehead**

In this painful novel, Colson Whitehead tells the story of a reform school for young boys. The novel is based on a reform school in the Florida panhandle. The school operated for over 100 years and destroyed countless lives in the name of "justice." *TIME* magazine named this one of the best books of the decade.

Amie's Required Reading on Race in America

The EEOC's guidance focuses largely on disparities in hiring, based on race. There are so many great books about the civil rights movement and race in America today. Here are a few of my favorites:

Beneath a Ruthless Sun: A True Story of Violence, Race, and Justice Lost and Found—**Gilbert King**

Gilbert King is a brilliant writer. His work is gripping and fact-filled, but easy to read and hard to put down. This must-read book tells the true story of a disabled man accused of rape by a ruthless and lawless sheriff in a small Florida town.

Devil in the Grove: Thurgood Marshall, the Groveland Boys, and the Dawn of a New America—**Gilbert King**

This 2013 Pulitzer Prize winner is masterful in documenting Thurgood Marshall's bold and courageous defense of four young boys—the Groveland Boys—who were accused of rape in the citrus groves of 1950s Florida.

March—**John Lewis, Andrew Aydin, and Nate Powell**

If graphic novels are your thing, this National Book Award winner presents Georgia Senator John Lewis's personal experiences during the civil rights movement.

***A Lawyer's Journey: The Morris Dees Story*—Morris Dees with Steve Fiffer**
This Alabama civil rights attorney changed history by repeatedly taking on the Ku Klux Klan in Alabama and establishing the Southern Poverty Law Center.

***The Lynching: The Epic Courtroom Battle That Brought Down the Klan*—Laurence Leamer**
When we think of the brutality of lynchings in America, we often envision the 1950s—not the more recent year when Princess Diana married Prince Charles, MTV showed its first video, and *The Raiders of the Lost Ark* opened in every theatre in the United States. Against the backdrop of the 1981 modern world, Michael Donald was lynched by the Ku Klux Klan in Alabama.

Amie's Required Reading on Fair Wages

***Knowing Your Value: Women, Money, and Getting What You're Worth*—Mika Brzezinski**
Written in 2011, this book is packed with advice from wildly successful women. It is a must-read for any woman in the workplace.

***The Grapes of Wrath*—John Steinbeck**
This novel will be illuminating for any person who has ever wondered why the United States has a federal law requiring payment of a minimum wage in American workplaces.

***Nickel and Dimed: On (Not) Getting By in America*—Barbara Ehrenreich**
Written by an undercover journalist who lived on her earnings from minimum-wage jobs, this book is over 20 years old—but the content still resonates today. For those lucky enough not to have to earn a living by working one (or more) low-wage jobs, this must-read will remind you that the working poor work very, very hard.

Bridges Out of Poverty: Strategies for Professionals and Communities—
**Ruby K. Payne, PhD, Philip E. DeVol, and Terie Dreussi-Smith, with Eugene
K. Krebs**

Solution-oriented folks should check out this volume. It's a great book-club
selection for industry groups, communities, and religious groups because it is
packed with discussion topics and practical long-term strategies for businesses
and individuals.

Amie's Required Reading (and Viewing) on Women in the Workplace and Gender Discrimination

***When Everything Changed: The Amazing Journey of American Women
from 1960 to the Present*—Gail Collins**

There are so many great books about women in the workplace—and this is
the best one I have read. Especially if you love history, you'll find it to be inspiring
reading.

On the Basis of Sex

If you want to learn about civil rights, gender equity, and the Notorious RBG
at one time, this biopic about Ruth Bader Ginsburg, starring Felicity Jones, is for
you.

***Knowing Your Value: Women, Money, and Getting What You're Worth*—
Mika Brzezinski**

This is an appropriate place to give a second shout-out to Mika Brzezinski's
excellent book.

Acknowledgments

My friend Carol Carlan gave me a box of 52 thank-you cards with instructions to write a thank-you note to a different person every week for a year. I am on the 52-week journey now, and it has opened my eyes to all of the things I want to express gratitude for on a daily basis. Not once have I struggled to find someone to thank for something.

It is fitting that I've spent so much time reflecting on gratitude this year because my heart is full of thanks for the people who have loved, supported, and mentored me from the day I suggested that maybe, just maybe, I would try to write a book to this very moment.

My gratitude begins with my perfect-for-me family. I don't have a fan club, but if I did, my husband, Scott, would be the president. He's my ride-or-die, my fiercest supporter, and my best friend. I am lucky to have a husband who unequivocally believes in my abilities—even when I don't. Scott, I am grateful for you Every Single Day.

I am also grateful for our children, Virginia, Tom, and Harry, who cared enough to constantly fake interest and excitement when I prattled on about topics for this book. Virginia, Tom, and Harry, thank you for never even considering the possibility that I would not finish this.

I am also blessed to have been born to parents who love the written word, who would drive an hour and a half to take me to Oxford Books "just for fun," and who were totally supportive when I wanted to major in English in college. Mom and Dad, thank you for never saying no to me in a bookstore.

I am lucky to have friends willing to take time to read drafts and who cared enough to tell me what was good—and what was not so good. Tracey Ellerson, Quint Studer, and Bert Thornton, thank you for your honesty and your willingness to help me succeed.

This book could not have been completed without the skill, professionalism, and absolute patience of my editor-turned-dear-friend, Dottie DeHart. Dottie,

I am grateful to you and the DeHart team for holding my hand from day one to today.

Finally, to the readers of this book, I'm grateful that you want to take care of the people who work with you. I hope I can play a small part in whatever makes another person's life better.

Endnotes

Introduction

1. Aditi Malhotra, "2023 U.S. Employment Law Changes to Consider," Replicon, February 9, 2023, https://www.replicon.com/blog/united-states-employer-law-changes/.

2. Ahmed Younies, "11 Employment Law Changes in 2024," HR Unlimited Inc., January 11, 2024, https://www.hrunlimitedinc.com/11-employment-law-changes-in-2024/.

Chapter 1

1. "Summary of the Major Laws of the Department of Labor," U.S. Department of Labor, accessed December 11, 2023, https://www.dol.gov/general/aboutdol/majorlaws.

Chapter 2

1. "Occupational Violence," The National Institute for Occupational Safety and Health, August 31, 2022, https://www.cdc.gov/niosh/topics/violence/default.html.

2. "Occupational Violence: Fast Facts," The National Institute for Occupational Safety and Health, August 31, 2022, https://www.cdc.gov/niosh/topics/violence/fastfacts.html.

3. "Occupational Violence: Fast Facts."

4. David Michaels, "Enforcement Procedures and Scheduling for Occupational Exposure to Workplace Violence," Occupational Safety and Health Administration, October 1, 2017, https://www.osha.gov/sites/default/files/enforcement/directives/CPL_02-01-058.pdf, 9.

5. "Workplace Violence," Occupational Safety and Health Administration, accessed December 12, 2023, https://www.osha.gov/workplace-violence.

6. "Senate Bill No. 553: Chapter 289," California Legislative Information, October 2, 2023, https://leginfo.legislature.ca.gov/faces/billNavClient.xhtml?bill_id=202320240SB553.

Chapter 3

1. Lorie Konish, "Pandemic Has Disrupted Retirement Plans for 35% of Americans, Study Finds," CNBC, October 12, 2021, https://www.cnbc.com/2021/10/12/pandemic-has-disrupted-retirement-plans-for-35percent-of-americans-study-says.html?&qsearchterm=pandemic+has+disrupted+retirement+plans.

2. Megan Brenan, "Women Still Handle Main Household Tasks in U.S.," Gallup, January 29, 2020, https://news.gallup.com/poll/283979/women-handle-main-household-tasks.aspx.

Chapter 4

1. "Enforcement Guidance on the Consideration of Arrest and Conviction Records in Employment Decisions Under Title VII of the Civil Rights Act of 1964, as Amended, 42 U.S.C. § 2000e et Seq.," EEOC Enforcement Guidance, April 25, 2012, https://www.eeoc.gov/sites/default/files/migrated_files/laws/guidance/arrest_conviction.pdf, 9-10.

2. "One in 31: The Long Reach of American Corrections," Pew Center on the States, March 2009, https://www.pewtrusts.org/~/media/assets/2009/03/02/pspp_1in31_report_final_web_32609.pdf, 5.

3. "What Do I Need to Know About…English-Only Rules," U.S. Department of Labor, accessed December 18, 2023, https://www.dol.gov/sites/dolgov/files/OASAM/legacy/files/20120321-FINALEnglish-Only-Rules-Factsheet.pdf, 1.

4. "Enforcement Guidance on the Consideration…," 11.

5. "Enforcement Guidance on the Consideration…," 18.

6. "Work Opportunity Tax Credit," Internal Revenue Service, August 31, 2023, https://www.irs.gov/businesses/small-businesses-self-employed/work-opportunity-tax-credit.

Chapter 5

1. Joseph R. Biden, "A Proclamation on National Equal Pay Day, 2022," The White House, March 14, 2022, https://www.whitehouse.gov/briefing-room/presidential-actions/2022/03/14/a-proclamation-on-national-equal-pay-day-2022/.

2. Greg Rosalsky, "How the Pandemic Is Making the Gender Pay Gap Worse," NPR, August 18, 2020, https://www.npr.org/sections/money/2020/08/18/903221371/how-the-pandemic-is-making-the-gender-pay-gap-worse.

3. Morgan Smith, "How the Pandemic Made the Pay Gap Worse for Low-Wage Workers and Women of Color," CNBC, March 15, 2022, https://www.cnbc.com/2022/03/15/the-pandemic-widened-the-pay-gap-for-low-wage-workers-and-women-of-color.html.

Chapter 6

1. "Handy Reference Guide to the Fair Labor Standards Act," U.S. Department of Labor, accessed December 14, 2023, https://www.dol.gov/agencies/whd/compliance-assistance/handy-reference-guide-flsa.

2. "Resources for Workers," U.S. Department of Labor, accessed December 14, 2023, https://www.dol.gov/agencies/whd/workers-resources.

3. "Fact Sheet #17A: Exemption for Executive, Administrative, Professional, Computer & Outside Sales Employees Under the Fair Labor Standards Act (FLSA)," U.S. Department of Labor, September 2019, https://www.dol.gov/agencies/whd/fact-sheets/17a-overtime.

4. "Back Pay," U.S. Department of Labor, accessed January 3, 2024, https://www.dol.gov/general/topic/wages/backpay.

5. "Code of Federal Regulations: Title 29," National Archives, December 18, 2023, https://www.ecfr.gov/current/title-29/subtitle-B/chapter-V/subchapter-A/part-516.

Chapter 9

1. "Title VII of the Civil Rights Act of 1964," U.S. Equal Employment Opportunity Commission, accessed December 15, 2023, https://www.eeoc.gov/statutes/title-vii-civil-rights-act-1964.

Chapter 13

1. "Charges Alleging Harassment Other than Sexual Harassment FY 2010 - FY 2022," U.S. Equal Employment Opportunity Commission, accessed January 31, 2024, https://www.eeoc.gov/data/charges-alleging-harassment-other-sexual-harassment-fy-2010-fy-2022.

Chapter 16

1. Stacy Jo Dixon, "Percentage of U.S. Population Who Currently Use Any Social Media from 2008 to 2021," Statista, July 27, 2022, https://www.statista.com/statistics/273476/percentage-of-us-population-with-a-social-network-profile/.

2. Stacy Jo Dixon, "Daily Time Spent on Social Networking by Internet Users Worldwide from 2012 to 2023," Statista, August 29, 2023, https://www.statista.com/statistics/433871/daily-social-media-usage-worldwide/.

3. Stacy Jo Dixon, "Average Time Spent Per Day on Select Social Media Platforms in the United States in 2023," Statista, September 12, 2023, https://www.statista.com/statistics/1301075/us-daily-time-spent-social-media-platforms/.

4. Rohit Shewale, "Social Media Users - Global Demographics (2023)," Demandsage, September 12, 2023, https://www.demandsage.com/social-media-users/#:~:text=There%20are%204.9%20billion%20social,platform%2C%20with%203.03%20billion%20users.

5. "Summary of the Major Laws…"

6. "Interfering with Employee Rights (Section 7 & 8(a)(1))," National Labor Relations Board, accessed December 13, 2023, https://www.nlrb.gov/about-nlrb/rights-we-protect/the-law/interfering-with-employee-rights-section-7-8a1#:~:text=Section%207%20of%20the%20National,of%20collective%20bargaining%20or%20other.

7. Anne Purcell, "Report of the Acting General Counsel Concerning Social Media Cases," National Labor Relations Board, May 30, 2012, https://apps.nlrb.gov/link/document.aspx/https://apps.nlrb.gov/link/document.aspx/09031d4580a375cd09031d4580a375cd.

Chapter 17

1. Anthony Martinez and Cheridan Christnacht, "Women Are Nearly Half of U.S. Workforce but Only 27% of STEM Workers," United States Census Bureau, January 26, 2021, https://www.census.gov/library/stories/2021/01/women-making-gains-in-stem-occupations-but-still-underrepresented.html.

2. Jennifer Cheeseman Day, "More Than 1 in 3 Lawyers Are Women," United States Census Bureau, May 8, 2018, https://www.census.gov/library/stories/2018/05/women-lawyers.html.

3. "Lawyers by Race & Ethnicity," American Bar Association, accessed December 14, 2023, https://www.americanbar.org/groups/young_lawyers/about/initiatives/men-of-color/lawyer-demographics/.

4. Mackenzie Bean, "Gender Ratio of Physicians Across 50 States," Becker's Hospital Review, February 13, 2020, https://www.beckershospitalreview.com/rankings-and-ratings/gender-ratio-of-physicians-across-50-states.html.

5. Linda Searing, "The Big Number: Women Now Outnumber Men in Medical Schools," The Washington Post, December 23, 2019, https://www.washingtonpost.com/health/the-big-number-women-now-outnumber-men-in-medical-schools/2019/12/20/8b9eddea-2277-11ea-bed5-880264cc91a9_story.html.

Chapter 19

1. "Charges Alleging Sex-Based Harassment (Charges Filed with EEOC) FY 2010 - FY 2022," U.S. Equal Employment Opportunity Commission, accessed January 29, 2024, https://www.eeoc.gov/data/charges-alleging-sex-based-harassment-charges-filed-eeoc-fy-2010-fy-2022.

2. "Enforcement Guidance: Vicarious Liability for Unlawful Harassment by Supervisors," U.S. Equal Employment Opportunity Commission, June 18, 1999, https://www.eeoc.gov/laws/guidance/enforcement-guidance-vicarious-liability-unlawful-harassment-supervisors.

3. "Enforcement Guidance: Vicarious Liability…"

4. "Enforcement Guidance: Vicarious Liability..."

5. "Enforcement Guidance: Vicarious Liability…"

6. "Enforcement Guidance: Vicarious Liability…"

7. "Questions & Answers for Small Employers on Employer Liability for Harassment by Supervisors," U.S. Equal Employment Opportunity

Commission, June 21, 1999, https://www.eeoc.gov/laws/guidance/questions-answers-small-employers-employer-liability-harassment-supervisors.

8. "Questions & Answers…"

9. "Enforcement Guidance: Vicarious Liability…"

Chapter 20

1. "Handy Reference Guide…"

2. "Board Rules Workplace Policies Limiting Wearing Union Insignia, Including Union Apparel, Are Unlawful Absent Special Circumstances," National Labor Relations Board, August 29, 2022, https://www.nlrb.gov/news-outreach/news-story/board-rules-workplace-policies-limiting-wearing-union-insignia-including.

Chapter 21

1. "Title VII of the Civil Rights Act…"

2. "Religion-Based Charges (Charges Filed with EEOC) FY 1997 - FY 2022," U.S. Equal Employment Opportunity Commission, accessed January 29, 2024, https://www.eeoc.gov/data/religion-based-charges-charges-filed-eeoc-fy-1997-fy-2022.

3. "Religion-Based Charges…"

Meet Amie Remington

Amie began her legal career handling property insurance claims…but that period was short-lived. While hanging from a seven-story building's roof to evaluate whether the soffit was damaged in a hurricane, Amie realized that property insurance claims might not be her calling.

Fortunately for Amie, shortly thereafter her mentor Tom Jenkins asked her to work on a sexual harassment/retaliation/gender discrimination lawsuit. That lawsuit was an extrovert's dream. It involved dozens of witnesses and depositions, and also provided a thorough introduction to civil rights in the workplace. Realizing that people were much more interesting than soffits, Amie was hooked. Since that time, she has focused her practice exclusively on labor and employment law and human resources.

During the past 25+ years, Amie has worked in private practice, served as general counsel to a 10,000 worksite employee professional employer organization, and worked as chief legal officer to a 70,000 worksite employee professional employer organization.

A lifetime Florida State University fan, Amie graduated cum laude with a B.A. in English. She went on to graduate with honors from Florida State University College of Law. Amie says the best part of law school was meeting her husband,

Scott. When she isn't working, Amie can usually be found at home on the Gulf Coast of Florida with Scott, their three children, and their very unruly puppy, Whistle.

Made in the USA
Columbia, SC
29 April 2025

57284408R00178